AMERICAN
COVENANT

ALSO BY YUVAL LEVIN

A Time to Build:
From Family and Community to Congress and the Campus,
How Recommitting to Our Institutions Can Revive
the American Dream

The Fractured Republic:
Renewing America's Social Contract in the Age of Individualism

The Great Debate:
Edmund Burke, Thomas Paine, and the Birth of Right and Left

Imagining the Future:
Science and American Democracy

AMERICAN COVENANT

HOW THE CONSTITUTION UNIFIED OUR NATION— AND COULD AGAIN

YUVAL LEVIN

BASIC BOOKS

New York

Basic Books
Hachette Book Group
1290 Avenue of the Americas, New York, NY 10104
www.basicbooks.com

Printed in the United States of America

First Edition: June 2024

Published by Basic Books, an imprint of Hachette Book Group, Inc. The Basic Books name and logo is a registered trademark of the Hachette Book Group.

The Hachette Speakers Bureau provides a wide range of authors for speaking events. To find out more, go to hachettespeakersbureau.com or email HachetteSpeakers@hbgusa.com.

Basic Books may be purchased in bulk for business, educational, or promotional use. For more information, please contact your local bookseller or the Hachette Book Group Special Markets Department at special.markets @hbgusa.com.

The publisher is not responsible for websites (or their content) that are not owned by the publisher.

Print book interior design by Amnet Contentsource

Library of Congress Control Number: 2023951811

ISBNs: 9780465040742 (hardcover), 9781541606104 (ebook)

LSC-H

Printing 1, 2024

For Cecelia, with love

As long as the reason of man continues fallible, and he is at liberty to exercise it, different opinions will be formed.
        —JAMES MADISON, Federalist 10

Hearken not to the unnatural voice which tells you that the people of America, knit together as they are by so many cords of affection, can no longer live together as members of the same family; can no longer continue the mutual guardians of their mutual happiness; can no longer be fellow citizens of one great, respectable, and flourishing empire.
        —JAMES MADISON, Federalist 14

CONTENTS

INTRODUCTION

THIS IS A BOOK ABOUT AMERICA, AND THEREFORE, IT IS A HOPE-
ful book. If that seems like a strange leap of logic to you, then
you are the right reader for this book. It aims to help you see why
America should make you hopeful, why it deserves your hope, and
how that hope might be vindicated.

To be hopeful about America is not to be optimistic about it.
Optimism, the expectation that good things will happen, is a pretty
silly attitude toward our fallen world. Assuming that all will be well
is not so different from assuming we are doomed. Optimism and
pessimism are both dangerous vices, because they are both invi-
tations to passivity. Hope is a virtue, and so it sits between those
vices. It tells us that things *could* go well and invites us to take action
that might help make that happen and might make us worthy of it
happening. It does not deny the obvious potential for calamity that
always casts a shadow over our future, but it holds out the possibility
of light and grace.

Hope about our country does not come easily to Americans
just now. Our capacity for it has been sorely tested in our time,

1

especially by deepening divisions in our society. Americans have never lost hope in the face of outside threats, but internal discord strikes at the roots of our strength and leaves us doubtful of our capacity for renewal. In times of division, we tend to equate the sheer multiplicity of American life—the fact that our society is teeming with different people who have different views and form different groups that want different things—with strife and breakdown. We assume that multiplicity must imply disunity. And since we know that our multiplicity is a permanent reality, we either rage against reality or grow despondent. This is one reason why our politics now overflows with melodramatic despair.

We have come to see other Americans as problems to be solved and so imagine that the obstacle to unity in our society is the existence of people who do not think as we do. Among other things, this has made us frustrated with our system of government because that system forces us constantly to deal with people who differ from us. Too many Americans are, therefore, persuaded that our Constitution is unsuited to our contemporary circumstances—that it assumes a more unified society than we now have, makes it too difficult to adapt to changing times, and so can only make our problems worse in this divided era.

But the Constitution is not the problem we face. It is more like the solution. It was designed with an exceptionally sophisticated grasp of the nature of political division and diversity, and it aims to create—and not just to occupy—common ground in our society. The problem is that we have forgotten that creating common ground is a key purpose of the Constitution and that it should be a key purpose of our own political and civic action. We have also lost sight of how the Constitution goes about creating common ground. It does so by compelling Americans with different views and priorities to deal with one another—to compete, negotiate, and build coalitions

in ways that drag us into common action even (indeed, especially) when we disagree.

This points to an even deeper problem underlying our contemporary frustrations with our system of government: we have not only lost sight of the importance of pursuing greater unity, but we have also tended to forget what unity in our free and dynamic society really involves. Unity doesn't quite mean agreement. Americans do have some basic principles in common—especially those laid out in the Declaration of Independence. But although those widely espoused principles impose some moral boundaries on our political life, there is enormous room for disagreement within those boundaries. This includes some significant disagreement about exactly what the declaration's principles actually mean regarding the nature of the human person and the proper organization of society, let alone disagreement about discrete political and policy choices in response to the needs of the day. Our politics is unavoidably organized around these disputes and requires us to take on common problems while continuing to disagree about questions that matter a great deal to us. But that disagreement does not foreclose the possibility of unity. A more unified society would not always disagree less, but it would disagree better—that is, more constructively and with an eye to how different priorities and goals can be accommodated. That we have lost some of our knack for unity in America does not mean that we have forgotten how to agree but that we have forgotten how to disagree. The parties to our various disputes now tend to talk *about* one another more than they talk *to* one another, and, so, even very active citizens actually spend relatively little time in active disagreement with others, let alone in efforts to overcome such disagreement for the sake of addressing some common problems in practice. This is the sense in which we have forgotten the practical meaning of unity: in the political life of a free society, unity does not mean thinking alike; unity means acting together.

How can we act together when we do not think alike? The United States Constitution is intended, in part, to be an answer to precisely that question. And it is a powerful and well-honed answer. Alleviating the disunity of contemporary America would, therefore, require not recklessly discarding our Constitution as an antiquated relic but rediscovering its fundamental purposes, grasping just how powerfully it speaks to some of our most serious contemporary problems, and finding ways to better put it into practice to address those problems. That is my aim in this book.

THE BOOK'S OPENING CHAPTER OFFERS A SENSE OF JUST WHAT OUR CONstitution actually is, because the Constitution is more than it seems. Now, we tend to view it as essentially a legal code, if not a judge's instrument. And the Constitution is a legal framework, to be sure. But it is also an institutional framework; a policymaking framework; a political framework in the highest sense of the political; and, finally, a framework for union and for solidarity. Although this latter unifying purpose of the Constitution was seen as vital by the framers of the document and was featured prominently in their case for its adoption, it is, for us, the Constitution's least familiar facet. It is also the one we most urgently need to recover and, for the sake of which, a broader constitutional restoration is essential. The remainder of the book will then elucidate that crucial facet of the Constitution in particular.

It will do so through chapters that explore the modes of political action envisioned by the Constitution, the ways in which it facilitates the formation of the people it governs, and then the several distinct formal and informal institutions and practices it puts in place. The book will ask how each of these was meant to function, how and why it now malfunctions, and what might be done about that

by reformers seeking renewal. We will find that the political vision of the Constitution is rooted in a republican ideal that we now barely understand and would do well to rediscover, because it speaks to a hunger we feel intensely but struggle to name.

As we consider the particular elements of our governing framework, we will see that Americans have weakened the capacity of the Constitution to unify us, not by accident but on purpose, out of an understandable but ultimately misguided sense of frustration with precisely the means by which our system of government pursues cohesion. Those means tend to slow down policy action and hold back narrow majorities so as to force them to accommodate minorities and grow. Our frustration with these modes of restraint is understandable, because we often think we know just what direction public policy should take but find ourselves held back and made to negotiate away our best ideas. But that frustration is misguided, because the rival constitutional vision to which it often drives us underestimates the need for unity and the difficulty of achieving it, and so it has worsened our divisions in the hope of facilitating more assertive policy action. The struggle between these two approaches to governing has shaped our constitutional debates for more than a century, and contrasting them will help us clarify the vision of politics and of the human person that underlies our Constitution.

Finally, the last chapter will reflect on what the understanding of the Constitution laid out in this book may tell us about the character of unity itself in a modern free society and what the framers of our system might have made of the challenges that our republic confronts in that regard today.

My aim is not to suggest that unity is the only purpose of the Constitution. The document is meant to enable American self-government on the terms demanded by the Declaration of Independence and in light of the imperatives of order, justice, liberty, and safety, among others. The preamble to the Constitution nicely

summarizes its formidable aims. But that list of objectives does begin with the imperative to "form a more perfect union," and the modes of governance the Constitution then creates again and again compel a fractious people to build coalitions and seek accommodations. The Constitution clearly prizes unity and solidarity highly among its ambitions—all of which are substantive moral ambitions and not merely procedural ones. It is vital now to see why and how it prioritizes unity and to understand the ways in which we today are failing to play our parts and might do better.[1]

I approach these daunting questions with humility, not only because the subject is vast but also because the character and meaning of the Constitution have been wisely explored by many greater scholars than me for well over two centuries. The argument laid out in these pages is not a comprehensive interpretation of the US Constitution but an elucidation of one important aspect of our system of government that deserves to be highlighted but tends to be neglected. It is meant as a supplement, not a substitute, to the work of the many eminent legal scholars, historians, political scientists, public officials, and countless other students of the American system who have taken up our Constitution as a subject. It seeks only to make a modest contribution to a vital conversation.

The first voices in that conversation were those of the authors of the Constitution themselves, a number of whom had a great deal to say about its meaning and intentions. I draw heavily on these and cite them often, but no voice will echo more forcefully or frequently through the pages to come than that of James Madison. As a participant in (and chronicler of) the Constitutional Convention and as a coauthor of the Federalist Papers, as well as at points later in his career, Madison was uniquely attuned to the challenge of division and the possibility of unity. Where Alexander Hamilton, for instance, was most concerned about threats to vitality and social order, and Thomas Jefferson was most concerned about threats to equality and

social justice, Madison was most concerned about threats to unity and social cohesion. Views like Hamilton's and Jefferson's fall into broadly familiar categories—very generally speaking, they are those of the Right and the Left at their best. But there is no one quite like James Madison in our political tradition. The cohesion he emphasized is actually a precondition for a politics in which the partisans of justice and the partisans of order can square off so that the country gets the best of both—and, in that sense, his was not a partisan vision, at least not with regard to this subject. He assumed that a large, free society will always be diverse and, so, will always have to work at holding together, and he wanted the Constitution to put that work front and center.[2]

This book seeks out the ways in which the Constitution bears the mark of that insight and so will hearken to Madison's voice more than to any other. This is not because any of his assessments are authoritative or indisputable, but because many of them are profound and brilliant and deserve our attention. We should always recall that much of what Madison and other framers of the Constitution wrote about the document had a rhetorical purpose. They were not scholars but statesmen, and they made arguments intended to persuade Americans to adopt the Constitution or understand it in a certain way. That means we should be attuned to their motives and aims, but it also means we should consider their arguments and see if we find them persuasive.

That requires us to take arguments seriously and, ultimately, to take politics seriously, which we Americans don't do enough in our time. It is all too easy to dismiss substantive political arguments as mere masks for interest or greed. And interest and greed are surely real and powerful. But it is impossible to see our politics close up (as I have done for my entire adult life) and not perceive that deliberation, persuasion, coalition building, and public-spiritedness are real and powerful too. Cynicism presents itself as sophistication, but it is

often very naïve about how political life really works. A realistic view of politics would consider both interest and argument, acknowledge that nearly all political actors genuinely believe they are acting in the best interest of the country, and remember that no one is right or wrong about everything. What follows will endeavor to approach the arguments made by the authors of the Constitution in that spirit.

The book, of course, also relies a great deal on the work of many later students of the Constitution, whose scholarship is gratefully cited throughout. But it also wrestles and contends with some of that work and takes sides in some of the disputes that have emerged within it.

Taking sides is essential to any effort like this book. I do not write as a disinterested neutral observer of American life but as a citizen who loves his country. I am a political theorist by training, and a public-policy analyst. I have worked over the years for several members of the US Congress and for a president of the United States. For the better part of the last two decades, I have toiled in Washington think tanks studying an assortment of challenges at the intersection of the theory and practice of American politics and editing a journal of public affairs.

I am also a conservative, and not a bashful or halfhearted one. My conservatism is rooted, first and foremost, not in opposition to progressivism but in a protective disposition toward the best of the inheritance of our civilization. Where I am critical of the Left, as I often am in this book, it is out of that motivation. And when I am critical of the Right, as I sometimes am in what follows as well, my critique begins there too. Protectiveness is not defensiveness, and I am not of the view that our Constitution is perfect or that its flaws should be shrouded and ignored. It was, as we shall see in some detail, the product of a patchwork of compromises. But just for that reason, I think it has been well adapted to the needs of a divided polity. In considering the Constitution, I begin from the premises that the

self-evident truths to which our country has been often imperfectly dedicated from the start remain as true as ever; that the Constitution has enabled us to work toward governing ourselves accordingly (and increasingly so in some important respects); and that the hard work involved in its preservation, improvement, and repair is, therefore, worth our best efforts.

This is not necessarily a partisan view, and what follows need not be a partisan argument. Our Constitution establishes the shared framework within which our partisanship should play out. But to let it do that effectively, we do need some shared understanding of just what the Constitution is and does, and the terms of that understanding have long been controversial. This book means to take part in that controversy. My understanding of the purposes of the American system of government, its strengths and weaknesses, its assumptions about human nature, its approach to political legitimacy, and its emphasis on social cohesion over administrative efficiency amounts to a distinct view of the Constitution. This book will argue that it was, in large measure, the view of the document's authors. But as we will also see, it has long been criticized by a competing progressive vision that considers the operation of our constitutional system too slow and cumbersome and not democratic enough. The book will describe and lay out that competing view from a variety of angles and take seriously its considerable strengths. But I ultimately argue that adherents of that view underestimate the dangers of division, and thus the importance of unity, even in a time when those should be painfully obvious. They view the Constitution as inadequate to the challenges of a modern, diverse, dynamic, democratic society, but they themselves have far too simple a conception of what such a society entails and requires. The Constitution is more sophisticated than these critics, particularly when it comes to the most daunting challenge that always confronts our politics: the challenge of legitimately balancing competing and opposing views without coming

apart, and especially of balancing majority rule and minority rights. On that front, I argue that the Constitution's critics are simply mistaken.

I, therefore, do not doubt that some readers will contest and disagree with the approach I take or with particular judgments and views I put forward. That may be because they don't see things my way, but also because they see things I do not. I only hope they might consider the possibility that the reverse might be true, too, so that what follows in these pages, by exposing something I have seen to someone with eyes to see it differently from me, might spark some insights that would not have otherwise occurred to either of us and will help us both approach the truth a little more closely than we had before.

That ambition and that attitude toward durable differences is implicit in the Constitution itself and was essential to the spirit in which it was authored. When presenting the finished document to the Confederation Congress that had called the Constitutional Convention, George Washington, who had presided over the proceedings, included a short note that made this point. "The Constitution, which we now present," he wrote, "is the result of a spirit of amity, and of that mutual deference and concession which the peculiarity of our political situation rendered indispensable."[3]

That kind of spirit is recoverable now, not by abandoning the factional and party differences that appropriately shape our politics but by engaging in that politics in ways informed by common premises and a common sense of gratitude. It is our great fortune that we get to share this country, and we should think about how to deserve, preserve, and become more worthy of that unearned gift. The problems we have are not entirely new, and many would have been all too familiar to the generation that first gave shape to our republic. We have inherited a lot of tools for dealing with these problems. But to use those tools effectively, we have to understand them, and

appreciate them. This book is, for that reason, essentially a work of gratitude—which is the deepest root of hope.

On October 15, 1858, during the last of his formal public debates with Stephen Douglas, Abraham Lincoln challenged his audience to recall these very reasons for gratitude and hope, even in a moment of maximal peril for the nation. The founding generation, Lincoln said, bequeathed to their successors a Constitution, "which it was hoped and is still hoped will endure forever," and which, when considered properly and in full, turns out to be a "great charter of liberty." In our day, which is full of its own perils, we should again work to get to know our Constitution, and we should come to understand (as Lincoln ultimately showed) that it is not only a great charter of liberty, but also a great charter of unity—an American covenant that can keep us together if we keep it together.[4]

Chapter 1

WHAT IS THE CONSTITUTION?

THE GREATEST OBSTACLE TO OUR UNDERSTANDING OF THE US Constitution is our familiarity with it. We know some of what there is to know about it so well that we struggle to see the rest. Americans who follow politics hear about the Constitution constantly, because our political life regularly overflows with constitutional controversies. In just the last few years, we have seen debates about emergency powers, election rules, abortion, public health, congressional districting, marriage, religious liberty, immigration, college admissions, financial regulation, and a seemingly endless parade of other crucial issues that have ended up as arguments about how to put into effect the 235-year-old blueprint for our government.

These have been important and necessary arguments. But to consider them together is to see that our constitutionalism—that is, the ways we understand, put into practice, and live out the meaning of our Constitution—has become too narrow. That narrowness is not only a symptom but also a cause of the dysfunction of our politics. Above all, it keeps us from seeing how the Constitution could be a vital resource for the renewal of our public life.

Most of those familiar controversies treat the Constitution as essentially the business of lawyers and judges and suggest that the stakes of our constitutional disputes are ultimately matters of personal rights and public policy. We, therefore, implicitly consider the Constitution a legal code that establishes what government in America can do to us and for us. This description is not wrong, but it is grossly incomplete. It keeps us from seeing the full scope of the ends and means of our Constitution, and, therefore, some of the ways in which it might be most valuable to us today if we took up the work of restoring and repairing it.

To broaden our view and to launch our exploration of the potential of the Constitution to help heal our divided society, we should start with a deceptively simple question: Just what is the Constitution?

On its face, the US Constitution is a document produced by a convention of delegates from twelve states (Rhode Island chose not to participate, though it ultimately accepted the outcome), which was called together in the summer of 1787 to address some serious deficiencies with the system of government under which the still newly independent United States of America had been living for much of the prior decade. The delegates quickly decided to essentially abandon that existing system and propose to the American people a new national system of government, which would be made sovereign over some distinct governing domains, while the states remained sovereign over others, and would consist of a representative legislature with two houses, an executive elected indirectly by the people, and an appointed judiciary. Once they agreed on some key details, they submitted the result to the congress that had called the convention, which then called for ratifying conventions in each state. Through those, the new system was ultimately adopted. The document they produced was a terse patchwork of compromises and ran to just a few printed pages. It has been amended twenty-seven times over the subsequent centuries, but ten of those amendments

were adopted (as a Bill of Rights) almost immediately after the system went into effect. Even including all twenty-seven amendments, the document runs to roughly seventy-five hundred words—about the length of an essay.

But of course, the Constitution is more than a document. It is also the system itself, brought into being by the words on the page and embodied in a set of offices, officials, institutions, laws, rules, norms, habits, and traditions. It is the essence of the American regime, which is, by now, one of the world's oldest and most durable democratic republics. And it decisively shapes the political ethos of our society and the character and dispositions of the American people.[1]

The Constitution can be all these things because it is, in essence, a framework—a structure or form that matches means to ends. And it is a complex structure, so that some of our differences about the nature of the Constitution are tractable differences of emphasis rather than more fundamental differences of principle. To capture its key facets, we can think about the US Constitution as comprising a five-part framework: a legal framework, a policymaking framework, an institutional framework, a political framework, and a union and unity framework. These are not alternative descriptions. They are all true of our constitutional system. But at different times, we tend to prioritize them differently, with serious consequences for how we understand our common life.

The first two frameworks, law and policy, are the most familiar of our ways of thinking about the purpose and character of the Constitution. The first tends to be the Right's foremost framework for constitutionalism and the second, the Left's. The next two, institutional and political, are less familiar but, in some respects, deeper ways to think about the nature of our national charter. Briefly considering, in this opening chapter, what each of those four entails and how they interact with one another to create the American constitutional order can help prepare us to consider the fifth and least familiar

framework of them all—to see the Constitution as a framework for national unity—which is our task in all the chapters to follow.

FIRST, WE MIGHT THINK OF THE CONSTITUTION AS A *LEGAL* FRAMEWORK— a duly enacted text that establishes a set of rules that can be put into effect by public officials and interpreted by judges in response to cases and controversies. The Constitution describes itself as "the supreme Law of the Land," and it certainly is, first and foremost, a legal document in this sense. It is crucial to see this facet of the Constitution first, because it sets out the fundamental character of the American system as subject to the rule of law.

The term *rule of law* is so commonly used that we rarely stop to hear what it really says. It says that the written law, rather than the will of any particular person or group in this moment, is the authoritative source of power in our system of government. The law can be changed, by methods that are themselves prescribed in the Constitution and the laws. But while it is in effect, the law is binding on all. Thomas Paine put this point powerfully: "As in absolute governments the king is law, so in free countries the law ought to be king." Our system is thus meant to be nomocratic—ruled by law.[2]

For this purpose, it is helpful that our Constitution is a written document. It is not just an evolved system known by its practice, like the British constitution, but a formalized system, defined by a written text and constantly measured against it. Written constitutions were common in the American colonies before independence, since those colonies began under formal charters. But they were not otherwise common among nations, and they only became more common thanks to the example of the US Constitution.[3]

There is something very lawyerly about the notion that a government should be defined by a formal, written charter in this way.

And indeed, before our country's independence, Americans had a reputation in England as a lawyerly people—disputatious, contractarian, and exacting. That is not to say we were, or are, a notably rule-following people—quite the contrary. But we have tended to understand our freedom as framed by clearly stated limits on what others, including our governments, can do to us or take from us. In that sense, our inclination toward liberty and our lawyerliness have always complemented each other.[4]

Indeed, the Constitution, understood as law, is above all a set of constraints or structured boundaries on power. Some of these are expressed as personal rights, in effect, defining protected spaces around individuals and communities into which others, or the government, may not enter. And some are expressed as definitional constraints on the institutions of government—placing a broad category of governing powers (like "the executive power" at the beginning of Article II of the Constitution) in an office but then shaping and defining the structure of that office so as to channel and contain that power. The text of the Constitution does not define what a legislator, an executive, or a judge are—it assumes a preexisting understanding of these terms, rooted in the common law and long-standing practice. But it sets explicit, written limits on what those constitutional officers can do with their powers in our particular system.

In both cases, the Constitution as law defines boundaries, and judges (as interpreters of the Constitution as law) patrol those boundaries and insist on their enforcement. There are exceptions: for instance, in some contemporary understandings of the Fourteenth Amendment, which see it functioning more as a set of guarantees than of constraints. And there is a vast space for public and private action within the boundaries sketched out by the Constitution, a space meant to be filled by the lawful actions of both public officials and citizens. But broadly speaking, the Constitution as law is a negative or protective instrument, a shield more than a sword.

And this makes sense, since the judge (unlike other constitutional officials) can only be called into action when a complaint or case presents itself—when someone can reasonably claim that a boundary has been transgressed.

That is not to say that the Constitution, even as law, is, therefore, purely procedural or devoid of substantive purpose. Limits necessarily speak of a purpose—they are there for a reason, and that reason is deeply rooted in an understanding of the ends of government. The powers of government and the limits on government created by the Constitution point in the same substantive direction. And the work of the judge, the interpretation of both statutes and the Constitution itself, is among the most important influences on the public life of our free society. Courts apply general laws or constitutional provisions to specific circumstances and resolve disputes about their meaning in ways that sometimes decisively set the direction of American history. They are the arbiters of legal meaning, and their independence and integrity continue to render them among the most trusted authorities in our public life. The Constitution's standing as our foundational legal framework is the first and foremost grounds of its significance for us.

And yet, there is no question that a view of the Constitution that takes in exclusively or largely its legal character would be a blinkered view. It would suggest that our system of government is, at its heart, a system of limits on government and that the problems with the constitutional system in our time are essentially functions of people doing things they shouldn't in ways that judges ought to stop. As we shall see, this is not what some of our most significant constitutional problems actually involve today. Much of what is wrong with our constitutional practice is not illegal, and the tendency to leave American constitutionalism to judges alone is frequently a form of dereliction.[5]

Ultimately, the Constitution is far more than a set of procedural boundaries not only because it is our highest written law but also

because it is more than just law. Ironically, contemporary critics (particularly on the Right) who argue that limiting the judiciary largely to policing procedural boundaries would lead to a constitutionalism devoid of moral substance have too narrow a conception of constitutionalism themselves. They identify the Constitution entirely with law and constitutional practice with the work of the judge. But judicial restraint is actually a means of protecting the space for legislative, executive, and civic action, and such action is far from morally neutral. To confuse the work of judges with the entire work of living out the Constitution is to undermine both the judiciary and the rest of our system.

The Constitution's role as law is essential to its fuller purpose, and it is reasonable to view the system as first and foremost a legal framework. It sets the boundaries of what our federal government may do, and those boundaries cannot be violated for the sake of other constitutional ends. But what happens within those boundaries is also constitutionalism, even if it isn't always law.

SECOND, THEREFORE, WE MIGHT THINK OF THE CONSTITUTION AS A *POLIcymaking* framework—a set of tools and authorities that enable a government to address practical problems by enacting statutes, implementing them, raising revenue, spending it, creating public programs, administering them, and taking policy action in response to needs and events. Our Constitution was adopted above all because its predecessor, the Articles of Confederation, was grossly inadequate as a policymaking framework, and the new system certainly established a far better one.

Policymaking is much of the substance of everyday governing. In this arena, the judge's role is muted, and the legislator and executive come to the fore. Their objective is to make law and to carry it out

in pursuit of substantive public goals. They are bound by the limits the Constitution imposes on the uses of government authority, but within those limits, they are meant to deploy that authority. The Constitution as a policymaking framework is, therefore, primarily a set of powers. Policies and programs direct those powers to meeting concrete public needs and satisfying specific public desires, and officials are judged as policymakers based on how well they do that.

The Constitution is rooted in an understanding of the great importance of effective governance, and the case for it has always put great emphasis on policymaking. Its framers believed that governmental incompetence undermines a society's self-confidence, and with it, the capacity for self-rule. In a memorandum laying out "The Vices of the Political System of the United States" in preparation for the Constitutional Convention, James Madison described the assorted weaknesses of American government largely in terms of a deficient capacity for policymaking. His concern was not that government in America was transgressing limits on its power but that it lacked the power to act. The Constitution would change that by creating a government empowered within its sphere.[6]

There is clearly a tension between the Constitution as a legal framework and the Constitution as a policymaking framework. While the legal regime is nomocratic, ruled by law, policymaking is (to use a term deployed by the British philosopher Michael Oakeshott), telocratic, or ruled by ends and goals. Uses of power framed above all by the substantive ends they seek to achieve will tend to trample procedural constraints—even when those constraints are shaped by ends of their own, like the protection of minority rights or individual liberties. A view of the Constitution that prioritizes the capacity of government to act must naturally chafe against a view that prioritizes boundaries on action. And so, policy-minded constitutionalism has long clashed with legally minded constitutionalism and insisted that any system of government assigned goals as

ambitious as those assigned to our Constitution must be granted powers sufficient to achieve those goals.[7]

But like a legalistic constitutionalism, this kind of policy-minded approach to our system tends to monopolize our thinking about the Constitution and crowd out other priorities. Approaching the Constitution as a policy instrument is plainly justified and crucial up to a point. Our system exists to enable a government to address public problems and meet national needs. But as Karen Orren and Stephen Skowronek point out in their important 2017 book *The Policy State: An American Predicament,* there is much more to government than policy. Government also exists to secure basic rights and to structure political relations, for example, and that requires us to think about the Constitution in terms other than policymaking. Arguments from policy, like arguments from law, cannot always simply trump other modes of constitutionalism.[8]

The authors of the Constitution clearly recognized this, and the American system, in particular, frequently de-emphasizes policymaking in relation to its other goals. The kinds of parliamentary democracies that prevail in Europe tend to prioritize muscular policy action. They often empower the majority coalition in the legislature to act fairly quickly and efficiently as long as its majority holds. That majority was chosen by the public to wield power, and so it should govern and then be judged again by voters. The American system almost never simply empowers any majority in that way but, rather, insists on restraints that slow and structure decision-making and require broad and durable coalitions, both within and across different institutions. We will consider why that is from several angles in the coming chapters, but one implication of this distinctly American constitutionalism is that it deprioritizes substantive policy outcomes and instead prioritizes structured decision-making and broad accommodations. It assumes that addressing a public problem is not a matter of finding the best technical solution but of finding a solution

that is most satisfactory to the relevant community on the whole. The goal is to address a problem in a way that people are happy with and feel is reflective of some understanding of their wishes and desires. For this reason, the American system often implicitly prefers doing nothing over enacting aggressive policy programs by narrow legislative margins. All four of the other ways of thinking about the character of the Constitution—as a legal, institutional, political, and unifying framework—militate in favor of such policy restraint.[9]

Frustration with that restrained or gridlocked character of the system often leads people to try to elevate policy outcomes above procedural constraints and institutional boundaries. Even constitutional officers themselves do this. The courts might prioritize Congress's *goals* (in health care legislation, for instance) over the letter of the laws it writes or over the separation of powers. A president might decide that his administration must change the immigration system or forgive student-loan debt even if Congress won't. Members of Congress might create a federal program that can fund itself without requiring regular appropriations. In each case, the people involved treat our system of government as a means to a policy end at the expense of its character or limits. Sometimes these actions are illegal. Sometimes they are merely contrary to the spirit of the Constitution. Either way, they express a desire to treat the Constitution exclusively as a policy instrument. It is such an instrument, but not exclusively.

ALTHOUGH THE LEGALISTIC AND THE POLICY-CENTRIC APPROACHES TO the Constitution are in tension in many respects, both pay attention, above all, to the powers that the system grants its different parts—whether with an eye to the limits or the uses of those powers. But if you consider the questions taken up by the framers at

the Constitutional Convention, you will find that they spent far more time thinking about structures than about powers. They were obsessed with institutional design.

Third, therefore, we might approach the Constitution as an *institutional* framework—a set of formalized bodies (a congress, a presidency, and courts) that each has a distinct structure and character and carries out a particular kind of work. Our constitutional system is made up of these interlocking institutions and is given its shape by their forms.

We are not used to thinking of political forms this way. Our usual approach to the separation of powers leaves us imagining that there is a fungible commodity called "power" that the different branches of our government exercise, so that the question is who has more or less of it. But our system does not just divide the power of the national government into three. It divides it among legislative, executive, and judicial institutions, each of which is expected to exercise its authorities differently, and for a different purpose. As James Madison put it in Federalist 41, "The Constitution proposed by the convention may be considered under two general points of view. The *first* relates to the sum or quantity of power which it vests in the government, including the restraints imposed on the States. The *second*, to the particular structure of the government, and the distribution of this power among its several branches."[10]

Congress generally frames and authorizes government action. It makes the laws that channel public power and allocate public resources. In a complex society like ours, this kind of framing work is necessarily the product of accommodation and compromise, and the work of the Congress is, therefore, necessarily plural: it is a work of many and involves conciliation among them.

The presidency, meanwhile, generally acts within the structures established by the laws that Congress frames. The purpose of the office is action, and its institutional design reflects that. The

president applies the sorts of power given to him by Congress (and, in some limited cases, directly by the Constitution) to the particular circumstances our society confronts and wields it in the moment to secure the nation and carry out its laws. He reacts to events, adjusts to pressures, and makes concrete choices among permissible options in complicated situations. Action like that is necessarily a singular endeavor, not a group activity, and carrying it off well requires energy, boldness, steadiness, focus, and ambition. The executive branch of our government is meant to enable those virtues in the individual chosen to exercise the power it possesses.

The judiciary then steps in after laws have been framed and actions have been taken and reviews them in response to cases and complaints to make sure that general rules have been applied appropriately in particular circumstances. It neither makes laws nor acts to execute them but assesses the behavior of others.

It is only a slight exaggeration to say that the Congress is expected to frame for the future, the president is expected to act in the present, and the courts are expected to assess the past. These boundaries are not perfectly clean, of course. "Experience has instructed us that no skill in the science of government has yet been able to discriminate and define, with sufficient certainty, its three great provinces the legislative, executive, and judiciary," Madison argued in Federalist 37. In fact, as he later noted in Federalist 48, to achieve the primary purpose of the separation of these branches—which is the prevention of abuses of power—it is actually necessary to intermix the branches a little at the margins. "Unless these departments be so far connected and blended as to give to each a constitutional control over the others, the degree of separation which the maxim requires, as essential to a free government, can never in practice be duly maintained."[11]

So the president not only has a veto power over legislation but is invited in the text of the Constitution to occasionally think like a legislator and recommend to Congress "such measures as he shall

judge necessary and expedient." Congress is given a role in foreign policy and exercises oversight over the entire federal bureaucracy, and the Senate has to approve treaties and confirm key presidential appointments to executive and judicial offices. The courts are more constrained to their own sphere, but they exercise a kind of over-sight, too, and can strike down both legislative and executive actions found to violate the Constitution or the laws.

This mixing of authorities is marginal, however. And rather than give each branch a real share of the kind of work the others do, the Constitution gives each branch some modest means to restrain the others in their own domains, as a defensive measure. This is ulti-mately intended to preserve the separation between the branches and insist on the differences between them. The most crucial of these differences are not about who has more or less power; they are fundamental distinctions of purpose, structure, and form. So they are best understood in institutional terms. That means we need to assess the health of our system not only by whether the various players in it are transgressing the boundaries established around their powers and using those powers to good policy effect but also by whether they are playing the sorts of roles assigned to them and exercising the *kind* of power they were given.[12]

When an administrative agency exercises an open-ended power to make general rules and enforce them in specific circumstances, it is acting legislatively and judicially even though it lacks a legislative or judicial form—and, so, is violating the structure and logic of our Constitution. This is one way to describe what is wrong with much of the modern administrative state: legislative or judicial actions with-out legislative or judicial forms. When a president says, "If Congress won't act, I will," he is threatening to violate the constitutional order. There are no properly legislative actions that an executive could properly carry out instead. When a judge creates a novel policy or right of action, he is acting in ways that may be permitted to other

constitutional officers but not to judges. He is exercising a share of the power of the government but in a form not appropriate to the particular institution of which he is part. Even if such actions are allowed by statutes or justified by loopholes that clever lawyers can describe to eager judges, they turn out to be counter-constitutional when we consider the Constitution from an institutional, and not a merely legal or policymaking, point of view. The institutional structures established by the Constitution call for certain forms of action and restraint by their occupants, and those constitutional officers should be appraised by how they play their parts.

Crucially, this means that an institutional approach to our system of government could help us see not only when one of the branches overreaches but also when it underreaches and fails to do its necessary work. As we shall see in later chapters, Congress today is plainly underactive. Its members often want to shirk responsibility for hard decisions, and tend to favor vague legislative mandates that describe popular goals but leave the tough governing details to bureaucrats and judges. That's generally not illegal, and courts can't do all that much about it. But an institutional perspective plainly shows it to be a constitutional dereliction that does serious harm to our system of government.

An institutional perspective can also help us understand the complicated balance that the Constitution strikes between the need to empower the government to govern effectively and the need to restrain it and avert abuses of power. That balance is ultimately maintained not by limits on the quantity of power granted to government but by the structures, forms, and formalities built into the institutions that deploy that power. The structural complexity that is so often frustrating to energetic reformers aims both to moderate and to legitimate uses of power, just as formality does in our social lives. Formalities are indirect, and constitutionalism seeks various means of making government action less direct or, as the great

constitutional scholar Walter Berns put it, "of doing properly what has to be done politically."[13]

Ultimately, such formalities also shape the character of our polity or the political personality of our society. And, so, they point us toward the next facet of constitutionalism.

FOURTH, THEN, WE MIGHT APPROACH THE CONSTITUTION AS A *POLITICAL* framework. This is the most capacious if also the most nebulous of the modes of constitutionalism we have considered. It refers to politics in its highest sense, not as a contest for power but as the common life of a community. And so it comes closest to the classical notion of a constitution, which is not so much the written charter of a government but, in Aristotle's terms, "a certain ordering of the inhabitants of the city," and "the way of life of a body of citizens." In this sense, the Constitution is almost analogous to the soul of a polity, and it describes the innermost character of our society and the meaning of citizenship and authority in its life.[14]

To understand the Constitution in such political terms is, therefore, for one thing, to contemplate the character of the regime we have. "Political constitutionalism," political scientist James Ceaser has written, "understands the Constitution as a document that fixes certain ends of government activity, delineates a structure and arrangement of powers, and encourages a certain tone to the operation of the institutions. By this understanding, it falls mostly to political actors making political decisions to protect and promote constitutional goals."[15]

It is by this light, and upon consideration of such questions of the proper tone of the operation of our institutions, that we can see some of the dysfunctions of our politics in recent years as constitutional problems. Failures of responsibility that involve

constitutional officers behaving like performers or mere seekers of celebrity, for instance, are increasingly common in all our political institutions. They don't always involve a violation of formal boundaries, and so they generally can't be addressed by litigation, but they nonetheless result from fundamental constitutional deformations—derelictions of responsibility and corruptions of political culture. Violations of constitutional norms that are not legally enforceable fall into this category too. Confronted with such behavior, we have to ask ourselves not only "Is this technically permissible?" but also something more like "Does this belong in our kind of politics?" That's a question that demands to be answered in terms of the purpose and goals of the Constitution, the sort of government it was aimed to create, and the sort of society it governs. Answers to it will be anchored in the ideals that shape our civic aspirations and in the common historical experiences that have forged us into a nation. They won't be as precise or confident as answers given by the courts to strictly legal questions, and they may be open to more debate and adjustment. But they are no less crucial for that.

Often what is at issue when the political character of the Constitution is at stake is not any one particular provision of the document but its overall tenor—what the great French political philosopher Montesquieu, who profoundly influenced the framers, described as "the spirit of the laws." As Alexander Hamilton wrote in Federalist 83, "The truth is that the general *genius* of a government is all that can be substantially relied upon for permanent effects. Particular provisions, though not altogether useless, have far less virtue and efficacy than are commonly ascribed to them."[16]

This spirit, or general genius, of the American republic can be hard to pin down sometimes, but it has a few broad characteristics we can certainly discern. It is, for one thing, rooted in the principles articulated in the Declaration of Independence—truths that are

foundational to the character of our society. The Constitution does not restate these truths, but they are a starting point for its essential republicanism. That does not necessarily mean that the Declaration can be used as an interpretive instrument by judges seeking to apply the Constitution in particular cases. There are rare occasions when this may be appropriate, if what is at issue in a case involves the broadest kinds of constitutional commitments. But the Declaration is most essential to the Constitution understood as a political framework, not a legal framework. It helps us understand the system's aims, even if it does not allow us to elucidate the legal meaning of specific provisions in the text. It makes sense of the spirit of the whole.[17]

The spirit of our Constitution is also given form by the ambitions laid out in its preamble. These also generally aren't enforceable as law but are political ambitions in the very highest sense. They describe the goods our government seeks to provide to its society, which are presumably the preconditions for the thriving of that society. And they remind us to think about our system of government not only in negative terms (in terms of what it protects us from and commits not to do to us) but also, and more so, in positive terms (in terms of what it offers us, demands from us, and commits to secure for us). Our constitutional debates often jump too quickly to the limits of our government, but the Constitution did not only limit the legislative, executive, and judicial institutions of our government—it first *created* them. Indeed, as we have just seen, in one respect it *is* those institutions. Its positive purpose logically precedes its negative limits, and while it is true that governments are instituted to secure our rights, it is also true that they are instituted to help meet our needs. The preamble to the Constitution offers a concise list of the needs our government seeks to meet: union, justice, domestic tranquility, the common defense, the general welfare, and security for the blessings of liberty. These are not modest ambitions. And they

are communal, not just individual. They describe the prerequisites for a thriving polity.

The spirit of the Constitution is also plainly democratic, in our modern sense of the term. It assumes that power is ultimately rooted in the people. Some historians have argued that the Constitution took a step away from the more radically democratic character of the Declaration of Independence, since it places restraints on majority power and recoils from any kind of radical or revolutionary politics. But the Constitution is actually much more democratic than the Declaration, which, after all, did not specify any particular form of government at all, made no reference or commitment to majority rule, and suggested that a wide variety of regimes could be legitimate if they were begun with the consent of the public. The Constitution is plainly committed to majority rule through representation sustained by regular elections. It builds upon the Declaration of Independence and completes it in a democratic direction. And it, therefore, stamps our political culture with an emphatically democratic temperament.[18]

At the same time, though, the Constitution is also clearly committed to the protection of minority rights and freedoms, and therefore does seek to restrain the uses of majority power. This, too, is evident in every one of its institutions and provisions, and is integral to the spirit of the regime it constitutes. As we shall see in the coming chapters, the tension between the imperative to empower majorities and the imperative to protect minorities (what we now might call the democratic imperative and the liberal imperative) and the attempt to combine the two is responsible for a great deal of the Constitution's structure and character.

That combination points to another political premise of the Constitution, which runs deep in America's cultural identity. Rather than placing the ultimate power of decision in any one place or portion of society—with elites or the public, legislators or judges, the national

government or the states or localities—the Constitution establishes a politics in which no one is in charge and, therefore, in some sense, everyone is in charge. This requires our political culture to be a culture of negotiation and accommodation and also makes our civic culture inclined toward self-help and independent-mindedness. These bedrock American political and civic traits preceded the Constitution, but were also reinforced by it and are inseparable from the political character of our society in the very highest sense. As we are finding in our time, their preservation or renewal depends on a certain kind of constitutional practice.

But at both the conceptual and the practical levels, the tension between democracy and liberalism is often also mediated in the constitutional system by republicanism. This is another essential element of the political framework of American constitutionalism, but one that has become less familiar to us over time. Republicanism is sometimes identified with its procedural implications and, especially, with representative as opposed to direct democracy. Indeed, James Madison, at times, defined it this way, referring to a republic as "a government in which the scheme of representation takes place." But republicanism, in both its classical and modern forms, runs far deeper than that. It is a civic ethic, not a system of government.[19]

At its heart is an idea of the human being and citizen that emphasizes our responsibilities to one another and to the common good. It counterbalances the democratic ethos because it values not just what we each want but what is good for all of us. It counterbalances the liberal ethos because it values not just rights but obligations. Such republicanism is the deepest political wellspring of the Constitution, but it has been largely lost to us. It has become so unfamiliar that we often mistake the consequences of its absence for symptoms of an excess of the dispositions it was meant to counteract— and so we argue that we have become too liberal when it might be more accurate to say that we are not republican enough. American

constitutionalism requires a distinctly republican virtue and cannot do without it. To be a free people, able to take advantage of the sort of system of government established by our Constitution, we need also to be a people with the kind of civic virtue that might, as Madison argued in Federalist 55, "justify a certain portion of esteem and confidence." Therefore, as we shall see in further chapters, the character of the souls of our citizens and leaders matters immensely and is of great concern to the constitutional system. A recovery of some sense of the meaning of republicanism will be necessary for any constitutional renewal, and such a recovery will require, in turn, a grasp of the Constitution as a political framework.[20]

But the political facet of the Constitution is not just the result of a collection of ideas and abstractions. It is also the product of an accumulated national history. America is not an idea; it is a nation, filled with men and women who live together and share in common a set of experiences, roots, and loves that render them into fellow citizens. The battles won and lost, challenges overcome, achievements and failures, triumphs and tragedies that fill the chronicles of American history also fill the hearts and minds of the American people. And our political character cannot help but be formed and framed by that life lived in common.

All of this is more vague and fuzzy than stark legal doctrines and institutional blueprints. It serves a different purpose than those do, but it is no less crucial to the meaning of our Constitution and to its effectuation in practice. The character of our Constitution as a political framework begins to help us see the enormously complicated and contradictory ambitions of our system of government. The framers sought a government that would be energetic but restrained, effective but limited, democratic but liberal and republican, responsive yet reflective, and representative of a vast and fragmented society yet able to focus on national challenges and address them. They approached the task by treating each of these seeming

contradictions as a potentially creative tension—a source of vigor and balance.

Perhaps the foremost risk inherent in that sort of approach is the risk of disintegration. And so the Constitution was designed to pursue these varied ends in ways that explicitly avoided disintegration and sought greater consolidation and unity. This is why the Constitution also has to be understood as structuring our solidarity—describing what it is that constitutes us as a people.

FIFTH AND FINALLY, THEREFORE, WE MIGHT THINK OF OUR CONSTITUtion as a *unity* framework. This idea is inherent in the very notion of a constitution and in the very term, which describes a whole constituted by constituent parts. It is evident, too, in the very first ambition articulated in the preamble, which is "to form a more perfect union." And it is apparent in the first-person plural in which the document presents itself, beginning with the fact that its first word is *we*.

But that *we* is aspirational as much as it is empirical. Not unlike the opening of the Declaration of Independence—which describes the Americans as "one people" connected by political bands with "another" and so implies that it speaks for an already existing distinct nation rather than for a new one being created—the Constitution opens by speaking on behalf of a united people when, in fact, the unification of that people is among its foremost goals. It is a goal the framers, and the public, knew would not be easy to achieve. The Articles of Confederation, which had structured the government of the United States through five years of war and five years of peace, were formally called "The Articles of Confederation and Perpetual Union." Yet they had clearly failed to foster union. The fearful prospect of disunity and even war among the states was quite real to late eighteenth-century Americans. And the need for union was the

first and foremost argument advanced by champions of the Constitution at the various state ratification debates. The first twenty-three of the eighty-five Federalist Papers were explicitly devoted to the need to preserve the union, and almost all the rest touch upon that subject too.

Sometimes the case for unity was advanced through aspirational descriptions, like the opening of the preamble, which insisted the Americans were already united but had to work to remain so. Charles Pinckney, a delegate to the Constitutional Convention from South Carolina, insisted to the delegates that "the people of the United States are perhaps the most singular of any we are acquainted with" because, "among them there are fewer distinctions of fortune, and less of rank, than among the inhabitants of any other nation." They were, to a unique degree, one people. John Jay, in Federalist 2, similarly asserted, "Providence has been pleased to give this one connected country to one united people—a people descended from the same ancestors, speaking the same language, professing the same religion, attached to the same principles of government, very similar in their manners and customs, and who, by their joint counsels, arms, and efforts, fighting side by side throughout a long and bloody war, have nobly established general liberty and independence." But there was more than a hint of wishful thinking in such assurances. It was no coincidence that unity was put forward as the first ambition of the reformed American regime in the preamble. Throughout the deliberations over the Constitution, a dark cloud of disunity hung in the air—disunity among the states, and among the people.[21]

James Madison was more alert to this danger than anyone else, and he did not think it could be dealt with by denial. The day after Pinckney's remarks to the convention, Madison rose to answer him directly and insisted that, while "it was true, as had been observed by Mr. Pinckney, we had not among us those hereditary distinctions of rank which were a great source of the contests in the ancient

34

governments, as well as the modern states," this was far from the whole story. "We cannot, however, be regarded, even at this time, as one homogeneous mass, in which every thing that affects a part will affect in the same manner the whole." The Americans were a divided people, he insisted, not only by state and regional identities but along economic and cultural lines that ran deep. These consistently rendered the nation into factions, and that tendency would only grow as America matured. "In framing a system which we wish to last for ages, we should not lose sight of the changes which ages will produce" on that crucial front in particular, Madison insisted.[22]

And the system the convention ultimately framed did indeed keep that challenge in sight. The Constitution was built with a keen awareness of the plurality and fractiousness of the American nation. It was offered as a way to live with the reality of our diversity and divisions, aiming to mitigate their downsides without harboring the utopian illusion of eliminating them. The key framers of the system hoped that the fact of the multiplicity of American life did not have to mean that Americans would be irredeemably alienated from one another, embittered and in conflict. They did not deny the reality of the diversity of interests and opinions in our polity, but they refused to believe that it had to mean that unity was impossible or not worth pursuing. Rather, the system they constructed presumes an idea of unity that takes such multiplicity for granted and attenuates disunity through common action.

All the other facets of the Constitution contribute to this one. Through the institutions it constructed, the boundaries it set, the ambitions it held out, and the spirit of the polity it helped instantiate, the system was plainly intended to help *forge* common ground in American life, and not just occupy such ground. It seeks to enable social peace, which cannot be taken for granted under modern conditions of pluralism. Social peace can offer a stable backdrop for political life. In a free society, it is not quiet but raucous. It cannot be

achieved by conquest or surrender but only by mutual accommodation. It is the condition of differing without rejecting one another's legitimacy—of disputing without being at war.

The very idea of a written Constitution that stands apart from regular legislation as the framework of a regime is rooted in the ambition to establish some such common ground in a permanently fractious polity. By drawing a distinction between views about the system of government and views about policy and interests, it stakes out space for agreement that can allow our disagreements to be dealt with more constructively. This does require some meaningful agreement about the framework itself, even as we disagree intensely about important political and policy questions. Charles Kesler makes this point especially persuasively in an important recent book. Our system can withstand a lot of discord, provided we share a general understanding of the character and purpose of the Constitution itself. That is why some restoration of such an understanding is an essential precondition to the recovery of our civic culture. But that culture, even in moments of relative unity, is a culture of disagreement. The breakdown of political culture in our day is not a function of our having forgotten how to agree with one another but of our having forgotten how to *disagree* constructively. And this is what our Constitution can better enable us to do. As a framework for unity, the Constitution functions as a means of rendering disagreement more constructive.[23]

It does this, above all, by rendering disputing factions in our politics into parties to a substantive debate about how to proceed together. In an essentially democratic system of government, this may be achieved by multiplying the number of factions in society (so that there is not a permanent majority faction) and by restraining the power of majorities (so that a narrow majority is not enough to win every argument). Our Constitution multiplies the number of factions in a variety of ways—beginning (as Madison famously

noted) with the sheer size of our republic but also extending to the profusion of modes of election and appointment to various offices and the variety of power centers and competing wielders of authority operating simultaneously. And it restricts the power of majorities through an assortment of mediating mechanisms that require agents of change to engage in a complicated dance of coalition building.

These counter-majoritarian restraints often feel not only frustrating but, in fact, divisive, because they force us to confront the reality of the existence of opposing views in our society, even when our side wins elections and makes appointments. But those divisions are there whether we confront them or not, and it is by being forced to confront them that we are moved to overcome them through negotiation.

The framers of the Constitution were exceptionally explicit about the need for such restraints on majorities, not only for the sake of building unity but also for the sake of avoiding dangerous mistakes in policymaking. In Federalist 71, Alexander Hamilton even imagined that the public, including those in the majority, might actually want such restraints and would be grateful for them:

They know from experience that they sometimes err; and the wonder is that they so seldom err as they do, beset, as they continually are, by the wiles of parasites and sycophants, by the snares of the ambitious, the avaricious, the desperate, by the artifices of men who possess their confidence more than they deserve it, and of those who seek to possess rather than to deserve it. When occasions present themselves, in which the interests of the people are at variance with their inclinations, it is the duty of the persons whom they have appointed to be the guardians of those interests, to withstand the temporary delusion, in order to give them time and opportunity for more cool and sedate reflection. Instances might be cited in which a conduct of this kind has saved the people from

very fatal consequences of their own mistakes, and has procured lasting monuments of their gratitude to the men who had courage and magnanimity enough to serve them at the peril of their displeasure.[24]

But we know from experience that most of the time, the public really does not like these kinds of restraints. And in our day, many citizens, activists, and even scholars of the law, particularly on the Left, are in open rebellion against these counter-majoritarian mechanisms and mediating layers between the people and the policy objectives they seek. Not only the Senate and the Electoral College but the courts and the Bill of Rights are now regularly under assault for being insufficiently responsive to democratic pressures. Their critics fail to see not only that these constitutional mechanisms are protective of minority rights—and are rooted in the painful truth, which echoes through the darkest chapters of American history, that majority rule can be an instrument of despotism—but also that they can contribute to unifying our society by compelling us to deal with one another. Frustration is frequently "the price of union," as the journalist and historian Herbert Agar noted in his famous book by that title.[25]

Such frustration is also often temporary. The process of dealing with one another, of being forced into arenas of contention and negotiation, often accustoms Americans, in time, to relating to one another across lines of difference. As our representatives negotiate on our behalf and reach accommodations with representatives of Americans with different interests and priorities, their rapprochements can come to be reflected back on us, and our sense of how problems are resolved can take on a more constitutional character. For this to work, though, our disputes do have to be resolved in democratically elected representative institutions, however slowly and painfully. Counter-majoritarian restraints must be exceptions to

the general rule of majorities. But this rule, too, is threatened now by critics, politicians, and voters, particularly on the Right, who are too quick to dismiss the necessity of majoritarian legitimacy and to gesture toward judicial supremacy even over what are essentially political disputes (not to mention to deny or ignore election results).[26]

The balance that the Constitution seeks between majority rule and minority rights is thus under attack from both directions in our politics. We know that this is happening in an era of particularly intense divisions in our society. And we assume that the rejection of the imperatives of our Constitution is one effect of that division. But we should see that it is also a primary cause of that division—that in order to be more unified, we need our constitutional system to function, and therefore, we must renew our commitment to it.

To grasp that unity is a core aim of the Constitution is to recognize that something has gone wrong in our practice of American constitutionalism. Rather than throw out the system or deform it to better suit today's grotesque civic vices, we should look to the logic of the Constitution for guidance toward constructive institutional reforms and healthier political habits.

If we actually want a more unified society, then we should view the Constitution much more as a solution than a problem. The nature of that solution is the subject of the chapters that follow.

Chapter 2

MODES OF RESOLUTION

THE CONSTITUTION HAS AN OPERATIONAL STYLE OF ITS OWN. The different rules and institutional arrangements it lays down, and the ways in which it seeks to have our government operate, fall into a pattern. Broadly speaking, they approach governing problems by setting competing interests and powers against one another so that those not only restrain one another but also are compelled into accommodations.

It would be easy to caricature that approach as substituting an almost mechanical proceduralism for any kind of morally substantive civic practice. But that would be to get things backward. This approach actually begins from the insight that, in order to be properly formative of healthy civic virtues, our politics must always be in motion—that the formation of citizens is a matter of establishing habits and that civic habits are built up by civic action. The different interests, priorities, and power centers set against one another in our system do not rest against one another like interlocking beams holding up a roof. Rather, they push and pull and tug at one another and unceasingly compete for position. They are living political actors,

not inanimate structural supports. And none can achieve anything lasting without dealing with the others, who are always in its way. The result is a peculiar style of politics, which feels frustrating and acrimonious at almost any given instant, but which can be remarkably dynamic in the long run.

Dynamic may not be the word that comes to mind when you reflect on the usual spirit of our politics. A sense of stalemate is frequently characteristic of American government and sets it apart from even the governments of many other modern democracies. Because our system tends to prioritize consensus building over decisive policy action, it is always in the process of struggling to get unstuck. But that sense of stalemate generally is not the last word in any political battle. It often characterizes just one phase in a long story of action and reaction, move and countermove, during which the various actors in our politics are gradually penned in, made to confront one another, and forced to wrestle toward some agreement. This leaves our political system always feeling unsettled—like no cause is ever truly won or lost. But it is also why that system is often able to create more winners than losers in divisive struggles. Because almost no victory is ever complete, almost no defeat is ever total either.

This pattern is no accident. It is a function of an implicit premise of the Constitution: that the diversity of interests and views in American society is a permanent reality. Our politics does not exist to extinguish that multiplicity but to allow us to live together, seek the good, and address public problems in the midst of it. The national motto—*e pluribus unum*, out of many, one—does not describe a one-time act of unification that occurred at the beginning of our republic, but the ongoing work of our society at all times. We remain many, even as we act together, so that common action is always the function of a process of accommodation.

In fact, one of the most original insights of the framers of the Constitution was that such processes of accommodation could turn our

multiplicity to our advantage by simultaneously allowing majorities to rule (thereby making our political life more legitimate) and protecting minorities from being trampled (thereby making our political life more just). This is not only a way of averting disaster; it is also a way of teaching justice in practice. The framers explicitly understood this idea to be an application of a set of modern innovations in political science. In Federalist 9, Alexander Hamilton described those innovations in structural terms:

> The efficacy of various principles is now well understood, which were either not known at all, or imperfectly known to the ancients. The regular distribution of power into distinct departments; the introduction of legislative balances and checks; the institution of courts composed of judges, holding their offices during good behavior; the representation of the people in the legislature by deputies of their own election: these are wholly new discoveries, or have made the principle progress toward perfection in modern times. They are means, and powerful means, by which the Excellency's of republican government may be retained and its imperfections lessened or avoided.[1]

This new way of thinking could transform not only the diversity of our vast society but also that vastness itself from an obstacle to republican government into a facilitator of it. Many theorists of republicanism had assumed that republics needed to be small and homogeneous—that their citizens would need to think alike in order to act together. In the early days of the Constitutional Convention, James Madison acknowledged that he had inclined to share this view and had almost come to "despair that a Republican Government could be established over so great an extent" as the new nation involved. But Madison soon came to believe that this extent was precisely what would allow the Americans to sustain a free society.[2]

In Federalist 10, building on precisely Hamilton's insight above, Madison did not so much summarize new discoveries in political science as announce his own. Small republics, he famously argued, were prone to majority tyranny. So not only is a durably just republican society possible in a large nation, but it may actually be possible *only* in a large nation:

> The smaller the society, the fewer probably will be the distinct parties and interests composing it; the fewer the distinct parties and interests, the more frequently will a majority be found of the same party; and the smaller the number of individuals composing a majority, and the smaller the compass within which they are placed, the more easily will they concert and execute their plans of oppression. Extend the sphere, and you take in a greater variety of parties and interests; you make it less probable that a majority of the whole will have a common motive to invade the rights of other citizens; or if such a common motive exists, it will be more difficult for all who feel it to discover their own strength, and to act in unison with each other.[3]

This was not an entirely modern innovation in political thought. Aristotle had actually proposed a version of this case, writing in *Politics* that larger polities would be more stable than small ones because they would have a broader middle class. But the boldness of Madison's proposal had to do particularly with his approach to social cohesion. He suggested that it was precisely by not being too unified that our society could hold together. Like Hamilton's vision, Madison's was durably dynamic: he was not after a stable end-state for our politics but assumed a continuous process of contention that would prevent any party from permanently winning control. The work of our national government, he implied, should be the work of holding together disparate social interests and forces by keeping them engaged in that contention.[4]

The key to this scheme is not just a set of institutions but a set of characteristic modes of operation intended to prevail within and between those institutions and help them deal with divisive tensions. We will consider the institutions themselves in the coming chapters. But we must grasp those modes of operation first because, through them, we can better understand why the institutions are framed as they are, and also hone a set of categories for assessing the contemporary successes and failures of American political life. Three such modes of dealing with differences stand out in particular in the workings of the Constitution: competition, negotiation, and productive tension. To understand how our system is faltering, we should consider how it is meant to work in these ways, and why.

FIRST, THE ETHOS OF *COMPETITION* FREQUENTLY CHARACTERIZES THE CONstitution's approach to clashing factions, interests, and ambitions. This is the most straightforward sense in which the system brings different political actors into contention with one another: it forces them into contests for support, influence, and power. In the process, it can both strengthen their capacity to appeal to a meaningful majority of Americans and diminish their ability to threaten the safety of minorities. As Christopher DeMuth has brilliantly shown, "the principle of competition underlies our political order."[5]

The democratic underpinning of the legitimacy of our republic is the competitive election, for instance. To win support, aspirants for office have to harness their ambitions to the public's desires. That requires knowing what voters want; helping them see why you and not your opponents could achieve it; and somehow standing apart in a contest of merit, skill, style, or experience. In this way, political differences can be transformed into competing arguments about national priorities.

Of course, elections are the essential feature of all democracies. But our system is in some ways uniquely formed to emphasize the distinctly competitive, rather than simply representative, character of electoral politics. The ground rules of American politics, which are not detailed in the Constitution but predated it and have then evolved around it, include winner-take-all congressional races and first-past-the-post rules for nearly all elections. These, together with the structure of the Electoral College (in which winning requires an absolute majority of electors, creating a powerful incentive to limit the number of serious candidates), has meant that our politics has almost always involved just two major parties. That means that each party is always working to build a broad coalition rather than to represent a narrow constituency and that the two parties compete for a band of persuadable voters who ultimately determine the outcomes of close elections. And it means that narrower factions in our politics have to participate in coalitions that are broader than their own memberships and, therefore, have to build the habit of presenting (and ultimately understanding) their own objectives in terms of a broader national interest and societal common good.[6]

The peculiar institution of the Electoral College, which we will further consider in chapter 6, also means that presidential elections are particularly focused on that persuadable swath of the electorate, even when (as in our time) that swath is quite narrow. Where a direct popular vote for chief executive would encourage each of the two major parties to focus on getting out its most devoted voters in the least politically competitive parts of the country, the Electoral College means there is little advantage to winning by an even wider margin in the safest states and that candidates, instead, have to focus on voters in the most competitive states, which tend to fall near the ideological middle. This is good for both national unity and the competitiveness of our politics.[7]

In recent decades, a variety of misguided political reforms and practices—and particularly the near-universal use of party primaries to choose candidates—have harnessed the power of competition to undermine unity rather than reinforce it and have driven our parties toward the margins of the electorate rather than toward undecided voters. But the simple fact that our system is rooted in electoral politics, so that durable power in American politics can only result from popularity with voters, gives every facet of our system of government a competitive character. (We will consider these reforms and practices and the related danger of declining competitiveness in some of our elections in chapter 8.)

The American system is also distinctly competitive outside the realm of elections, thanks to the structure of the Constitution. In most other democracies, winning an election means controlling the agenda for a time. But in the American system, winning an election only grants you the ability to compete for such control with other actors in the system, some of whom have been elected by overlapping but not identical electorates, and all of whom can make their own claims to legitimate authority.

A key purpose of this unending competition is to prevent abuses of power. This is achieved, as James Madison put it in Federalist 51, "by so contriving the interior structure of the government as that its several constituent parts may, by their mutual relations, be the means of keeping each other in their proper places." Elections do offer some protection against such abuses, and Madison saw those as preeminently important. "A dependence on the people is, no doubt, the primary control on the government," he wrote. "But experience has taught mankind the necessity of auxiliary precautions." Those precautions must be realistic about human nature, and so they need to establish competitive relations between various actors and institutions in our system. "Ambition must be made to counteract ambition," Madison famously argued. "The interest of

the man must be connected with the constitutional rights of the place."[8]

For this reason, the government is divided into three distinct and coordinate (if unequal) authorities that frequently get in one another's way. The legislature (which was understood by the framers to be the most powerful and, therefore, most dangerous branch of any republican government) is then further divided into two houses that are often set against each other. The work of the judiciary, which oversees an essentially adversarial legal culture, also involves a kind of competitive principle in which parties to disputes must advance their strongest legal and constitutional arguments, and the courts are frequently arenas for competition between the other two branches as well. As we shall see, competition is not the only principle behind the separation of powers. But it is one crucial principle behind it, and our regime was meant to be suspended in unending contention between different claims to authority, legitimacy, and priority, both to make it accountable and to render it limited and just.[9]

Similarly, the relations between the different levels or layers of government—the national government created by the Constitution and the state and local governments that preceded it and retained much of their authority under it—were, to a significant degree, intended to be competitive. The states compete intensely with one another, using their tax laws, regulatory policies, and other forms of governing leverage to attract residents, businesses, and investors. In recent decades, as Christopher DeMuth noted, "states with relatively low taxes, efficient government, and business-friendly laws prospered and attracted new residents and jobs at the expense of states with less attractive policies," even when the latter states (like California) had other significant advantages, such as natural beauty or a more pleasant climate. States also compete with the federal government, often challenging federal laws or policies in the courts or using their leverage to impose effectively national standards (in

environmental protection or consumer safety, for instance) that the federal government has declined to pursue.[10]

The Constitution's approach to the protection of some core political rights is also rooted in competitive assumptions. The First Amendment, for instance, protects the capacities of individuals and groups in our society to participate in the competition of ideas (through the freedoms of speech and of the press), to compete for adherents (through the freedoms of speech and religion), and to engage in competition among interest groups in our politics (through the freedoms of association, petition, speech, and the press).

The Constitution's power over the regulation of interstate commerce is intended, perhaps above all, to permit free and fair competition in America's commercial economy. The Constitution's nationalization of patents, copyrights, and portions of bankruptcy and contract law was meant to establish protections of property and a level playing field for commerce across state lines. Indeed, the Constitutional Convention was called in no small part in response to state protectionism, which restricted competition across the economy in ways that had created intense conflicts. The Constitution assumes, supports, and regulates a commercial economy in which competition is an engine of prosperity and also a source of greater unity and peace.[11]

This is true of the role of competition in our system more generally: Competition is simultaneously a means of constraint and a source of energy, and because it is both of those things, it can also serve the cause of unity. Competition compels competitors to make themselves appealing, and therefore, to accommodate themselves to the priorities of others precisely in pursuit of their own ambitions. And in governing, the imperative for competition forces you to face reality—to change when you lose and adapt when you fail so as to grow stronger by learning from diverse approaches and ambitions. Competition improves the quality of our national life by making

competitors smarter and better adapted, even as it makes them more solicitous of potential voters, consumers, and adherents. It can foster unity by turning opponents into rivals in a common pursuit and so subjecting them to common rules and harnessing their desire for victory to the advancement of a common good.

Not all these supports for competition have worked as intended, needless to say. And not all are in good order now, as we shall see in different ways throughout the coming chapters. But there is no question that competition is a fundamental mode of resolution deployed by the constitutional system again and again and is, therefore, essential to understanding the logic and design of the system.

COMPETITION IS NOT THE ONLY WAY TO DEAL WITH DIFFERENCE AND division in our system, however. A second and equally crucial mode of turning disagreement into strength is *negotiation*. In key moments, our system forces differing interests and ambitions to deal with one another—often literally to make deals with one another. Bargaining and accommodation are invaluable tools for resolving disputes peacefully, not so much by determining which side is stronger as by reaching an accord between them and so building common ground. But the American system does not assume that the instinct for bargaining will come naturally to citizens or even to their representatives. Rather, it forces people with differing interests and views to engage with one another by making some degree of bargaining unavoidable.

This prejudice in favor of negotiation can easily be mistaken for another example of the ethic of competition, but it is not the same. The president and Congress, for instance, don't simply compete with each other—they do different sorts of work, yet neither can durably do its work without bargaining with the other. The two houses of

Congress are in competition, in a sense, but they do not put different options before a third party to see which will be most attractive; they have to negotiate and compromise with each other before anything can be accomplished by the branch of our government that they compose together.

Often, competitors are driven to bargain when the results of their contest are not conclusive, and none of them quite wins or loses. The American system of government is designed to make sure this happens often, by creating competing power centers and multiple consent requirements. As James Madison wrote in a letter to Thomas Jefferson, it is often the case in our system that, "neither party being able to consummate its will without the concurrence of the other, there is a necessity on both to consult and to accommodate."[12]

Consultation and accommodation are also the essence of coalition building—the process of turning multiple minorities into a single majority. Coalition building is essential in any representative democracy to some degree, but the American system stands out for making such negotiation unavoidable and for requiring it to take part not only among political parties but also within, between, and beyond them. Crucially, even majorities, unless they are unusually broad, need to negotiate with minorities before they can act. This is a frequent source of frustration and of accusations that our system is insufficiently democratic. But the Constitution recognizes that majority rule can sometimes be a principle of oppression, not just of legitimacy. So rather than simple majority rule, it seeks something closer to consensus rule through a variety of counter-majoritarian requirements and mechanisms. This is a means of manufacturing common ground in society—of producing consensus that otherwise would not exist. The counter-majoritarian processes and institutions in our system are all, in one way or another, intended to advance this purpose. This is why they are often so frustrating, but also why they are so frequently essential.[13]

We should not mistake consensus for harmony. Consensus really just describes a broad and durable majority, and such majorities are often built by tense, adversarial, and even antagonistic negotiating processes. They require different parties to the process to seek common ground by downplaying differences, moderating demands, aligning aims, and accepting trade-offs. This is an inherently frustrating process. Indeed, its purpose is to frustrate potentially tyrannical majorities and turn them into more public-spirited majorities. It is a common mistake in American politics to let such frustration become an impetus for championing pure majoritarianism—and so to view consensus government as an inferior and undemocratic alternative to simple majority rule. In reality, consensus government is a way to make majority rule a force for unity rather than division, and frustration is a means of forcing stubborn partisans to negotiate, rather than letting them seek to dominate. The result is more than an expression of the will of a majority; it is a process of conscious mediation that begins in will but proceeds toward greater rationality.

The mix of institutions in our system and the different ways in which officials are elected and appointed within them also mean that we never really have a simple and durable majority in American life but always face an ever-shifting arrangement of majorities and minorities. This is particularly evident in our time. In the three decades since the mid-1990s, for instance, the same American public has elected three Democratic presidents and two Republican ones, eleven Republican House majorities and four Democratic ones, and eight Republican Senate majorities and seven Democratic ones. When each side has won one of these victories, it has inevitably expressed frustration at its inability to simply carry out its agenda. This has often led to arguments for a simpler majoritarianism in our election system (in opposition to the Electoral College, for instance, or to the structure of the Senate). We will see why such desires are

misguided in the coming chapters, but clearly, even if they were heeded, they would not result in durable policy paths in this closely divided era. Simple majoritarianism is of no use when there aren't simple majorities. Only negotiated settlements could garner durable support even as partisan control of the institutions changes hands. This is why our system is built to enable negotiation on behalf of complex majorities and the building of coalitions among representatives that might then make for greater unity among the factions they represent in the larger society. The habits involved in building such coalitions accustom us to negotiating, accommodating, and finding ways to live together—which makes them helpful well beyond politics too.[14]

Ultimately, the purpose of these requirements for consensus is to build and broaden majorities, not to frustrate them. The Constitution embraces the essential justice—indeed the inescapable necessity—of majority rule. But it also works to create the conditions for consensus, so that majority rule might be protective of minorities, too, and might be productive of stable, durable, and effective government. This does require restraining small, ephemeral majorities. But that is done ultimately in the service of empowering a more considered and therefore effective majority rule. As Harry Jaffa put it:

Because men are by nature equal; because, that is, no man is by nature the ruler of another, government derives its just powers from consent—that is, from the opinion of the governed. But government based upon the consent of all must operate upon the only practicable approach to unanimity, namely, the rule of the majority however defined; and majorities can take shape or form only in and through the process of discussion. It is for this reason that discussion is indispensable to the democratic process; but the principle of discussion can never be separated from the principle of majority

rule; nor can the principle of majority rule be separated from the principle of the natural equality of political rights of all men.[15]

Such "discussion," and the negotiated politics it makes possible, must happen in Congress above all. The Constitution clearly envisions Congress—its first and foremost branch of government—as an arena for bargaining and accommodation. The institution is built to be representative of key constituencies in American society but also to refine and elevate the wishes of those constituencies through negotiations among representatives. As we shall see, a functional Congress is essential to a functioning American constitutionalism, and congressional dysfunction is now at the heart of our system's broader problems.

Although negotiation can function as a search for shared commitments in this sense, it is not fundamentally a search for truth so much as for mutual accommodation. Negotiated compromises are never ideal outcomes, but they are broadly acceptable and, thus, legitimate outcomes. A politics that puts bargaining at its center assumes a broad base of moral legitimacy—it assumes that most political questions will not be fundamental questions of right and wrong but prudential questions of better and worse. There are limits to that assumption and, therefore, to a politics of negotiation. Some means and some ends must be out of bounds in the politics of a decent society, and just which those are is a question that must itself be fought over at times. But functional societies will only rarely encounter those boundaries and should want to avoid treating normal political questions as if they were fundamental or existential moral questions. We should want to resolve most disputes by negotiated settlements. And the ethos of our Constitution is clearly directed that way rather than toward theoretical simplicity or ideological purity. This doesn't make it ungrounded in moral principle but, rather, reflects its view of the nature of politics. Truth is not determined by interest-group

negotiations. But the truth of human dignity demands political institutions that provide free and equal people with an effective government that represents them, meets their civic needs, and lets them pursue the common good free from oppression or violence. A politics of consensus building through negotiation among elected representatives offers a chance to do just that.

This can be disappointing, because we implicitly expect that politics in our modern, scientifically and technologically advanced era might have gotten beyond the give-and-take of the bazaar. But that expectation is badly misguided. The most significant political questions are not technical questions, and the give-and-take of negotiation across lines of difference is actually an advanced and impressive social achievement. The alternative is not expert administration but disorder and social breakdown. As the sociologist Daniel Bell once put it, "Politics is haggling, or else it is force."[16]

And yet, even though negotiation is not philosophical investigation and moral truth does not answer to election returns, it would be a mistake to view a politics of negotiation as purely procedural or prudential. Such a politics is formative of habits that tend to turn our attention toward the common good by compelling different factions in society to make their case (and in time, even to understand their case) in terms of the broader interests of society. In order to persuade others to go along with you, in negotiation, just as in a competition for votes, you have to show them that what you want would be good for them, too, and so to present your own interest in terms of a broader good and a broader truth. As James Madison wrote, "In the extended republic of the United States, and among the great variety of interests, parties, and sects which it embraces, a coalition of a majority of the whole society could seldom take place on any other principles than those of justice and the general good."[17]

Moreover, the process involved in such negotiation is inherently deliberative regarding that general good. Deliberation and

negotiation temper the will of the parties involved, and the result is a more deliberated will, which is better suited to guiding political action. The point of such a process is not just social peace. You can always achieve peace by surrendering, but that would be no one's idea of a successful politics. The point, rather, is a peaceful social order—a mode of living together that better enables all to flourish. Negotiation points toward such an order both by letting more people and groups be part of the process of political action and by legitimizing outcomes that are less than ideal—enabling people to feel that, even when things do not turn out quite as they'd hoped, the outcome is fair and just and better than it might have been. This is particularly important for legitimizing majority rule.

For that purpose, the relatively slow pace of negotiated settlements is crucially important. That placid pace of our system of government is frequently aggravating, of course, but it is crucial to the capacity of a politics of negotiation to form us toward a pursuit of the common good. This is what the great French analyst of America Alexis de Tocqueville had in mind in describing the American republic as "a conciliating government, in which resolutions ripen for a long time, are discussed slowly, and executed only when mature."[18]

This capacity of negotiation to orient competing parties toward a common good was evident in the framing of the Constitution itself. As Herbert Storing noted, various factional differences at the Philadelphia Convention were expressed as different emphases regarding the good of the whole, not as narrow partisan interests. The bigger states at the convention, for instance, wanted their size to let them dominate the new republic, but they argued for union and explained why they believed it would be good for all. The small states wanted more influence than their size would proportionally afford them, but they argued for the importance of local distinctions—for states as such—for reasons they believed would speak to everyone. These were partisan angles on the good of the whole, but they were serious

arguments about the good of the whole, and they expressed genuinely held convictions, as well as partisan interests.[19]

In fact, the experience of the convention as a whole illustrates the unifying power of a politics of negotiation. The fact that the Constitution was the result of a patchwork of compromises arrived at through deliberation has often been used to insist that there is no coherent logic behind the document. But that argument assumes that deliberation is merely a way to balance interests, rather than also a way to seek a practical truth rooted in principle. Because in reality negotiation acts to orient rival parties toward a common aim, the fact of its being arrived at deliberatively is a reason to take the Constitution more seriously, not less, and to view it as especially well adapted to facilitating a politics of constructive bargaining. The framers, according to Martin Diamond, "successfully balanced the rival claims of theory and practical necessity. Despite the compromises which produced it, the Constitution is an essentially logical and consistent document resting upon a political philosophy that remains profoundly relevant." It stands as evidence that principle and practice can be reconciled by negotiation and that we can sometimes better approach political truths through the practice of politics itself.[20]

The same may be said of the various ways in which the Constitution has been amended and our constitutional practice has evolved over time. Because the Constitution creates a politics of negotiation, its own evolution (especially when it has proceeded through amendment and legislation rather than judicial fiat) has largely happened through negotiation and in the course of the practice of politics. Such a practice can involve a kind of mutual moderation that homes in on workable common ground. At the Constitutional Convention, Benjamin Franklin described how this can work (referring to the efforts of the convention itself) in terms drawn from carpentry: "When a broad table is to be made, and the edges of the planks do not fit, the

artist takes a little from both, and makes a good joint. In like manner here, both sides must part with some of their demands in order that they may join in some accommodating purpose."[21] This kind of process characterized the formation of our Constitution and is at the very core of our practice of constitutionalism, when we practice it properly.

BUT COMPETITION AND NEGOTIATION DO NOT EXHAUST THE MAJOR modes of resolution embraced by the Constitution. A third approach—less familiar and more novel than these—characterized the responses of the framers to some of the most contentious and difficult of all the challenges they faced. When the need to balance competing concerns was most acute, and especially when they faced a stark choice between two approaches or institutional forms, they often opted to create a composite that took in both, rather than give up on one for the sake of the other or shave both down until they fit. We might call this approach an ethos of *productive tension*—it is the instinct to respond to an either/or question by embracing the antinomies and answering, "Yes, both."

The Constitution does this, for one thing, at the level of principle, embracing at once liberalism and republicanism, individualism and communitarianism, majoritarianism and the protection of minority rights, consolidation and decentralization. This makes the American system a scourge of fastidious political theorists but is also responsible for its extraordinary durability and for the dynamic character of the system, which is always answering its own excesses and seeking balance without ever settling down.

But the Constitution also employs this method at the practical and institutional level. Nearly every fundamental structural question confronted at the Constitutional Convention was ultimately

resolved in this peculiar way. Would the system empower the small states or the large ones? It would empower both, and leave them ever struggling for balance. Would the president be a glorified clerk or an elevated head of state? He would be both and, therefore, neither. The few and the many, the city and the country, freedom and order, equality and excellence, representation and administrative efficiency— to each of these stark choices, the Constitution says, "Yes, both," and as a result, it creates a regime, a democratic republic, that (as the very term suggests) lives in constant tension with itself yet is capable of extraordinary feats.[22]

This dialectical institutionalism allows the American system to respond to its own failures by shifting its weight without losing its balance. It enables us to benefit from seemingly contradictory commitments while limiting their costs and downsides. This peculiar character of our system is rooted in a particular way of thinking about politics: it looks to countervailing interests and pressures as counterbalances that enable stability, and more profoundly, it seeks an active balance—peace but not quiet—as a core goal of political life. It is rooted in a recognition that, in practice at the very least, our regime is always going to be far from perfect; that it is, however, better than the alternatives provided its excesses are corrected; and that such correction requires it to confront constant friction, endless criticism, and continuous resistance. Such tension is not easy to sustain, as the tension itself is almost no one's explicit aim. But by crafting a system that simultaneously embodies rival approaches to key questions, it can hope to create what the political philosopher Joseph Cropsey aptly called a "temperate equilibrium of error."[23]

Keeping countervailing principles in tension creates a kind of sustained indecision about key structural elements of the system—not a third option or a middle point but a way of letting rival approaches keep pushing and pulling interminably. This yields a dialectic but not a synthesis. It allows for not so much a harmonizing of competing

goods as a kinetic political existence. It does not equate stability with stasis but with bounded action so that it expects our politics to always be in motion, or even in the midst of going too far, yet it has confidence that things will not get altogether out of hand because an offsetting push that calls on a competing principle of action is always in the offing.

The Constitution takes this approach not to secondary matters but to the most essential and controversial of its concerns. The tension between majority rule and minority rights, for instance, is addressed by energetically advancing both. As James Madison wrote in Federalist 10, the necessity of majority factions and the dangers they bring make for a kind of paradox: "To secure the public good and private rights against the danger of such a faction, and at the same time to preserve the spirit and the form of popular government, is then the great object to which our inquiries are directed. Let me add that it is the great desideratum by which this form of government can be rescued from the opprobrium under which it has so long labored, and be recommended to the esteem and adoption of mankind."[24]

The paradox may be resolved, not by withholding power from both majorities and minorities, but by giving it to both. As Alexander Hamilton said at the convention, "Give all power to the many, they will oppress the few. Give all power to the few, they will oppress the many. Both therefore ought to have power, that each may defend itself against the other." This is one reason why everyone in American politics always feels as though they are acting defensively, because even aggressive action, even starting a fight, is an essentially defensive measure in a system with competing power centers.[25]

One of the most divisive questions at the Constitutional Convention—the question whether representation in Congress should be equally divided among the large and small states or should follow population—was also resolved in this peculiar way.

Our bicameral Congress is a way of saying yes to both options. The differences among the states on this question seemed insurmountable, as they were rooted in both strong interests and powerful arguments. But on June 29, 1787, after weeks of debate on the question, Connecticut delegate William Johnson rose to argue that "the two ideas embraced on different sides, instead of being opposed to each other, ought to be combined; that in one branch the people, ought to be represented; in the other the States."[26]

Combining opposing ideas in the structures of our institutions, rather than decisively settling the dispute between them or even finding a middle ground, was also the way in which the equally fundamental question of the relation of federal and state power came to be treated. As Madison put it in Federalist 39, the result of the convention on this front was "in strictness neither a national nor a federal Constitution, but a composition of both." As we shall see in chapter 4, this composite character of American federalism is perhaps its most essential feature. Frustrating as it often is, sustaining that character rather than resolving the dispute between state and federal power in one direction or another will be crucial to the unity of our society in the years to come.[27]

Similarly crucial questions about balancing power between the three branches of the federal government were also left constructively unresolved, so that tensions between the branches would always characterize American government. Congress both is and is not meant to dominate the system; the president both does and does not command the administrative bureaucracy. Most tensions around such questions do not ultimately result from a lack of clarity about the meaning of the Constitution's text. They cannot be fully resolved by judicial interpretation. They are inherent and intentional. They are meant to set the tone of our politics and to encourage public officials to identify with their institutions and play the roles assigned to them by the system, since those roles are their sources of leverage in

an ongoing contention for authority and influence. This, too, does not work quite as intended today. But grasping just what the intention was and just what isn't working now is the only way we can hope to determine how to improve our constitutional practice.

THIS EXTRAORDINARY APPROACH TO THE STRUCTURING OF A REGIME IS the function of a more general appreciation for the complex and paradoxical character of our society. Political life is not a series of geometric proofs and applications. It requires us constantly to live with tense contradictions, and to see them as sources of strength. The Constitution was created under those very pressures and has therefore been well suited to dealing with them. Its methods for doing so implicitly acknowledge the need to forge some unity amid disagreement by establishing arenas for contention and creating structures of accommodation.

By embracing conflicting aims together, by compelling political combatants into negotiation, and by putting differing interests into competition, our system drives us to engage with one another precisely where we disagree, and so to build common ground through common action at the very heart of our disputes. Those are not ways of eliminating differences, or even quite overcoming them. But they are ways of making it possible for citizens to act together when they don't think alike, and therefore, of making civic unity more achievable.

These modes of resolving problems do not just get us through disagreements. They are unavoidably formative of our public life. They help mold the American character and have clearly had a hand in shaping the peaceful dynamism that characterizes so much of the American experience. The absence of that peace and that dynamism in growing swaths of our experience cannot help but suggest

the waning of these constitutional habits. And the importance of these habits suggests that restoring our capacity for peaceful dynamism will require renewing our practice of constitutionalism. That practice is not mere procedure. It can serve as the foundation of a joint pursuit of the common good through the forging of common ground and the formation of people well suited to living together. And that work of forging and formation occurs through the life of our society. It does not need to have been perfected before we can live together. Its continuing perfection is the product of our living together, and it is, in that sense, always a work in progress—and a work we pursue by practicing the Constitution's characteristic methods of resolving disputes.

This is one reason to believe that a revived constitutionalism might help heal our divisions. It is also a reason to consider not only the shape of the Constitution but also the ways in which it shapes all of us as citizens.

Chapter 3

THE CONSTITUTED PUBLIC

THE CONSTITUTION NOT ONLY GIVES FORM TO THE GOVERNING institutions, laws, and political practices of our society, it also shapes the American people. Our collective self-consciousness as citizens—our sense of who we are as a nation and as particular political communities—is a function, in no small part, of how the constitutional system arranges representation and facilitates public action. And the instincts, habits, characters, and souls of individual Americans are inevitably influenced by our society's ways of governing itself.

A lot of premises Americans take for granted—about what we owe one another, how important decisions should be made, who is responsible for what and accountable to whom—are functions of constitutional forms. We bring these with us well beyond politics too. Americans can regularly be found insisting on free speech around the dinner table, running school meetings by rules of order established for congressional debates, or otherwise importing into private life the peculiar forms of our constitutionalism. But constitutional formation reaches deeper still. Our sense of what is fair or just,

our national instinct for competition, and our knack for building and joining civic institutions, among many other traits of our national character, all speak to a kind of republican formation facilitated to a great extent by our constitutional tradition.

This peculiar reality, which we easily forget, means the stakes of our constitutional debates are even higher than they seem. On the one hand, a deformed constitutionalism can deform our society, undermining our capacity to treat one another as dignified equals and to take our common life seriously. On the other hand, a renewal of our constitutional system depends on some civic virtues that we can only hope to form with the help of that very system. Our sort of society—an enormous and diverse liberal democracy—not only requires a particular kind of citizen, it also tends to form a particular kind of citizen. Ideally, those two kinds would be the same, or at least very similar, so that our regime could produce the sorts of citizens it needs in order to thrive. But that alignment has never come easily and will not happen by itself. From the beginnings of our constitutional order, this has meant that our political life has needed both to function in ways that might mold the virtues it requires in the people and to rely on and protect institutions of formation outside of our politics (like families, schools, civic and religious groups, and more) that can forge those virtues. Meeting that need requires us to be keenly aware of it, which we often are not. Our society's capacity for unity and solidarity, therefore, depends on our seeing more clearly how our Constitution shapes us and how to put it into practice in ways that will form better citizens.

BEFORE CONSIDERING THE MODES OF PERSONAL FORMATION BY WHICH our Constitution shapes *each* of us, it is worth thinking through the modes of political formation by which it molds *all* of us—transforming

the mass of the American people into an ordered democratic public and a set of electorates that ultimately direct our public life. That process is crucial to facilitating unity in our republic.

This is an underappreciated fact about every democracy: the structure of the institutions of government creates the contours of the electorate. We tend to think of an election as something like a census of views—an occasion to measure an external reality called public opinion so that we can use the result to determine who should hold political power. We imagine that the public is always divided in a certain way and that elections merely let us see exactly how. But public opinion has to be formed before it can be measured, and it is formed not only on the basis of people's innate preferences but also in response to the shape of the political system and its work. People don't just walk around with a strong opinion about who their state's next governor should be. They form that opinion in response to the question put to them at election time and the choice of answers presented to them. If the question were put differently and the range of options looked different, the same people could well make very different choices. And the questions put to voters are functions of the institutions that need to be populated and of the methods of election that apply to each—or, in other words, they are functions of the structure of the Constitution.

In fact, the nature of those questions in America is rather distinct. In most democracies, voters in elections for national office are asked a question about politics, which roughly amounts to "Which party do you support?" In the United States, such voters are asked a question about government that sounds more like "Who should be your state's next US senator?" These are related questions: both parties and candidates for office run on particular policy platforms, and voters weigh those heavily when choosing. We do have parties in America, of course. As we will see in chapter 8, those parties shape our public life in crucial ways. But the questions we put to voters at

election time are generally questions about persons and positions, so that our system forms the electorate around the demands of particular offices. That form sometimes cuts across party allegiances. Even in our polarized era, it is not all that unusual for the very same voters, on the very same day, to elect a US senator from one party and a governor from another.

The Constitution also creates distinct, if overlapping, electorates for the different elected positions in our system. Members of the House and members of the Senate, even when they represent the same places, represent differently formed constituencies in those places; a statewide election and a district-wide election are, at least in many states, quite different matters. Senators were originally appointed by their state legislature until the Seventeenth Amendment took effect in 1913. But even under the direct election of senators, the broader scope of their constituencies and the nature of the Senate as an institution have meant that the electorates created by Senate races differ substantially from those created by House races.[1]

The president is chosen by still another kind of electorate. Thanks to the Electoral College, our presidents are chosen by virtue of the number of states in which they can win popular majorities and the relative sizes of those states' populations. As noted in chapter 2, one consequence of this is that presidential races are focused on competitive states, and therefore, on competitive slices of the electorate and of the issues facing the country, rather than on the voters and issues with which each party is most comfortable. Election campaigns naturally follow the lead of the voters whom the candidates most need to win. This fact often escapes the notice of opponents of the Electoral College, who insist that, because Electoral College results sometimes fail to mirror the result of the overall national popular vote, our presidential elections are not representative. In fact, a presidential race fought as a national popular-vote election would look very different from one fought over the Electoral

College. Candidates would run differently, focus on different parts of the country, and appeal to different voters. Its outcome would not necessarily look like the aggregate national popular-vote tallies we see in today's (Electoral College–based) elections. The national vote total in an election in which the outcome is decided by the Electoral College amounts to an answer to a question that voters were not asked. It's an incidental byproduct of the actual election and does not describe an actually existing electorate and so does not tell us more about public opinion than the official result of the presidential election. An election structured differently would produce a different electorate.

The shapes of key governing institutions and modes of election create the voting public in every democratic system. If we wanted a more proportionally representative system or a more direct democracy, we could put one into place, but we would still be creating the electorate in such a system, not merely measuring it. Two different election systems don't just measure the same majorities and minorities in two different ways that are somehow more or less democratic or representative. Rather, they bring into being two different sets of majorities and minorities, with two different sets of aims in mind.

The particular aims that guide the ways the American system creates electorates are rooted especially in the concerns we have already seen the framers express about the dangers of majority factions and the necessity of a balanced regime. Conjuring distinct majorities around distinct and varied questions put to the public offers another way for our system to multiply competing power centers. American government, with its crosscutting layers of institutions, clearly has an unusually large number of elections, and these call into being a profusion of majorities of different sizes, characters, and priorities. Again, the system allows us to avoid becoming too divided by preventing us from becoming too unified. It seeks to keep in place a dynamic and multipolar competition, even in our

two-party politics. Where the mixed regimes of the ancient world were meant to represent deep structural divisions in their societies, the American regime, built for an egalitarian nation, in some respects works to *create* divisions and distinctions in an effort to maintain a unifying balance between majority rule and minority rights. The same voters can be part of several majorities and minorities at the same time, which helps to keep democratic citizenship from devolving into mob rule.

This is one reason why our system functions almost entirely through representation rather than the direct involvement of voters in deciding substantive policy questions. In Federalist 63, James Madison argued that what really stands out about the American republic, in comparison to its classical predecessors, is "the total exclusion of the people, in their collective capacity, from any share" in the administration of government. The American public does not rule collectively but only indirectly through elected representatives. This is not because elected leaders somehow form an elite of individuals superior to members of the broader public, but because the structure of a representative institution is inherently better suited to yielding more balanced and less divisive political action than the structure of direct democracy would. As Madison wrote in Federalist 55, regarding the far more direct democracy of ancient Athens, "Had every Athenian citizen been a Socrates, every Athenian assembly would still have been a mob." The mediating layer of representation can transform a mob into a public and only then empower government to act on its behalf. This makes it more likely that, in Madison's words, "the cool and deliberate sense of the community" will ultimately prevail. (This is also one reason why issue referenda, in which specific policy questions are put before the public directly, are at odds with the logic of our system and undermine its capacity to elevate public opinion and promote greater unity.)[2]

But our Constitution creates the democratic public in an even more basic sense, and not just on Election Day. Its institutions and procedures act to transform general preferences and dispositions into particular aims in our politics and so to transform public opinion from a disorganized jumble into a coherent terrain of priorities. The great twentieth-century sociologist Robert Nisbet described this as a transformation from "popular opinion" to "public opinion," which in turn speaks of the difference between "the mass or crowd" and an "organized community." Transforming the former into the latter was a key purpose of the framers of the Constitution. "Few things seem to have mattered more to the architects of the American political community than that government should rest upon public opinion, upon public consent and affirmation," Nisbet wrote. But by this, they did not mean mere aggregated whims. "Hence the strong emphasis in the Constitution and in *The Federalist* upon the whole set of means whereby government, without being in any way severed from the will of the people, would respond to this will only as it had become refined through subjection to constitutional processes."[3]

These processes, in James Madison's words, "refine and enlarge public views." They allow for a distinction between momentary popular impulses and durable public opinion, relying on a set of institutions built to require a popular view to be firmly held by a significant majority for an extended period before it can become a root of public action. The institutions of the American regime, therefore, give form and structure to public opinion—in effect, subjecting our republic to the will of the constituted public but not to the whim of the impulsive crowd. This contributes to the unity of our society by shaping discrete political factions around concrete public challenges and so, in essence, giving us a unified set of questions over which to be divided. The vast and complex mass of public challenges that a modern society must confront is thereby filtered into a few key choices, and the electorate's preferences regarding those then give

direction to our public life and shape the competition and negotiation in which our representatives engage. The crowd must be transformed into the public before our peculiar constitutional politics of unity can do its work.[4]

A working constitution also forms the people into a democratic public in one additional way—by building up our national spirit and investing our sentiments in the preservation of our social order. A government that works well and allows us to reduce the intensity of our tensions and divisions comes, in time, to earn our respect, and that enables us to more easily think of ourselves as one nation, as Alexander Hamilton argued in Federalist 17. James Madison thought this was one reason to avoid changing our system of government too frequently or sharply. As he put it in Federalist 49, since every appeal to the people to transform the system "would carry an implication of some defect in the government, frequent appeals would, in a great measure, deprive the government of that veneration which time bestows on every thing, and without which perhaps the wisest and freest governments would not possess the requisite stability." That veneration, which makes stability possible, also makes greater unity possible, and it does both by enabling the public to understand our government as well rooted and established and by attaching our patriotism to our constitutional order rather than just to our particular party. The importance of such sentimental attachment should not be underestimated, Madison wrote: "In a nation of philosophers, this consideration ought to be disregarded. A reverence for the laws would be sufficiently inculcated by the voice of an enlightened reason. But a nation of philosophers is as little to be expected as the philosophical race of kings wished for by Plato. And in every other nation, the most rational government will not find it a superfluous advantage to have the prejudices of the community on its side."[5]

By forming the public, therefore, the Constitution also renders Americans more public-spirited and patriotic and more inclined to

view one another as fellow citizens, even across lines of political difference. By being formed together, we come to understand ourselves as belonging together.

THIS EMPHASIS ON THE SPIRIT OF THE CITIZEN POINTS US FROM THE WAYS in which the Constitution forms the public to those in which it also forms the characters and souls of individual Americans.

This has always been a hotly contested question. Because our free society permits its citizens broad latitude to set the courses of their own lives and to pursue their understandings of the good, Americans have always wanted to imagine that our laws do not impose a moral outlook on us or require a particular kind of character of us. But the law is a teacher, unavoidably, even when what it teaches is freedom and tolerance. And the political system of a society that seeks to advance a way of life marked by great personal freedom actually makes greater demands of the characters and souls of its citizens than would living in a tyrannical regime. A nation that gives citizens a lot of freedom requires a lot of responsibility from them. For such a society to remain cohesive, it requires a particular sort of public-spirited responsibility, and it must work to see that the forms and institutions of its public life can help to inculcate that spirit and enable it to endure.

There are times in the writings of the framers of the Constitution when they seem to think this isn't necessary and, instead, appear to take a much more cynical view of the relation of the regime they proposed to the character and soul of the citizen. In one particularly Machiavellian passage of Federalist 51, for instance, James Madison wrote that the Constitution despairs of trusting in responsible leaders and citizens and so aims to substitute structural balancing mechanisms (like the separation of powers and assorted checks on power)

for good intentions on the part of people in power. As he put it: "This policy of supplying, by opposite and rival interests, the defect of better motives, might be traced through the whole system of human affairs, private as well as public. We see it particularly displayed in all the subordinate distributions of power, where the constant aim is to divide and arrange the several offices in such a manner as that each may be a check on the other that the private interest of every individual may be a sentinel over the public rights." In this way, people's selfishness, rather than their public spirit, can be channeled to advance the public good.[6]

Madison thought these kinds of constitutional constraints were essential, because moral constraints would be inadequate. As he wrote in Federalist 10, virtue won't hold back a majority faction intent on abusing its power. "If the impulse and the opportunity be suffered to coincide, we well know that neither moral nor religious motives can be relied on as an adequate control." Alexander Hamilton suggested much the same in Federalist 9, arguing that the sorts of failures of morality and character that led to the downfall of the ancient republics need not be an argument against modern republics only because of innovations in the design of governing institutions that can render their consequences less destructive.[7]

But this sort of cynicism was never the last word. The mechanisms of checking and constraint were, as we have seen, intended especially to sustain the dynamic balance of the constitutional system, and both Madison and Hamilton argued repeatedly that without such a balance, neither freedom nor union could be sustained. But while that balance was a necessary condition of the durability of the system, it was not a sufficient one. The framers clearly assumed that a distinct set of virtues in the people was essential to the kind of government they were proposing as well. These prerequisite virtues were not the very highest kind of human excellence, but they were a demanding set of republican commitments.

In the course of the Virginia ratifying convention, as his own neighbors were deciding whether to approve the new Constitution, James Madison rose to answer a charge from opponents of the document who insisted that it left far too much of an opening for corruption among elected officials. That objection, Madison insisted, was rooted in expectations of public officials that were far too low. "I have observed that gentlemen suppose, that the general legislature will do every mischief they possibly can, and that they will omit to do every thing good which they are authorized to do. If this were a reasonable supposition, their objections would be good," Madison said. But such a charge was unfair and unfounded. At the same time, Madison went on, he also did not think the country's leaders or its people would be perfect:

> Nor do I go on the grounds mentioned by gentlemen on the other side—that we are to place unlimited confidence in them, and expect nothing but the most exalted integrity and sublime virtue. But I go on this great republican principle, that the people will have virtue and intelligence to select men of virtue and wisdom. Is there no virtue among us? If there be not, we are in a wretched situation. No theoretical checks, no form of government, can render us secure. To suppose that any form of government will secure liberty or happiness without any virtue in the people is a chimerical idea.

The public's judgment, as refined by the electoral and institutional arrangements of the regime, could be relied on to drive responsible decisions much of the time. But it could be relied on because there is virtue in the public. If that were not the case, Madison argued, no amount of clever institutional design could suffice as a substitute.[8]

Hamilton offered much the same observation, arguing in Federalist 76 for a kind of middling view of human nature as the foundation

for confidence in republican government and rejecting the extreme pessimism that characterized some of the Constitution's most hostile critics. "This supposition of universal venality in human nature is little less an error in political reasoning than the supposition of universal rectitude," he argued. "The institution of delegated power implies that there is a portion of virtue and honor among mankind, which may be a reasonable foundation of confidence; and experience justifies the theory." And this applied not only to the public at large but to elected leaders too. They would not be perfect models of virtue, but neither would they be simply low and reckless. "A man disposed to view human nature as it is, without either flattering its virtues or exaggerating its vices, will see sufficient ground of confidence" in such leaders to expect them to do their duty in properly constructed institutions. The arrangement of checks and balances in the Constitution would not be a substitute for their virtue but an inducement to their putting it into practice.[9]

In fact, meeting the challenge of drawing reasonably virtuous people into public service was a key purpose of the Constitution, and an assumption of the possibility of virtue in democratic leaders, alongside a recognition of the difficulty of sustaining such virtue, lay at the heart of some of its key provisions. Madison put it plainly in Federalist 57: "The aim of every political constitution is, or ought to be, first to obtain for rulers men who possess most wisdom to discern, and most virtue to pursue, the common good of the society; and in the next place, to take the most effectual precautions for keeping them virtuous whilst they continue to hold their public trust." This extraordinary statement combines an earnest ideal with a realistic anthropology and proposes to achieve a high political purpose in light of some low human realities.[10]

Such an ambition can be realized only because those human realities are not irredeemably low and because the Constitution is not rooted in cynicism or dismissiveness about the need for a virtuous

citizenry. This is nowhere clearer than in Madison's insistence in Federalist 55 that even concerns about the potential for abuses of power (concerns he obviously shared, as we have seen) must have some limits if any kind of free government is going to be possible. He wrote:

> The sincere friends of liberty, who give themselves up to the extravagancies of this passion, are not aware of the injury they do their own cause. As there is a degree of depravity in mankind which requires a certain degree of circumspection and distrust, so there are other qualities in human nature which justify a certain portion of esteem and confidence. Republican government presupposes the existence of these qualities in a higher degree than any other form. Were the pictures which have been drawn by the political jealousy of some among us faithful likenesses of the human character, the inference would be, that there is not sufficient virtue among men for self-government; and that nothing less than the chains of despotism can restrain them from destroying and devouring one another.

This is a rousing case for the possibility of a free society and for a politics that is much more than a cynical balancing of vices. And it offers us a crucial hint about the particular kind of virtue that our free society requires and must somehow work to produce and sustain. It is, in Madison's words, "republican government" that presupposes (and, therefore, demands) certain particular moral qualities in the citizen. Each of the passages just quoted recurs to this idea of republicanism in one way or another in describing the moral underpinnings of the American regime.[11]

That emphasis on republicanism is no coincidence. It points to the substantive heart of the kind of formation our institutions mean to facilitate, and to the sort of citizen they seek to mold.

REPUBLICANISM IS A DIFFICULT CONCEPT FOR US TO DEFINE, BECAUSE IT isn't really part of our political vocabulary anymore. Some elements of it have been subsumed by other broad conceptual categories like liberalism and democracy, while others have altogether fallen out of use. But republicanism was also hard for the generation that framed our Constitution to define, and for almost the opposite reason. For many of them, it was such an essential idea and one taken for granted to such a degree that it was difficult to distinguish it from their basic political identity.[12]

Some of the major disagreements about the ratification of the Constitution were fought as disputes about which side was more truly republican, and those debates can make it difficult for us, at a distance of more than two centuries, to get a firm grasp on what the various combatants meant by republicanism. The anti-federalists, who opposed ratification, accused the Constitution of being inadequately republican, especially because the national government it proposed would be too far removed from any particular community's life to be defined by the moral character of a living polity. Republics could only really succeed on a small scale, in their view, because they required a great deal of common ground and common purpose. This view, which was widely shared by republican theorists for centuries, led the anti-federalists to fear that the proposed Constitution would not be rooted in such a communal spirit, and in fact would tend to undermine that spirit by drawing power away from the small republics—the individual states—that had, until then, constituted the union.[13]

As we have begun to see and will explore in greater depth in chapter 4, the champions of the Constitution responded to this argument by insisting that only an extended republic—on the scale of the American nation—could actually defend republican principles in a durable way. But in doing so, they sometimes deployed a definition of republicanism that was far too narrow. In Federalist 10, most

notably, James Madison defined a republic simply as "a government in which the scheme of representation takes place." This is not only an absurdly constrained definition, it also contrasts a republic to a democracy (which Madison took to involve direct participation by the public in the administration of the government, as opposed to representation) and so suggests that what stands out about republics is how little their citizens are involved in politics. While it may have served Madison's purpose in responding to a specific anti-federalist critique, this is a definition that ultimately obscures more than it reveals.[14]

In fact, involvement in politics is an essential feature of what both the framers and their opponents had in mind when talking about republican citizenship. Throughout their writings, including in many of Madison's own references to republicanism (like those quoted earlier in this chapter), they suggested that a republican ethic is an ethic of civic engagement and obligation. And they implied that republicanism is best contrasted not with democracy but with monarchy. As political scientist Martin Diamond noted, a republic, in this sense, is a regime in which politics is the domain of the public and not the private preserve of a monarch. A republic consists of citizens rather than subjects. It expects a lot of these citizens, and in return, it regards them as free and equal participants in national life. There can be aristocratic republics or oligarchic republics, in which the citizenry is narrowly defined yet broader than a single ruler. But the American republic has always been, in principle (and gradually became in practice), a democratic republic, in which the political has been the domain of a broadly defined body of citizens—indeed, the very "we the people" who articulate the Constitution.[15]

Republicanism has roots that extend to the classical world and especially to preimperial Roman life, which was a rich source of inspiration, models, symbols, and ideals for the early American republic. In an important recent book, Michael C. Hawley argues

that classical republicanism rested on the pillars of popular sovereignty, liberty, and natural law. That combination begins to distinguish republicanism from liberalism—which emphasizes the rights of the individual and treats popular sovereignty as a kind of amalgamation of those rights. Republicanism treats popular sovereignty—the rule of the people—as the achievement of a particular kind of public that takes ownership of its common life and responsibility for its shared fate, and that keeps politics grounded in a collective moral vision.[16]

In the classical republic, that commitment was sustained by the solidarity of a small community, which shared not only a common history but also, generally, a common religion and culture. The history of republicanism (and its demise in Rome and in the early-modern European republics), therefore, suggested to some Americans in the founding era that republicanism could not survive the growth or diversification of a community. But the distinctly modern republicanism of the framers, while it has deep roots in that classical vision, is modern precisely in the sense that it presumes a larger public and a significant degree of internal multiplicity. Andy Smarick of the Manhattan Institute has nicely summarized five core premises of the ethic that has characterized American republicanism since the founding era: that citizens are equal and self-governing; that they must exhibit civic virtue and actively take ownership of the fate of the community; that representative democracy is the primary means of making public decisions; that public life should advance the common good; and that government should be active but limited.[17]

This is a rough sketch, to be sure, but it can help us see both how the republicanism that underlies the Constitution is connected to classical republicanism and how it is distinct. It describes a set of ideals that clearly informed the thinking of the framers of the Constitution and, indeed, that ran so deep for them that they never even articulated it as a discrete worldview but, rather, embodied and

exemplified it. Those ideals begin with the core truths articulated in the Declaration of Independence, which are the foundational presumptions of the American political order. Without at least some general agreement about these, no American polity is imaginable, and no constitutional system could be sustained. It proceeds from these to an idea of the citizen and of the character of government that are less self-evident and more open to ongoing dispute, and which require sustained work and commitment.

Such republicanism is compatible with the early-modern ideal that we now call classical liberalism up to a point, but it is by no means interchangeable with it. It does not treat liberty as autonomy, for instance, but as self-rule, both individual and communal. This emphasis on self-rule translates into an emphasis on the community's capacity to legislate for itself—and therefore, as we shall see, into an emphasis on the legislative power more generally. This emphasis on communal self-legislation, though rarely explicitly laid out, was crucial to the thought of the American founding. The first six grievances against the British laid out in the Declaration of Independence, for instance, describe not a denial of personal rights but constraints on the capacity of the colonies to make their own laws. And the demands of communal self-rule also shape the concerns or fears of the framers—which were not only liberal but also republican fears. As Herbert Storing stated, perhaps the most complicated aim that the framers set out for American citizens is "not to protect themselves against political power but to accept the responsibility of governing themselves."[18]

American republicanism also assumes an aptitude for forbearance and self-control that is essential for resolving disputes and sustaining unity but is not necessarily implicit in the liberal ideal of the citizen. Although liberalism cannot endure without such restraint and self-command, its core principles do not articulate a case for it. Indeed, it might not be too much to say more generally

that liberalism requires a kind of citizen that only republicanism can produce, so that our liberal society requires some republican institutions to sustain itself. Leo Strauss nicely captured this relationship between the two when it comes to the crucial question of freedom, writing that, in both the modern and classical sense, "the liberal man cannot be a subject to a tyrant or to a master, and for almost all practical purposes he will be a republican."[19]

A similar dynamic connects liberalism and republicanism regarding the challenge of diversity in modern politics. Like modern liberalism, modern republicanism assumes multiplicity and diversity, not only as a mark of freedom but also of civic health and rationality as well. As James Madison wrote in Federalist 50: "When men exercise their reason coolly and freely on a variety of distinct questions, they inevitably fall into different opinions on some of them. When they are governed by a common passion, their opinions, if they are so to be called, will be the same." Entrenched disagreement, and even partisanship in society, are consequences of freedom itself— understood not only as autonomy but also as self-rule. We should neither expect nor want partisanship ever to be extinguished, "because an extinction of parties necessarily implies either a universal alarm for the public safety, or an absolute extinction of liberty."[20]

Yet even as it assumes immense diversity, republicanism presumes a set of core virtues and ideals that must hold a society together. At the heart of modern republicanism is an idea of the human being and citizen rooted in the highest traditions of the West: that we are each fallen and imperfect yet made in a divine image and possessed of equal dignity; that individuals are social creatures meant to live together; that living together requires a commitment to pursue the common good; and that this pursuit in a free and, therefore, diverse society requires of the citizen selflessness, accommodation, restraint, deliberation, and service. These commitments still leave enormous room for disagreement, though not infinite room. Yet even if we do

not have explicit and formal agreement about this idea of the human person throughout our society, our political institutions are founded in and embody this view, and therefore, in the course of our practice of constitutionalism, they will tend to teach us this view even when it is countercultural—as it frequently is. A defense of constitutionalism in America is inherently a defense of this republican anthropology, while hostility to constitutionalism is often rooted in hostility to this view of the human person and the nature of society.

These are, to be sure, only the beginnings of a sketch of the meaning of republicanism in our constitutional practice. The coming chapters will aim to fill it in further. But the importance of renewing our grasp of the republican ideal can hardly be overstated. In our time, when republicanism is no longer an implicit touchstone, and indeed, when it is nearly lost from our vocabulary even where we continue to practice it, a fuller articulation of republicanism could clarify some key disputes and vital needs. It seems likely, for instance, that most of the problems now attributed to an excess of liberalism by some on the American Right would be better understood as resulting from a shortage of republicanism, and therefore, that addressing them would require not an overthrowing of an element of our political heritage but a recovery of one that has been nearly lost.

A better understanding of republicanism could also help us see that a recommitment to the way of governing ourselves sketched out by the Constitution would be very far from morally neutral or purely procedural. Our constitutional practices and boundaries are not ends in themselves but, rather, elements of a broader and deeper vision of politics. That republican vision can help us see what it would take to both establish and sustain meaningful individual and communal self-rule. It aims at a politics of common action and of solidarity achieved by engagement and accommodation, not hostility and exclusion. In this sense, seeing how the Constitution can serve

as a means of greater unity in our society also involves seeing more clearly what the republicanism that underlies it might consist of.

But the Constitution is not just an *expression* of that republican worldview. It is intended to inculcate it and to convey it to citizens, so that life under the kind of regime created by the Constitution can be understood in part as a *formation* in republicanism.

THE CONSTITUTION CAN ENABLE SUCH FORMATION THROUGH THE WORK of its institutions, when those are working reasonably well. The law is a teacher, both in principle and practice, but it teaches even principle through its practical operation. The politics of a constitutional republic are in this respect a form of civic education, and a more powerful and enduring form than the mere teaching of facts about history or government.

This practical civic education gradually shapes the minds and souls of citizens by habituating us to a particular set of expectations and instincts about politics. As it teaches us about the mechanics of government, it teaches us that life in a diverse society consists of constant engagement across lines of difference and that those differences are often ultimately less significant than they appear and less significant than our common commitments. It can inculcate in us an instinctive sense of responsibility—that public problems are our problems and not other people's and that, in many cases, they can best be resolved by acting together to take them on. Such acting together, in turn, can teach us patience and restraint: Taking part in any process of common action, from serving on a church committee to speaking at a city council meeting to lobbying a legislator, gives us practical experience in the formalities of democratic life and in the forming of coalitions with people who don't share all our priorities. We learn to listen to others so that we may be heard and to stick to

our cause through assorted complications and delays. These are all essential liberal-democratic habits, rooted in core republican virtues.

But of course, there is also a downside to our institutions molding us to think and act as they do. When those institutions break down, as a number of them have in our time, their deformations become our deformations. When arenas of substantive civic contention in our politics become replaced by arenas of performative partisan playacting, a generation of Americans who have known no other kind of politics come to mistake political expression for civic action, and to lose some of the core habits of republican citizenship. And when the institutions of our republic offer support and protection for abuses of power—like abuses of racial or political minorities—our laws can come to teach a sort of evil as a way of life.

Such deformations are rooted in corruptions of the ethic of the American system. Although these corruptions are all too common, the fact that they are corruptions does offer some ways to combat their formative power. The fundamental premise of our regime—that majorities should rule but minorities must be protected—shapes every facet of the constitutional system, as we have already begun to see, and it can therefore also shape the souls of citizens. Countermajoritarian mechanisms like the separation of powers, the Bill of Rights, or our independent courts are not merely procedural, and they are not merely protections of individuals against the power of the government. They are not even merely protections of minorities against the power of majorities; they also protect majorities from themselves. They guard all Americans against the seductive lie that majorities get to define the standard of justice. In Federalist 51, James Madison powerfully explained this crucial point:

> Justice is the end of government. It is the end of civil society. It ever has been and ever will be pursued until it be obtained, or until liberty be lost in the pursuit. In a society under the forms of which

the stronger faction can readily unite and oppress the weaker, anarchy may as truly be said to reign as in a state of nature, where the weaker individual is not secured against the violence of the stronger; and as, in the latter state, even the stronger individuals are prompted, by the uncertainty of their condition, to submit to a government which may protect the weak as well as themselves; so, in the former state, will the more powerful factions or parties be gradually induced, by a like motive, to wish for a government which will protect all parties, the weaker as well as the more powerful.[21]

The operation of our institutions tends to teach this lesson, and when it fails to teach it, then those in our society willing to articulate it can point their fellow citizens to the principles underlying our Constitution, which plainly teach it too. The frustration that so often defines the experience of taking part in American politics is a teacher of justice. It tells us that having a few more votes than the opposition does not allow us to do anything we want. Majorities must answer to principles that stand above majority rule. Even within the bounds of those principles, majorities still need to persuade, which means they still need to advance their aims and interests within the framework of a broader common good and to help others see how the majority's aims could meet their own needs too.

Sustaining that framework means sometimes valuing the processes by which our system acts above the outcomes we desire. This requires a kind of commitment to the Constitution and veneration of the law that do not come naturally but can be achieved by the experience of living under a system of government we respect. As Charles Kesler put it, "This means that the people must not only rule through the law, but be ruled by the law: they must come to love the law, and in particular the fundamental law, the Constitution, more than they love their own sovereign authority. Or, more precisely,

they must come to identify their rule with the majestic authority of the Constitution." This kind of formation of the citizen's soul cannot be achieved by merely teaching civics in the abstract. But it can be achieved by a combination of rhetoric and experience, by teaching constitutionalism, and by living it.[22]

Such formation involves, especially, an education in restraints on democratic appetites. And that is an education essential not only for democratic citizens but also for democratic leaders. Public officials are, of course, also shaped, as individuals, by the structures of the institutions in which they operate, like any other citizen. The structures of our institutions are not only meant to channel the ambitions and will of powerful leaders in the direction of the public good, but also to mold those leaders, even to shame them, into acting the parts assigned to them by the Constitution.

In Federalist 57, responding to concerns that members of Congress might exempt themselves from the laws they enact, James Madison sketched out the complicated interplay between the structure of the system and the characters of the people involved:

> If it be asked, what is to restrain the House of Representatives from making legal discriminations in favor of themselves and a particular class of the society? I answer: the genius of the whole system; the nature of just and constitutional laws; and above all, the vigilant and manly spirit which actuates the people of America, a spirit which nourishes freedom, and in return is nourished by it. If this spirit shall ever be so far debased as to tolerate a law not obligatory on the legislature, as well as on the people, the people will be prepared to tolerate any thing but liberty. Such will be the relation between the House of Representatives and their constituents. Duty, gratitude, interest, ambition itself, are the chords by which they will be bound to fidelity and sympathy with the great mass of the people.[23]

At the heart of this interplay, and not to be underestimated, is an idea of honor and, therefore, of shame. The offices created by the Constitution come with certain obligations, and the republican character of the larger society implies powerful expectations attached to those obligations. A failure to uphold the office should, therefore, lead to disgrace. The framers expected public officials to uphold constitutional norms most of the time, and they expected voters to punish officials who failed to do so, because failing to do so would be disgraceful.

This has never been a foolproof protection against derelictions of responsibility, to put it mildly. We have learned in our own time, as prior generations have in theirs, that some public officials and some voters will be shameless and will remain unmoved by these constitutional sentiments. Although our system seeks to arm itself against the danger of the debasement of democracy into demagoguery, its protections are far from perfect. As political scientist Bryan Garsten expressed recently:

> To allow oneself to be shamed is to admit that you are subject to and ruled by society's arbiters of what is acceptable. Demagogues, as a rule, insist that they will not be so ruled; that is part of their democratic appeal. Shame is a constraint, and so is an affront to freedom. Shame condemns from a moral high ground, and so is an affront to equality. The demagogue follows these impoverished understandings of freedom and equality and concludes that conventions and laws are for suckers. Part of his pernicious influence is to persuade even his opponents that moral and constitutional scruples are forms of weakness.[24]

Our politics in recent years has been one big lesson in the truth of this description. And yet, it is a lesson that points us back to the Constitution and the ethic it works to impart. We have increasingly failed

to be formed in the ethic of republican constitutionalism because we have increasingly failed to insist on the practice of republican constitutionalism, at the level of the citizen and of the public official, of the individual and of society as a whole.

Many of our most dangerous civic vices now are the result of this degradation of our regard for and confidence in the structure of our system of government. And those very vices then contribute to the further degradation of that regard and confidence. A vicious cycle like that can only be broken by a concerted change of attitude, and therefore, of behavior. Our institutions aren't going to change before our expectations do, only after. And so, a recovery of our civic health— and especially of our capacity for unity despite our differences—has to begin with a recovery of our commitment to the ethic and the practice of American constitutionalism. Our system can help form us to be better citizens, and our practice of citizenship can, in turn, help form our system to be more effective and unifying. The vicious cycle can be transformed into a virtuous cycle. But given the condition of our politics, we, as citizens, must move first by coming to better understand our Constitution and to better live it out.

THE NATURE OF THE VIRTUES REQUIRED FOR SUCH A RENEWAL MEANS WE have to consider one further kind of civic formation that our Constitution makes possible. The operation of our institutions can teach us some essential truths and habits, but the free society requires more of its citizens than its politics alone can teach them. To put it another way: our politics requires a kind of person it does not produce by itself, and so it must depend on other institutions of our society to produce that person. It has to make room for, and to offer essential protections to, a set of preliberal and prerepublican institutions of formation—familial, communal, religious, civic, and educational.

To see how it does that, we need to grasp that the idea of rights in our political tradition is deeper than it seems. We generally think of rights as inhering in individuals. The language of the Declaration of Independence suggests as much, and our practice of the politics and jurisprudence of rights often involves the protection of individuals from the power of the government. But in fact, many of the most significant rights explicitly protected by the Constitution are communal rights, best understood as protecting minority communities and their formative institutions from the power of majorities or protecting the capacity of citizens to participate in public life.

All the rights enumerated in the First Amendment are in this category, for instance. They cannot be exercised individually, but only communally. No one practices their religion entirely on their own. The freedom of speech is of no use to someone stranded alone on a desert island. The freedom of the press and the right to petition are freedoms to take part in public life. The freedom of assembly is obviously not an individual freedom. All of these describe boundaries on the power of the federal government, acting on behalf of a majority, to constrain the ability of minorities to participate *communally* in our national life. And as a practical matter, a lot of what is protected in this way has to do with the work of forming better human beings and citizens. Individuals, families, and communities are enabled by these rights to live according to their ideals and raise their children as they believe best. Much of the work of producing republican citizens is the work of the family, religion, and civil society, and our Constitution protects the preconditions for that work—securing the private sphere so that society might benefit from the human beings produced there. This is a more sophisticated idea of freedom than the kinds of shallow and individualistic political theories often used to defend it. In this arena, as in so many others, the practice of American life runs far deeper than the theories we normally deploy to describe it.

As it was understood by the framers' generation, the Bill of Rights did not create this privileged place for civil society but merely secured it. The rights it describes are mostly prepolitical, and the activities they protect are essential prerequisites for republican politics. We have lost sight of this fact in our time, partly because the Bill of Rights has become largely a focal point for litigation. Like much of the rest of the Constitution, it has come to be thought of as a lawyer's tool. Yet even understood in legalistic terms, the Bill of Rights is a powerfully formative tool as well. As it protects the space for crucial prepolitical institutions, it also teaches the citizenry to acknowledge the importance of these institutions, or at least to confront their significance.[25]

This teaching function was essential in persuading James Madison of the value of a Bill of Rights. Madison had originally opposed the idea, seeing it as unnecessary and potentially counterproductive. He first changed his mind only because a Bill of Rights seemed necessary to secure the ratification of the Constitution in some key states. But by the time he became the author of most of the provisions of the Bill of Rights in the first Congress, Madison was a genuine advocate of the idea. As Michael Zuckert has argued, the reason had a lot to do with the potential of the Bill of Rights to shape the souls of American citizens:

> Madison shifted from viewing the matter in structural terms to pedagogical ones. Bills of rights in the republican context, he had come to believe, should not be thought of primarily as a means to appeal to the people against an oppressive master, but rather a means to convince the people not to become oppressive masters. After all, if republicanism means government by the great body of the people, why shouldn't some effort be made to teach them to respect the rights their rule should secure, and to train them to use their power rightly and wisely? Why not take more seriously the

idea of rule by the people and work to shape the people into a body fit to rule?[26]

Much the same can be said of a number of other critical assertions of rights in later amendments to the Constitution, and perhaps especially the Thirteenth, Fourteenth, and Fifteenth Amendments, which were adopted after the Civil War. These amendments, like the Bill of Rights, certainly had crucial practical implications: they prohibited slavery, extended citizenship to anyone born or naturalized in the United States, and guaranteed equal treatment under law and the right to vote to all citizens, regardless of race. But they have also had crucial pedagogical implications. They put into practice the ideals articulated in the Declaration of Independence, limiting the power of majorities in our democracy for the protection of minorities, and they force our society to always be asking itself whether it is living up to those ideals sufficiently.

There is plainly a tension between the ways in which the First Amendment and the post–Civil War amendments go about their tasks—both practical and formative. That tension is nicely captured by the distinction between the opening words of the First Amendment ("Congress shall make no law") and those of the second sentence of the Fourteenth Amendment ("No state shall make or enforce any law"). The First Amendment protects the core formative institutions of civil society by, among other things, allowing states and local communities to regard those institutions in a variety of ways, in line with their priorities and ideals. But the post–Civil War amendments insist that there must be some limits on the powers of the states to go their own ways. Some principles are national principles. The original text of the Constitution gestured in this direction in Article IV, Section 4, which says that "the United States shall guarantee to every State in this Union a Republican Form of Government." But the later amendments, as well as the Supreme

Court's gradual application of the restraints on government in the Bill of Rights to the state governments, have put some meat on the bones of that guarantee. They have meant that, while (as we shall see in the next chapter) federalism has remained a vibrant and essential feature of our system of government, our constitutional rights *as rights* mostly guard the space in which private formative work can be done, and mostly do so uniformly across the country.[27]

ALL THESE WAYS OF CONSTITUTING THE PUBLIC—AS AN ELECTORATE, AS organized bodies of citizens, and as individuals and communities equipped for self-government—are crucial to the continued functioning of our constitutional order. This formative work is an underappreciated facet of American constitutionalism, but seeing it more clearly is vital to understanding how our Constitution can better unify our society.

Needless to say, these various mechanisms of formation do not always work as intended, and many of them are not working well at all in our time. Their breakdown has a lot to do with the sorry condition of our political culture. But because we do not often think about the formative aims of the Constitution, we have not paid enough attention to the ways in which the deformation of our practice of constitutionalism also deforms us as a democratic public and makes it harder for us to hang together. Seeing how our institutions, norms, and constitutional habits shape us will help the work of diagnosing the dysfunctions of the institutions of our system in the coming chapters and will help to point toward remedies, and so toward renewal.

Grasping the centrality of civic formation to American constitutional practice will also help us to resist the inclination to approach our system of government from the top down. The unifying work

of our Constitution unavoidably begins with our multiplicity, and so it begins with us as individuals, with our communities, and with the states we live in. The Constitution created a national government, but it did not simply nationalize American politics. In pursuit of a productive tension, it both did and did not allow the states to remain self-governing sovereign actors in our system. Just as it leaves much room for civil society to do its work, it also provides enormous leeway (within the bounds of the basic rights of citizens) to state and local governments, which do most of the work of governing our society.

Federalism, the system by which power is divided, shared, and distributed among the layers of our government, therefore, connects our examination of the modes of American constitutionalism with an examination of the discrete institutions of the American system of government. Considering its character and its evolution will help us better understand the governing vision of the Constitution and will help us begin to see (as we will also find in examining our other institutions in the coming chapters) the ways in which the conflict between that vision and a rival ideal of American government that has emerged out of frustration with the Constitution has shaped our most intense public controversies. A healthy federalism is essential to the capacity of our Constitution to better unify our diverse and often divided society, but what a healthy federalism would look like is a question that has also divided Americans from the beginning.

Chapter 4

FEDERALISM

THE RELATIONSHIP BETWEEN THE STATES AND THE NATION WAS the most contentious question at the Constitutional Convention of 1787. It was the question that had brought the convention about in the first place, since the practical inadequacies of the existing American confederation showed themselves particularly as failures of the national congress to assert meaningful authority and as failures of coordination and cooperation among the states. It was the question that brought out the sharpest divisions among the delegates, too, because it forced them to decide whether the United States should be a confederation of thirteen essentially independent political units or one national state with thirteen powerful administrative subdivisions. There were adamant voices on both sides of that question, but in the end, the convention avoided coming down firmly on either side—instead inventing a new kind of "compound republic" by incorporating elements of both approaches into nearly every facet of the system it proposed.[1]

That fateful choice made the Constitution possible, but it also made continuing tension between partisans of the national and

state governments inevitable. Such tension broke out immediately after the adoption of the new constitutional system, at first mostly over economic policy but soon enough over slavery and race—that is, over whether the fundamental truth that all human beings are equal, which our country had declared before the world in the moment of its birth, could be embraced by only some states and openly scorned by others. The partial resolution of that question in the Civil War led to a recalibration of the relations between the states and the national government, which was the most significant of all the changes our Constitution has undergone in its history. But the question was only partially resolved, and many subsequent divisions and tensions in our society's life—about race, economics, and increasingly about moral and cultural differences too—have played themselves out as intergovernmental frictions between state and federal authorities.

This dynamic obviously bears on the capacity of our Constitution to facilitate greater unity and cohesion, but not in a straightforward way. On its face, administrative centralization would seem to be a unifying force, since it brings disparate places under one political umbrella. Yet forced uniformity is frequently an invitation to recalcitrance and sectionalism. Fidelity to the local can be an obstacle to national identity, yet it can also be the root of a national spirit. So in our search for greater unity, Americans must still continually ask ourselves how centralized we want our government to be. There is no denying, however, that, while American government has grown more centralized in recent decades, the American people have grown more divided. The history of federalism suggests that this is no coincidence and that alleviating our disunity will require us to lower the temperature of our national politics a little by better distinguishing between national and state responsibilities in the years to come.

THE VERY TERMS *FEDERALISM* AND *FEDERAL* ONLY REALLY TOOK ON THEIR current meanings in the debate about the Constitution. Prior to the Philadelphia Convention, *federal* referred to a confederation of essentially independent, sovereign entities and was generally contrasted with *national.*

So for instance, on May 30, 1787, the fifth day of the convention, Virginia delegate Edmund Randolph proposed a package of three propositions to organize the delegates' further work:

1. That a Union of the States merely federal will not accomplish the objects proposed by the articles of Confederation, namely common defence, security of liberty, & genl. welfare.
2. That no treaty or treaties among the whole or part of the States, as individual Sovereignties, would be sufficient.
3. That a national Government ought to be established consisting of a supreme Legislative, Executive & Judiciary.[2]

With an admirable deadpan, James Madison recorded in his notes of the convention the exchange that then took place between Randolph and South Carolina's Charles Pinckney: "Mr. Charles Pinckney wished to know of Mr. Randolph whether he meant to abolish the State Governments altogether. Mr. Randolph replied that he meant by these general propositions merely to introduce the particular ones which explained the outlines of the system he had in view."[3]

This brief exchange amounted to a kind of microcosm of the tumultuous several weeks that followed in Philadelphia. The delegates had gathered because the confederation under which Americans had lived since the American Revolution was not working. But those very delegates, and the people they represented, could not agree about whether they were aiming, therefore, to establish a single political entity or merely to revise the terms of the compact

between the states. Proponents of a strong national government were repeatedly accused of wanting to abolish the sovereignty of the states, and their replies (at least at first) involved an extraordinary amount of hand waving and misdirection. They even came to call themselves "federalists" rather than "nationalists" so as to take possession of the popular term their opponents might well otherwise have claimed.

To begin with, these federalists clearly were nationalists. James Madison proposed to give Congress a "federal negative"—essentially the power to veto any new state law. It was never quite clear how this would have worked, but Madison seemed to have wanted approval from Congress (or perhaps just the Senate) to serve as the "necessary final step" in the enactment of any new state legislation, thereby giving federal legislators a standing power of oversight over the legislative process of every state. And he was not alone in this view—his proposal was ultimately defeated, but it was not treated as ridiculous. Alexander Hamilton went even further, arguing early on at the convention that, "I have well considered the subject, and am convinced that no amendment of the confederation can answer the purpose of a good government, so long as state sovereignties do, in any shape, exist." In order to avoid the pitfalls that always undermine confederations, he insisted, "we must establish a general and national government, completely sovereign, and annihilate the state distinctions and state operations; and unless we do this, no good purpose can be answered."[4]

If nothing else, this radically centralizing view demonstrated how important national unity was to some of the key framers and how prominent it was in their thinking. That view even seemed to be winning the day at first, but its opponents among the delegates soon marshaled firm opposition, and it became clear that neither side would have the numbers to prevail. We now tend to think of the alignment of forces at the convention as dividing the larger states

(like Virginia, New York, and Pennsylvania) from the smaller ones (like New Jersey, Delaware, and Maryland). But that is not how these debates broke down. The line of division was substantive, not simply geographically self-interested, and several state delegations (including Virginia's) were internally divided on the question of the relative powers of the state and national governments. The same pattern later emerged at the various state ratifying conventions.

One source of resistance to the centralization of power ran deep in the political soul of the early republic. The political life of colonial America had been an exercise in local control by necessity: since London was far away, the Americans developed habits of decentralization, relying on their colonial legislatures to take on most of the tasks of governing, with the exception of setting military and trade policies. For many Americans, the necessity of local control had been a key argument for independence, at least as vital as the broader theoretical arguments laid out in the opening paragraphs of the Declaration of Independence. They took up arms, as they saw it, to vindicate the authority of their locally elected legislatures in most domains. The specific complaints against the British in the second half of the Declaration advanced just that vision of political life.

But the deepest and most energetic defenses of state power (both at the convention and at the state ratifying conventions) focused on what political scientist Martin Diamond called the "small-republic" argument—the view that only relatively small and cohesive political communities could remain durably free, while a vast nation with a centralized government would inevitably devolve into a tyrannical empire. The case for powerful and sovereign state governments was, in this sense, closely related to the case for republican civic ideals and democratic political forms. As Diamond put it: "First, those who opposed the adoption of the Constitution charged that it violated state sovereignty and created a consolidated national government; it was insufficiently federal. Second, they claimed it

had undemocratic, dangerously oligarchic tendencies; it was insufficiently republican. The two charges were connected by the belief that, because the new system was insufficiently federal, it must be insufficiently republican. In short, the small-republic belief underlay the ratification debates."[5]

At the heart of this small-republic belief was an argument about unity and cohesion. Its adherents, who would become known to history as the anti-federalists, were exceptionally alert to the challenges of attaching the people's allegiances to their fellow citizens and to their government, making that government meaningfully responsible to those people, and forming the kinds of citizens required to both rule and be ruled in a free society. All three goals, they thought, necessitated a relatively small polity. Centralizing power would only facilitate abuses of power.[6]

The first argument—the historical case for local control—was relatively easily answered by the federalists on the basis of the sheer dysfunction of American government under the Articles of Confederation. No one at the convention, and few Americans more generally, thought the existing system made for effective government. The colonial experience of the Americans had indeed suggested that local governance in many arenas could be sustainable if just a few key political tasks—especially the management of diplomacy, defense, and economic affairs—were managed jointly or left to a central authority, but clearly that was not working in the newly independent nation. The central authority would need to be much stronger than the Articles of Confederation allowed for in order to perform that role. Some renegotiation of authorities between the states and a national government was, therefore, in order on practical grounds, even if the long history of colonial rule from London was to be the model.

But the small-republic argument was not so easily answered. Rooted deep in the history of republican political thought and practice, and well adapted to both the puritan moralism of some

Americans and the yeomen independence of others, it was a point of view that felt like common sense to a lot of the people involved in the debates over the Constitution.

The federalist response to that argument came to revolve around an insight that James Madison developed in the course of the debates about the Constitution, which we have begun to consider from a couple of angles already. Simply put, Madison argued that the very goals set out by the small-republic anti-federalists were the reason to pursue a larger republic. He did not think it was true that smaller republics were inherently better suited to enabling the government to be responsible to the people, to be representative, and to be formative of good citizens. Madison thought that smaller republics actually tended to constrain liberty, to give majorities too much power to dominate minorities, and so to fall into despotism. For him, a larger republic on a national scale could facilitate a greater range of forces and interests and so more effectively compel cooperation across factional lines and avoid abuses of power. It was a solution to the distinct problems of republicanism, not just a response to the practical necessities of the American situation. It would allow for a durable and dynamic balancing of social pressures and for a politics of accommodation that would be better for the republican cause. Indeed, Madison came to argue that only a larger republic could actually achieve what the small-republic critics wanted. "In the extent and proper structure of the Union, therefore," he concluded in Federalist 10, "we behold a republican remedy for the diseases most incident to republican government. And according to the degree of pleasure and pride we feel in being republicans, ought to be our zeal in cherishing the spirit and supporting the character of Federalists."[7]

Madison's solution was ingenious and elegant, but it was also convenient. At the convention, it spoke to delegates who understood the depth of the practical problem they were commissioned to

solve but needed some way to assuage the principled concerns of the anti-federalists. Madison's case for it in several debates among the delegates seemed to be genuinely persuasive, especially to the Connecticut delegation. But it did not persuade them to adopt the radical hostility to the states that characterized the early views of Madison, Hamilton, and some other federalists. Rather, it opened the path to a middle ground on federalism, which, in a classic example of the Constitution's logic of productive tension, embraced elements of both of the competing views about state and national power at once, even where they contradicted each other.

The most familiar implication of this middle-ground approach and the heart of what became known as the "Connecticut Compromise" at the convention had to do with representation in Congress. Here, there really were some tensions between small and large states that had to do with securing power in the new system. Rather than simply giving every state the same level of representation in Congress or varying the sizes of state delegations based on population, the Constitution ultimately did both—the first in the Senate, and the second in the House.

But on the question of federalism, the compromise was more complex and the different approaches more thoroughly intertwined. The differing views came to be resolved into one core question: Would the national government govern the people directly, with the states serving at most merely as its administrative arms? Or would the national government govern only the states, and only in a few discrete areas, while the state governments alone would then have direct contact with the people? Here, the convention worked its way toward a novel concept: the state governments and the national government would both govern the people directly but with regard to different matters. Broadly speaking, the federal government would govern the economy, diplomacy, and defense—which may sound like a short list but (especially given the reach of economic policy)

encompasses a great deal. And the states would continue to govern everything else, including deploying the core police powers that constitute most of what government does. When state and federal laws came into conflict, federal law would generally be supreme, and the Constitution itself would be "the supreme law of the land," as the document puts it in Article VI. But such conflicts would be rare, the framers hoped, because the federal government was assigned to govern in only a select number of areas. As a practical matter, most governing would still be done by the states, and they would remain sovereign even as members of the union.

This would be a complicated arrangement. In Federalist 39, Madison described it this way: "The proposed Constitution, therefore, is, in strictness, neither a national nor a federal Constitution, but a composition of both. In its foundation it is federal, not national; in the sources from which the ordinary powers of the government are drawn, it is partly federal and partly national; in the operation of these powers, it is national, not federal; in the extent of them, again, it is federal, not national; and, finally, in the authoritative mode of introducing amendments, it is neither wholly federal nor wholly national."[8]

The federalists thought it was essential that the national government not depend on the states for the execution of its laws. As Alexander Hamilton wrote in Federalist 16, any genuine government "must carry its agency to the persons of the citizens. It must stand in need of no intermediate legislations; but must itself be empowered to employ the arm of the ordinary magistrate to execute its own resolutions." Within their distinct spheres, the federal government and the state governments each have full sovereign authority. But their spheres are separate—or at least they are intended to be.[9]

This structure was achieved by implicitly accepting the priority of the states but the superiority of the federal government. A doctrine of enumerated and delegated powers is implied in the body of

the Constitution, and is spelled out in the Tenth Amendment, which says that "the powers not delegated to the United States by the Constitution, nor prohibited by it to the States, are reserved to the States respectively, or to the people." So in essence, the states are taken to have started out with all the customary powers of government, but then the Constitution delegated some of those to the central government and restrained the states from invading those delegated powers. But unlike federal powers, the extent of state powers is not enumerated. Only limits on those powers are enumerated. As Madison put it, "The powers delegated by the proposed Constitution to the federal government are few and defined, those which are to remain in the State governments are numerous and indefinite." This default assumption of state authority long helped to protect the American system from the powerful pull of centralization in modern government. It has become attenuated in our time, as we shall see, but it still contributes to an exceptionally decentralized mode of governance in America.[10]

It is, however, a complicated balance to maintain—more difficult even than the separation of powers within the federal government. As Madison acknowledged in a 1792 essay:

It must not be denied that the task of forming and maintaining a division of power between different governments is greater than among different departments of the same government; because it may be more easy (though sufficiently difficult) to separate, by proper definitions, the legislative, executive, and judiciary powers, which are more distinct in their nature, than to discriminate, by precise enumerations, one class of legislative powers from another class, one class of executive from another class, and one class of judiciary from another class; where the powers being of a more kindred nature, their boundaries are more obscure and run more into each other.[11]

This peculiar balancing act, which was the product of grudging and gradual compromise from both directions, amounts to a genuine middle ground. It is a novel arrangement, with no real precedent in the history of republics—"without a model," as Madison put it, "and to be explained by itself, not by similitudes or analogies." It answers neither to the theory of the small-republic anti-federalists nor to the radical nationalism of the federalists. "As far as either of them is well founded," Madison wrote in Federalist 37, "it shows that the convention must have been compelled to sacrifice theoretical propriety to the force of extraneous considerations." But it turned out to offer some powerful advantages, which are essential to understanding the strengths of the Constitution, and its capacity to build national cohesion.[12]

For one thing, the Constitution's novel federalism is an extension of its broader approach of averting abuses of power by setting powers against one another. As Madison argued in Federalist 51, "In the compound republic of America, the power surrendered by the people is first divided between two distinct governments, and then the portion allotted to each subdivided among distinct and separate departments. Hence a double security arises to the rights of the people. The different governments will control each other, at the same time that each will be controlled by itself."[13] This approach assumes some degree of jealousy and competition between the states and the federal government, just as between the branches of each. Yet at the same time, it can permit our national politics to specialize in national challenges. "The federal Constitution forms a happy combination in this respect," Madison wrote, "the great and aggregate interests being referred to the national, the local and particular to the State legislatures."[14]

When it comes to those particular and local questions, the dual nature of American government allows for a diversity of governing approaches to coexist at once, even to compete, without having to be resolved into a single national approach. This makes it possible

for some of the most contentious of all governing issues—crucial questions of religion, education, morals legislation, criminal law, and much else—to be addressed in different ways in different places. That can sometimes lower the temperature of our national politics a little without diminishing the importance of those governing questions, enabling intense divisions to be contained while Americans cooperate across lines of difference on other matters.

We sometimes think of such substantive diversity as a modern phenomenon and imagine the early republic as far more unified. But that was not the view of the generation that adopted the Constitution. The challenges of political diversity were very much on the minds of the framers and were at the heart of the arguments advanced by both sides of the debate over the nature of American federalism. The federalists backed a stronger national state because they worried that, without such a union, the diversity of the nation would pull it apart. The anti-federalists opposed centralization because they worried that too strong a union would fail to represent the multiplicity of the society and that, according to Herbert Storing, "a national government would be compelled to impose a crude uniform rule on American diversity, which would in fact result in hardship and inequity for many parts of the country." That uniformity would be particularly harmful to the task of civic formation, they thought, because such formation assumed an intense homogeneity that can only be achieved at the state or local level. National homogeneity in a vast society could only be achieved on terms so thin and shallow as to be inadequate foundations for real civic life. Both sides thus took a multiplicity of political (and up to a point moral) views for granted and sought to govern well in light of it.[15]

The middle ground discovered by the convention ended up opening some unexpected vistas for unity in American life by balancing these concerns. It allowed the state governments to remain significantly more republican (and so more focused on civic formation

in light of majority views) than the national government, which could be somewhat more liberal (and so more focused on protecting minority rights and social peace). And it afforded moral minorities the opportunity to pursue their visions of the good within a broader union by building communities in more friendly jurisdictions. Here, too, the logic of restraining the dangers of factionalism by multiplying their number implicitly came into effect.

But this unifying potential took time to emerge, and it was by no means the first face of American federalism. At the outset, especially because the federalist compromise was achieved by excluding Black Americans from the circle of citizenship (indeed even of humanity) and leaving open the question of slavery, the balance of power between the states and the federal government was extremely uneasy and contentious and was shadowed by a growing threat of dissolution and, ultimately, civil war.

SIGNIFICANT TENSIONS FIRST AROSE ESPECIALLY AROUND TRADE AND economic development. These were delegated to the national government, but the national debate about them quickly devolved into regional disputes that raised questions about the viability of a national economic policy. By the first decade of the nineteenth century, American politics had become regionalized, with the northeastern states opposing the economic policy of the ruling Jeffersonians so intensely that there was open talk of secession among New Englanders. Jefferson's new Democratic Party ultimately won that struggle at the ballot box—indeed, it won so decisively that the Federalist Party essentially ceased to exist by the mid-1810s. But the Jeffersonians also learned some hard practical lessons, both economic and geopolitical, and gradually moderated their economic views. That first threat of secession was serious, but it lifted.

It was with regard to a much more consequential question, indeed a morally existential question, that the original federalist compromise ultimately ran aground: the question of slavery and race. Slavery was legal in most states at the time of the Constitutional Convention, but it was practiced on a mass scale only in the South. The delegates were divided on the issue, but the southern states (especially Georgia and the Carolinas) made it clear they would not permit the status quo on slavery to change much. The convention, therefore, went out of its way to avoid taking up the issue of slavery—addressing it only in three specific contexts where it was simply unavoidable, given the powers the new Constitution would delegate to the national government.

The first was a function of Congress's power to regulate international trade. Some southern states were concerned that this power might be used to end the transatlantic slave trade, on which they insisted they still depended. And indeed, some northern delegates did want the new national government to prohibit that trade. The delegates ultimately decided that Congress should not be altogether denied the authority to restrict the transatlantic slave trade, but that it should be required to leave it alone for two decades, until 1808, by which time the southern states believed they would be less dependent on the continuing importation of slaves. There was real discord over this approach. James Madison, although he was a Virginian and owned slaves himself, thought the global slave trade should be ended sooner and that "so long a term will be more dishonorable to the National character than to say nothing about it in the Constitution." Gouverneur Morris, a New York delegate and opponent of slavery, wanted the Constitution to state specifically that a delay in Congress's power to restrict the slave trade was inserted at the insistence of Georgia and the Carolinas so that it would be clear that other states did not agree. In the end, the delay was adopted—and Congress

ultimately did end that wicked trade as soon as the Constitution permitted it, prohibiting the importation of slaves to the United States in 1808.[16]

Second, there was also no way to avoid the question of slavery when determining representation in Congress—since the southern states wanted men and women held in bondage to count as part of state populations for purposes of representation. They would have denied citizenship to enslaved people but used their numbers to empower their enslavers. The northern states wanted to exclude enslaved people from being counted so that slave states would not end up with more power than free states. In the end, they drew on a compromise embedded in the Articles of Confederation's rules about how the states were taxed, and counted three-fifths of the enslaved population of any state for purposes of representation. But even in codifying that compromise, the convention could not bring itself to speak openly of slavery—referring instead (in a section later nullified by the Fourteenth Amendment) to the free persons living in each state and "three fifths of all other persons."[17]

A third implicit reference to slavery also turned out to be unavoidable: the question whether an enslaved person escaping into a state where slavery was prohibited would, thereby, become free needed to be resolved before some southern delegates would support the Constitution. To appease them, the convention determined that escaped slaves could not be made free by the laws of the state to which they escaped. But on this front, too, the compromise language (later made moot by the Thirteenth Amendment) avoided describing what it really meant to do. It read: "No Person held to Service or Labour in one State, under the Laws thereof, escaping into another, shall, in Consequence of any Law or Regulation therein, be discharged from such Service or Labour, but shall be delivered up on Claim of the Party to whom such Service or Labour may be due."

Such obviously evasive language has long suggested to some readers of the Constitution that the framers were ashamed of the document's entanglement with slavery, or even that they implicitly hoped that evil institution would fade away with time, and left room for that to happen in the system they created. There is some evidence to support that view. Some of the framers (including some southerners) clearly did want slavery to end, even if they were prepared to compromise with its defenders for the sake of making a constitution possible. In the course of the debate about Congress's power to restrict the slave trade, North Carolina delegate Hugh Williamson told the convention that "both in opinion and practice he was against slavery; but thought it more in favor of humanity, from a view of all circumstances, to let in South Carolina and Georgia on those terms, than to exclude them from the Union." In the same discussion, James Madison argued that it would be better to keep the language touching on the slave trade vague because he "thought it wrong to admit in the Constitution the idea that there could be property in men."[18]

Abraham Lincoln advanced this view of the framers' intentions too. In an 1854 speech, Lincoln drew his listeners' attention to the very fact we have just seen: "At the framing and adoption of the constitution, they forbore to so much as mention the word 'slave' or 'slavery' in the whole instrument." He thought this suggested that the framers viewed slavery as a disgrace:

The thing is hid away, in the Constitution, just as an afflicted man hides away a wen or a cancer, which he dares not cut out at once, lest he bleed to death; with the promise, nevertheless, that the cutting may begin at the end of a given time. Less than this our fathers could not do; and more they would not do. Necessity drove them so far, and farther, they would not go. But this is not all. The earliest Congress, under the constitution, took the same

view of slavery. They hedged and hemmed it in to the narrowest limits of necessity. . . . The plain unmistakable spirit of that age, towards slavery, was hostility to the principle, and toleration only by necessity.[19]

That may well have been true of many of the framers, even some of the southerners among them. But clearly some delegates were intent on protecting slavery and were willing to scuttle the effort to adopt a constitution to do so.

Taking in the convention's treatment of the subject as a whole, it is hard to generalize regarding the framers' views of slavery, but it is impossible to avoid the simple fact that the Constitution treated slavery as a state issue. Because the new national government would govern the American people directly rather than governing the state governments, the framers sought to establish clear lines of demarcation between state and national matters. The exceedingly limited mentions of slavery in the Constitution stand out not only for their evasive language but also for the fact that they all treat slavery as a matter for the states. Enslaved people are described as "held to Service or Labour in one State" or as residents of a state, and even the power to restrict the international slave trade was described in the final document in terms of "the Migration or Importation of such Persons as any of the States now existing shall think proper to admit."

This was a way to prevent disagreements over slavery from derailing the convention and destroying the union. It was also an application of the basic logic of the middle ground the convention had reached regarding relations between the states and the national government. But it was ultimately unsustainable. Slavery was such a profound moral evil and so obviously at odds with the fundamental principles of the American republic that it proved impossible to treat it as a matter to be left up to different Americans in different places

to resolve in different ways. As new states joined the union in the early nineteenth century, the question whether they should permit or prohibit slavery created endless tensions, and the precarious compromises that kept these tensions from exploding the union proved, in time, to be simply unmanageable.

In 1858, Abraham Lincoln put his finger on the core problem and on the sheer impossibility of applying the accommodative logic of federalism to the particular question of human bondage in America. Drawing on New Testament imagery, he told the Illinois Republican Convention in Springfield:

> A house divided against itself cannot stand. I believe this government cannot endure, permanently half slave and half free. I do not expect the Union to be dissolved—I do not expect the house to fall—but I do expect it will cease to be divided. It will become all one thing, or all the other. Either the opponents of slavery will arrest the further spread of it, and place it where the public mind shall rest in the belief that it is in course of ultimate extinction; or its advocates will push it forward till it shall become alike lawful in all the States, old as well as new, North as well as South.[20]

This was one issue where federalism simply would not be good enough. Lincoln was right, as usual. But it would take a civil war, the temporary dissolution of the union, and its reintegration by force to even start on a path toward resolution.

In the wake of the war, the basic character of the federalist compromise of the Constitution was transformed. The prohibition of slavery and the securing of equal treatment under law regardless of race more broadly were added to the powers specifically delegated to the federal government by the Thirteenth, Fourteenth, and Fifteenth Amendments. The extension of a guaranteed right to vote to Black Americans (in the Fifteenth Amendment) and later to women

(in the Nineteenth Amendment) further extended the range of federal authority. These did not exactly alter the policies of the national government as determined by the original Constitution—which, of course, did not prohibit Blacks or women from voting; only the laws of some states did that. But it altered the balance of federalism and the meaning of the American union.[21]

In time, the logic of the Fourteenth Amendment, in particular, also gradually came to be understood (by judges, legislators, and citizens) to require the securing of the other individual and communal rights articulated in the Bill of Rights, not only against federal power but also against the power of the states. The freedoms of speech and religion, and the various protections afforded to citizens in those early amendments, came to be applied by courts to the actions of state legislatures and officials.

This rebalancing of federalism did not go smoothly. The attempted reconstruction of the South on these new foundations, following the Civil War, was soon abandoned for the sake of political expediency. Vicious and often violent racism persisted, and far into the twentieth century was routinely defended on the grounds of "states' rights." The federal civil rights statutes of the 1950s and 1960s, which were rooted in the post–Civil War amendments, brought enormous federal power to bear against these persistent evils and made a tremendous positive difference. But those statutes also created complicated new uncertainties in American federalism and raised thorny questions about whether the protection of Black Americans could serve as a template for the use of federal power in other arenas and on behalf of other groups of Americans that are very far from analogous—whether, in essence, the federalism of the Constitution should be abandoned altogether and not just reconceived to account for a distinct and grave moral wrong.

That question has been unavoidably entangled with a broader critique of the character of the American Constitution. That critique

emerged in the course of the nineteenth and twentieth centuries under the banner of progressivism and also, at first, had much to do with objections to the federalist middle ground in particular.

PROGRESSIVISM BEGAN AS A RESPONSE TO THE MASSIVELY DISRUPTIVE social change let loose on American life by industrialization and the growing scale of the market economy in the nineteenth century. As industrial capitalism drove movements of population from farms to cities and drew millions of immigrants to American shores, dense urban poverty presented novel challenges to our society. Those same economic forces also brought about the emergence of immensely powerful corporations in a number of sectors—oil and coal, steel and railroads, finance, and more—which exercised unprecedented economic and political power. American progressivism began as a loose movement of journalists, activists, social reformers, academics, and politicians who first sought to draw attention to the dire consequences of these changes and, in time, argued for new approaches to public policy to address them.

The progressive critique took a variety of forms, but as it coalesced into a political movement, it came to focus especially on the inadequacy of American government to the scale of these new challenges. The progressives insisted that, for the protection of workers, consumers, and citizens, corporate power required a regulatory response that the American regime was simply ill-equipped to offer. And the structure of the Constitution was the primary reason for that insufficiency. Herbert Croly, a journalist and leading progressive intellectual, argued that, while the Constitution had shown a sophisticated grasp of the dangers of concentrated political power, it was totally blind to the dangers of concentrated economic power, and its restraint of political power through decentralization and

competing power centers left it incapable of answering the challenge of corporate power. To meet that challenge, the framers' constitutionalism would need to be largely abandoned, and Americans had to embrace a much more centralized and consolidated approach to government—one that would empower elected officials to govern in the public interest with far fewer constraints.[22]

Federalism, in time, became a primary target of this critique. Although some early forms of progressivism were friendly to diverse uses of local power (and indeed involved state-level activists resisting a kind of conservative nationalism), by the early twentieth century, as an ambitious progressive political program took shape, progressivism had itself become largely a nationalist movement. The logic of that approach was articulated with particular force by Theodore Roosevelt. In 1910, by then a former president contemplating running again, Roosevelt delivered what came to be known as his "New Nationalism" speech, laying out a comprehensive progressive agenda. After defining the challenge of restraining corporate interests for the public good and describing the American system of government as cumbersome and fragmented, he said, "The New Nationalism puts the national need before sectional or personal advantage. It is impatient of the utter confusion that results from local legislatures attempting to treat national issues as local issues. It is still more impatient of the impotence which springs from over-division of governmental powers, the impotence which makes it possible for local selfishness or for legal cunning, hired by wealthy special interests, to bring national activities to a deadlock."[23]

This argument amounted to a rejection of the core logic of the federalist compromise. The progressives' focus was on economic issues, which were, in fact, delegated to the federal government by the Constitution. But they argued that this delegation defined the economic sphere too narrowly and that effectively regulating

American economic life actually required national policymaking on the full range of domestic issues. They believed that, in an industrial market economy, the power to regulate interstate commerce should amount to a power to regulate almost everything. The federal courts, after first resisting this view, gradually embraced it in time, and federal power became increasingly expansive.

Although the progressive critique of the Constitution was fundamentally rooted in an economic argument, it amounted to a rejection of the deepest assumptions underlying the framers' constitutionalism. For the sake of more effective regulation in the public interest, it called for undoing the intricate balancing mechanisms of federal power, exhibiting a great deal of confidence in the capacity of public officials to use power responsibly and remarkably little concern about the dangers of concentrated political power. This approach also conceived of national unity quite differently than the framers of the Constitution did: rather than forging common ground among rival factions through the common work of arriving at negotiated accommodations, the progressives assumed that greater consolidation under centralized leadership would yield a more united society. The president was the central figure in this revised theory of American government. In fact, Roosevelt pointedly placed Congress last in his reconception of the work of the three branches, insisting, "This New Nationalism regards the executive power as the steward of the public welfare. It demands of the judiciary that it shall be interested primarily in human welfare rather than in property, just as it demands that the representative body shall represent all the people rather than any one class or section of the people."[24]

There was little sensitivity, in this view, to the tension between majority power and minority rights—in fact, progressivism implicitly assumed that more populist governing mechanisms with fewer restraints on majorities would actually result in more technocratic expert rule by elites, which would yield more rational governance.

Such rational governance would have to reach beyond the few domains assigned to the national government and enter into more comprehensive regulation of American economic life.

The framers of the Constitution had sought to assure their anti-federalist critics that the federal government would not be in a position to wrestle most governing power from the states in this way. Alexander Hamilton even argued that the sorts of people who would seek power at the national level would never want to involve themselves in the minutia of state and local issues, writing in Federalist 17:

> The regulation of the mere domestic police of a State appears to me to hold out slender allurements to ambition. Commerce, finance, negotiation, and war seem to comprehend all the objects which have charms for minds governed by that passion; and all the powers necessary to those objects ought, in the first instance, to be lodged in the national depository. The administration of private justice between the citizens of the same State, the supervision of agriculture and of other concerns of a similar nature, all those things, in short, which are proper to be provided for by local legislation, can never be desirable cares of a general jurisdiction. It is therefore improbable that there should exist a disposition in the federal councils to usurp the powers with which they are connected; because the attempt to exercise those powers would be as troublesome as it would be nugatory; and the possession of them, for that reason, would contribute nothing to the dignity, to the importance, or to the splendor of the national government.[25]

This remarkable argument has not stood the test of time at all. Progressivism sought to transform the constitutional system into a national regulatory regime that would take on precisely the governing issues that the federalist compromise left in the hands of the

states, and that would do so by also abandoning the essence of the separation of powers.

The progressives understood that this would require some amendments to the Constitution, and the impedimentary role assigned to the state legislatures in the amendment process moved them to even greater hostility toward federalism. They wanted to make American democracy more direct and unmediated and, at the same time, more subject to centralized control. They did have some success, securing constitutional amendments for the direct election of senators and for a national income tax in 1913. But they were also stymied in many important respects—which only heightened their impatience.

Ironically, despite their hostility toward federalism, the progressives actually made more progress in the states than in Washington. Many state legislatures adopted processes for enacting state laws and even changing state constitutions by initiative and referendum. Assorted progressive transparency requirements that went nowhere at the national level were adopted in the states. So were proposals to make judges elected (or subject to recalls). Many states adopted laws making their attorney generals and other cabinet officials directly elected, too, and rendered their constitutions far easier to amend. The sorry effects of many of these reforms in our time speaks to the wisdom of the framers' quite different approach, but the fact of these reforms is a testament to the transformative legacy of the Progressive Era.

Yet even as it thrived in many states, progressivism sharpened its hostility toward the framers' notion of a compound republic. In the course of the twentieth century and into the twenty-first, the progressive economic critique of federalism became melded with the logic of the civil rights legislation discussed above into an expansive rejection of the logic of federalism and the traditions of constitutionalism. This joining of forces was not preordained. Progressivism,

in its early phases, was often drenched in vicious bigotry and racism. But as it matured, progressivism increasingly embraced a more egalitarian vision and also realized the potential of combining a technocratic case for centralization with a morally infused case for aggressive federal action into a transformative agenda that proposes an alternative to the entire logic of American constitutionalism.

That agenda dismisses the framers' skepticism about power, indeed their broader vision of human nature and social thought, without bothering to refute it or contend with it much at all. As we shall see in the coming chapters, its focus extended well beyond federalism, offering a critique of each of the core institutions of the American system, and even a kind of rival constitutional vision rooted in a peculiar mix of radical democracy and elite self-confidence. It is a vision that assumes a preexisting unity waiting to be represented at last rather than assuming durable differences that need to be negotiated and assuaged.

This view began with a hostility toward federalism for a reason. The republican logic of the Constitution and its approach to the question of unity in our diverse society finds perhaps its fullest expression in the peculiar federalist structure of the American regime. The pursuit of greater national cohesion in our time, therefore, has to begin by grasping the potential of the framers' federalism (duly amended by the lessons of the struggles against slavery and racism) to allow us to be more unified by allowing us to remain more diverse—and so by loosening the hold of the progressive political vision on our self-understanding.[26]

AS WE HAVE BEGUN TO SEE FROM SEVERAL ANGLES, THE PURPOSE OF OUR national government—and the purposes of the institutions that compose it—is not to put into effect a single, unified policy vision but to

enable our society to take on common challenges through common action, despite the fact that Americans sometimes do not all share one such vision. This is why the central institution of our national government is not the executive (which puts an agenda into action) but the legislature (which negotiates through durable differences). It is also why the range of governing questions assigned to the national government (which must ultimately negotiate toward one particular course) should be kept reasonably narrow, while those left to the states (which can sometimes pursue different and competing courses at the same time) should be made as broad as is reasonably possible.

It is, therefore, also why we should not think of the states and the national government as collaborating in one joint governance effort but as governing in different domains. Generally speaking, the states and the federal government are not intended to cooperate, and "cooperative federalism" (which has usually involved the states serving as deputized agents of federal action, often in return for federal dollars) is at odds with the logic of the Constitution. By that original logic, states can cooperate or compete with one another, and the federal government should secure the preconditions for both to work smoothly, but state and federal action should be mostly kept apart.

That logic holds enormous promise for better addressing our contemporary challenges. Americans have obviously grown more divided in recent decades, but our mode of governance has not grown fragmented. On the contrary, our politics and government are now more centralized and more national than they have usually been in our history. That a more divided America has a more consolidated government is not a coincidence. And a less consolidated government could well help us grow less divided.

The nationalization of our politics is clearly a key part of the story of polarization and division in American life—as both cause and effect. The issues that dominate local and state politics tend to

be more practical and immediate than our national debates and so lend themselves better to bargaining and accommodation. National issues now too often reach us as abstractions and seem to require us only to identify with one political tribe or another. By allowing national debates to dominate our perception of politics, we therefore deny ourselves the opportunity to deal with people who differ from us and end up, instead, just talking about such people at a distance and with members of our own camp.

But even more fundamentally, a politics that tends to emphasize symbolic debates over practical governance leads us to mistake expression for action and so to understand the very fact of the existence of people with different views from ours as a problem to be solved. The fact that someone, somewhere, is saying or doing something I profoundly disagree with is not inherently a problem for me or for our society. Given how diverse our society has always been, we should want a system of government that lets us live with such differences. But living with multiplicity does not come naturally. We need a lot of help from our political culture and our institutions before we can tolerate diversity. Letting differences exist without having them become existential problems requires some sophisticated modes of civic and political life. In some cases, that must involve keeping some questions beyond the reach of majorities altogether—as the Bill of Rights does, for instance. But in some domains, simply relegating differences to the private sphere and insisting that they have no public implications will not do. With regard to those matters, federalism offers a crucial avenue of action.

There is a role for government in providing some support to Americans looking to live in accordance with their understandings of the good life, yet there will always be differences about what sorts of support should be lent and to what kinds of understandings of the good life there are. Letting people in one part of the country live out one sort of answer to these questions while others elsewhere live

out another is a tremendous source of flexibility and strength for American society. There is no real alternative to legislating morality. But by allowing most such legislation to happen at the state or local level, we can allow for a lot of variation in how different places approach that formative moral task. The Constitution's guarantee of republican representative institutions in every state and of the freedom to move from place to place in our society makes it possible to give states (and within states, to give localities) a lot of leeway when it comes to determining the character of different political communities.[27]

There are limits to what local majorities should be able to legislate, of course. We have seen, for instance, that slavery posed such a limit and that the continuing imperative to combat racism does too. The Bill of Rights points to others. So should the need to sustain a common economic market across our society and the need to preserve our national security. The moral convictions of the American people may lead the nation to conclude that further matters must be resolved nationally, and we will always debate whether and when such limits should be set, and even whether the Constitution requires them. But when we can, in good conscience, we should want those limits to be relatively broad so that different communities can approach deeply meaningful questions differently. Allowing for diverse modes of self-government allows us to live together across difference and so also to share in common an idea of the common good that makes room for a great deal of substantive moral diversity.

Prioritizing the preconditions for that variety of political forms could help turn down the temperature of our national politics without ignoring or dismissing crucial moral and political questions and without leaving minority communities in our society feeling permanently excluded or subordinated. When decisions are made closer to the level of the community and the individual, more Americans can

feel included in the work of self-government. In this sense, perhaps the highest purpose of federalism is forging legitimacy by making greater civic participation and representation possible. The goal of a policymaking process is very often not just finding the right answer to a public question, but finding an answer that is most satisfactory to the relevant public, and which the people affected feel reflects an understanding of what matters to them. Public policy presents us not with engineering problems but with political ones.

We often understand such political problems through our communal identities and not simply as individuals, and in this respect, too, a revival of the original logic of federalism has a lot to offer us. The key dividing lines in American life today are not regional, as they once were. They tend to be ideological but not quite individualistic; they involve questions about how our communities live their lives. For that reason, they can be best answered in the form of a diversity of communities and not just of options for individuals. A robust federalism allows for a multiplicity of communal forms. As Peter Berger and Richard John Neuhaus put it in their classic communitarian manifesto *To Empower People,* "the goal of public policy in a pluralistic society is to sustain as many particularities as possible, in the hope that most people will accept, discover, or devise one that fits."[28]

We have already seen that some of our most essential civil rights—like those protected by the First Amendment—are ultimately communal rights in this respect. The federalist division of powers enables us to vindicate those rights in different ways, and not only in our private lives. It makes it possible for us to take seriously the idea of communal liberty, which has always been essential to the larger American ideal of liberty but has never been sufficiently articulated in our political thought. Our communal liberties are frequently crucial to our pursuit of happiness as individuals and to our sense of satisfaction. But the Constitution's protection of these

liberties leaves room for different approaches to the relationship between public policy and communal priorities in areas like education, welfare, religion, morality, and culture. Expressing these different approaches as different governing decisions in different places can contribute to the sense of allegiance that members of different communities feel for our larger society. But insisting that they be resolved in one way for the entire nation is more likely to deepen our divisions.

Individual rights and communal rights are sometimes in tension, to be sure. Our Constitution does provide some protections to individuals from oppression by the communities of which they are a part. But it also offers protections to communities from oppression by political majorities in the larger society. Here, too, it is crucial that there is not just one majority in American life, which wields public power by itself. There are numerous overlapping and competing majorities, each with real but limited power. By adding geographic depth to this institutional framework, American federalism enables it to be both more representative and more protective.

It is vital to see, however, that this does not mean that the federalism of the Constitution prefers the local to the national as a matter of principle, or even of prudence. Federalism is not localism. And it is not subsidiarity—a vital concept from Catholic social thought that contends that power should be kept as close to the people it touches as reasonably possible. Because American federalism leaves most governing authority in the hands of the states, it can often point in the same direction as subsidiarity. But at the heart of federalism is a separation of authorities rather than a layering of them. The national government does not quite support or encircle the states. It does not stand above them on most occasions, but beside them. It acts on the people directly, just as the states do, but regarding different public concerns.

This separation of authorities serves some pragmatic and practical purposes. It allows for experimentation and for keeping governing mistakes relatively contained. As legal scholar Michael Greve has put it, "If government has to screw up, as invariably it will, it's best not to do it all over the place, all at once." It sometimes allows for more direct accountability and transparency, although the demise of local journalism has meant that it is now often easier to know what is happening in Washington than in our state capitals. Above all, this separation of authorities allows for greater social peace, cohesion, and unity. This was its purpose and can still be its great benefit for us.[29]

THE ABILITY OF AMERICAN FEDERALISM TO SERVE THIS PURPOSE HAS BEEN constrained in our time, however, by a tendency to conflate state and national authorities. For almost a century now, we have seen national political ambitions increasingly pursued through the national deployment of state governing powers. In education, health care, welfare, housing, and other key domestic arenas, Congress has made vast federal funds available to the states in return for states' acting as administrators of federal programs. The result has been an intentional confusion of state and federal means and ends, which has advanced the nationalization of our politics, enervated state politics, and consolidated American government into an increasingly unitary policymaking framework. By now, this is the norm. It is what we think federalism means, but it is a federalism that cannot hold us together.

There have been benefits to these measures, to be sure. Federal goals have, in some cases, been better advanced by making use of the reach and experience of state officials. The involvement of the states and, in some cases, also the diversity of forms of implementation

made possible by letting states experiment with different uses of federal dollars, has sometimes made these programs more effective, more popular, and easier to enact. The federal government has also taken great fiscal pressures off the states—immense federal borrowing (and the support it makes possible, both in normal times and during national emergencies and economic downturns) allows the state governments to balance their budgets without heavy borrowing of their own.

But the costs have been enormous. Twisted combinations of state and federal authorities have made for poorly designed and administered public programs and for confused chains of authority and accountability—especially in health care, education, and welfare. And the full range of domestic issues has been effectively nationalized so that we now argue about them as large, unitary questions and, therefore, think of them in partisan, divisive, and increasingly abstract terms.

This cannot change quickly. But it can change over time if we understand the unifying purpose of American federalism and grasp the need to distinguish and separate state from federal domains. We may decide we can no longer limit the federal government merely to economic regulation, core civil rights, and foreign affairs. Some renegotiation of the properly national domains is certainly legitimate, particularly if it is undertaken by Congress rather than through regulatory or judicial action. But those domains that are national ought to be exclusively so, or as close to exclusively as we can get, and those that are left to the states should belong to them.

Given the nature of the American health care system, for instance, there is certainly an argument for nationalizing the Medicaid program, which is now an incoherent amalgam of state and federal funds and authorities. On the other hand, there is surely a case for taking the federal government entirely out of the business

of regulating and funding education. That is mostly a state domain already but should be more nearly exclusively so.

There is also a growing need for Congress to revisit the aims of the civil rights laws enacted in the middle of the twentieth century, which (through litigation and regulation) have evolved away from their original purposes in ways that no one could claim were intended by their authors. How far the frameworks developed for combating segregation and protecting Black Americans in light of centuries of racist oppression should be applied to other communities and other arenas of American life and how much of the federalist compromise of the Constitution should be abandoned for that purpose are questions that Congress alone is empowered to decide. Taking up that work would take courage, but it would vindicate the just intentions of the civil rights champions of the last century alongside those of the framers of the Constitution.

Reformers of American federalism should, in other words, look to disentangle state and federal governance as far as they practically can. This would not necessarily make for better-administered public programs in every case, though it likely would in some. But there is every reason to think that a more robust federalism would allow us to be more cohesive, less divided, and more at home in our society. By reducing the quantity of divisive questions that need to be resolved at the national level and providing some space for a diversity of answers to such questions in the forms of different individual choices and communal practices, federalism offers us a framework for political life exceptionally well adapted to the challenges our society now confronts.

While it limits the capacity of our national government to impose uniformity, federalism also limits the degree of uniformity required for our diverse society's politics to function. And while it sometimes creates intense national tensions, it often functions as a release valve for intense national tensions. Federalism brings

a Madisonian logic to bear on our divided society, rooted in the premise that a pattern of competing power centers and crosscutting affiliations can make possible a unifying politics of common action across lines of difference.

This is the logic of all our institutions and their peculiar approach to unity. Just as that logic helps us see why federalism permeates our politics, it can also help us see why the national government is structured as it is—beginning with why Congress comes first.

Chapter 5

CONGRESS

THE UNITED STATES CONGRESS IS THE PRIMARY AND PREDOMI-
nant institution of the American system of government. This is
true whether the Congress behaves accordingly or not. When the
system works well, it is usually because Congress is more or less
doing its job. When the system is dysfunctional, it is often because
Congress is dysfunctional—as it plainly has been in our time.

The framers of the Constitution believed that there was really
no alternative to this centrality of the legislature in a republican
regime. They took some steps to mitigate the dangers of legislative
overreach and to encourage the institution to function as an arena of
constructive bargaining and effective deliberation rather than simply majority will. They also emphasized the promise of legislative
centrality, which has especially to do with its potential to promote
national unity in a vast and multifarious society. A government with
a functional Congress at its center would be a government with bargaining and negotiation at its center, and our society stands to benefit a great deal from such a government. But when Congress is not
functional, there is no alternative venue for such accommodation,

and the system's capacity to engender unity and forge common ground is sorely diminished.

There is now widespread agreement that Congress is broken. But there is much less agreement regarding just what it is that Congress is failing to do. The problem is not that Congress is failing to pass the legislation that one party or another wants but that Congress is failing to facilitate cross-partisan accommodation and negotiated outcomes. By grasping its dysfunction in these terms, we can see our way to a clearer diagnosis of Congress's twenty-first-century deficiencies and toward a practical and unifying agenda for reform.

"IN REPUBLICAN GOVERNMENT, THE LEGISLATIVE AUTHORITY NECESSAR- ily predominates," James Madison wrote in Federalist 51. "The remedy for this inconveniency," he continued, "is to divide the legislature into different branches; and to render them, by different modes of election and different principles of action, as little connected with each other as the nature of their common functions and their common dependence on the society will admit." Much of the framers' basic approach to the creation of the Congress is rooted in these two sentences. They assumed and asserted the supremacy of the legislature but recognized that this was not entirely a good thing.[1]

Madison's observation was not just descriptive but also prescriptive. It is of the essence of republican government that the legislature should predominate, because the legislature is the branch whose work is fundamentally representative of the public. A government in which the legislature does not predominate is not a republican government. So the government created by the Constitution was meant to be dominated by the legislative branch and should be understood to be failing if it is not dominated by Congress. Yet this fact and, in this sense, republican government itself is inconvenient in some

important respects, because legislatures are prone to certain characteristic problems—and especially to the excesses of unjust majorities.

The framers worried deeply about those problems. Looking around the state governments, in Federalist 48, Madison concluded that "the legislative department is everywhere extending the sphere of its activity, and drawing all power into its impetuous vortex." The state constitutions had created relatively weak governors, since Americans had just gained independence in a revolution fought, in some measure, against the power of a king. But as a result, they created excessively strong legislatures, which often left them at the mercy of majority factions that could be mercurial and reckless. The legislative branch also has some inherent power advantages over the other branches of government in a republic. It can claim to speak for the people; its powers are generally not carefully delimited; and it controls the purse, which makes the rest of the government dependent on its decisions. Simply put, as Madison argued in Federalist 49, "the tendency of republican governments is to an aggrandizement of the legislative at the expense of the other departments."[2]

The Constitution does not pretend it can nip this tendency in the bud. It abides and embodies the supremacy of the legislature, and indeed, it implicitly identifies congressional power with the power of the national government as a whole. The document could have been written to define the scope of the federal government's reach and jurisdiction in one article and, only then, in separate articles, to establish the three branches of the government intended to operate in those domains. But that is not what it does. Instead, the scope of federal power is defined within the portion of the Constitution that creates the Congress. Article I, Section 8 says, "The Congress shall have power to" tax, borrow, regulate commerce, set rules for bankruptcy and naturalization, coin money, establish a postal system, protect copyrights, create courts below the Supreme Court, declare war, raise armies, and make laws to bring into effect "all

other Powers vested by this Constitution in the Government of the United States, or in any Department or Officer thereof." In effect, this suggests that federal power is congressional power. Congress is to deploy it through its acts of legislation, and the other branches are to act within the frameworks Congress creates or to interpret and apply them. As Hamilton wrote, "Government implies the power of making laws."[3]

The Constitution also gives Congress unparalleled authority over both the other branches. If it can muster large enough majorities, Congress can remove even the highest-ranking executive and judicial officials, while neither of the other branches has the power to remove a member of Congress. Each House of Congress makes its own rules, but Congress can legislate much of the scope, budget, and organization of the other branches. The familiar notion of "coequal" branches is largely an invention of modern presidents. In a number of Federalist essays, Hamilton and Madison used the term *coequal* to describe the relations of the states with one another, the taxing powers of the state and federal governments, and the relations of the two houses of Congress, but never the relations of the three branches of government. Rather, the branches are described as "coordinate departments." Each has its own separate article of the Constitution, and they exist alongside one another. But they are not equally powerful.

This centrality of Congress is essential to the legitimacy of the regime and to its claim to republicanism. Republican government is representative government, and although the other two branches are ultimately accountable to the people, only Congress is designed to be representative of them. But that very centrality poses grave dangers of excessive legislative ambition and majority power, and the Constitution tries to mitigate its potential abuses. One way to do that, as Madison suggests above, was to divide the Congress into two chambers elected in somewhat different ways and, therefore,

creative of and responsive to somewhat different constituencies. Senators were originally chosen by the state legislatures, which distinguished their interests from those of directly elected members of the House. But even with a directly elected Senate, the two chambers—because they are of different sizes and because states and districts are not the same—will generally be different enough to create some internal friction that can hold back aggressive but narrow majorities in either house. It only takes a quick walk across the Capitol Building on any random day when both houses are in session to see that they still have quite different characters in our time. This certainly impedes the legislative process in many cases, but it seemed to Madison, Hamilton, and others that it would avert legislative recklessness more frequently than it would obstruct essential measures.[4]

Another crucial check on Congress is the separation of powers itself. The idea of distinguishing and offsetting the legislative, executive, and judicial authorities was championed in the English political tradition mostly as a way to restrain the monarch, and so the executive power. There was some discussion of preventing potential executive excess in the Philadelphia Convention and throughout the ratification process too. But for the leading champions of the Constitution, the chief appeal of the separation of powers was clearly to restrain the legislature. As Alexander Hamilton stated in Federalist 71:

The tendency of the legislative authority to absorb every other, has been fully displayed and illustrated by examples in some preceding numbers. In governments purely republican, this tendency is almost irresistible. The representatives of the people, in a popular assembly, seem sometimes to fancy that they are the people themselves, and betray strong symptoms of impatience and disgust at the least sign of opposition from any other quarter; as if the exercise of its rights, by either the executive or judiciary, were

a breach of their privilege and an outrage to their dignity. They often appear disposed to exert an imperious control over the other departments; and as they commonly have the people on their side, they always act with such momentum as to make it very difficult for the other members of the government to maintain the balance of the Constitution.[5]

For this reason, the Constitution created executive and judicial branches at the national level that were stronger and more independent than those found in most of the states. Federal judges are given exceptional independence through life tenure in good behavior, and Congress's capacity to push them around (for instance, by threatening to lower their pay) is strictly constrained. The executive is not only rendered unusually independent, he is also given a peculiar capacity to interject into legislative action—particularly through the veto power, but also by allowing the president to propose legislation to Congress, and therefore inviting the executive to sometimes think like a legislator and so introducing a powerful influence on Congress's work that would be distinct from the voice of the political majority. Presidents have in fact turned out to be crucial drivers of the congressional agenda thanks to this power.

The framers seemed to understand these authorities as distinctly defensive, to be used as shields by presidents and judges against what they expected to be constant pressure from Congress, and so in essence from political majorities in the larger society. This would make for better administration and adjudication, keeping those vital functions apart from the important but mostly distinct goal of representation. But the separation of powers would also improve the capacity of Congress itself to function as a deliberative body, by guarding it from the temptation to become overly involved in administrative minutia or the nuances of legal disputes.

That point is key to grasping the framers' conception of the legislature: the risk of excess legislative power is a danger to Congress, and not just to the other branches, because Congress has a crucial role to play not only in framing the uses of federal power but also in facilitating the cohesion of the American nation.

IN THIS SENSE, LEGISLATIVE POWER WAS BY NO MEANS ONLY A CAUSE FOR concern for the Constitution's authors. Although the centrality of the legislature raises the specter of majority tyranny, it also makes possible not only greater legitimacy through representation but also greater national unity through distinctly legislative modes of accommodating differences. The fact that republican government is fundamentally legislative government is the foremost reason why it is possible for a vast and diverse republic to hold together and forge meaningful cohesion.

This is in part because of the nature of representative institutions in a pluralistic society. As John Adams argued, a representative assembly "is the only instrument by which the body of the people can act; the only in which their opinions can be known and collected; the only means by which their wills can be united, and the strength exerted, according to any principle or continued system." And by representing our plurality, our national legislature can allow for negotiations among the key factions that compose that plurality. This is a commonly misunderstood source of cohesion. Many observers of our democracy seem implicitly to believe that a unitary representative of the electorate as a whole (like a popularly elected president) would better hold us together by embodying our unity. But that view assumes away our diversity, and implies that we are unified but not adequately represented. The opposite is surely closer to the truth. Because we are a diverse society, representing us

requires a plural institution, not a unitary one. And that institution, by reflecting the key factions and divisions that define our polity, could also allow for the accommodation and negotiation of some of those differences. Indeed, the president's role—which is fundamentally administrative and not representative—would not be possible if Congress did not first transform the multiplicity of views and interests surrounding some particular policy question into a more nearly unitary aim and purpose. The executive would have nothing to administer if Congress did not legislate first.[6]

We have already seen in chapter 3 that James Madison took this to be perhaps the primary advantage of representative institutions. Representatives in a legislature can refine and elevate public sentiments and passions and give them forms that are more amenable to negotiated accommodations so that they may be turned into coherent governing objectives. According to Joseph Bessette, "The theory of deliberative democracy that undergirds the American constitutional order rests on the central proposition that there are two kinds of public voice in a democracy—one more immediate or spontaneous, uninformed, and unreflective; the other more deliberative, taking longer to develop and resting on a fuller consideration of information and arguments—and that only the latter is fit to rule." The former is transformed into the latter, above all, through the accommodative work of the legislature, and that transformation does not happen when Congress is not functioning well. In such times, we seem to be ruled by the more immediate and unreflective passions of the public more directly.[7]

When Congress does work reasonably well, its accommodations not only refine public sentiments, they can also be reflected back onto the factions of the public that members of Congress represent, helping to mitigate tensions in the larger society. As legal scholar Adam White has put it, "When legislators representing diverse people and values meet on equal footing to debate and deliberate, the

product is informed by values of toleration. The legislative process's inherent tendency toward compromise and moderation is itself a crucial institution for the perpetuation of tolerance."[8]

Such accommodation cannot happen directly between the members of the public who are parties to the conflicts that roil our public life at various times, but it can happen among their representatives. Congress can, thereby, legitimate bargains and negotiate settlements in ways that are simply not possible outside the legislative context. Court decisions and administrative actions are sometimes products of deliberated compromises or of some plausible vision of what a compromise might involve, but they are inherently dictated by elite institutions that are not representative of the parties to a conflict but stand above them. Accommodations reached in Congress are intrinsically more likely to be palatable to the nation in the long run.

The bicameral structure of the Congress can help in the negotiation of tensions between elite and populist pressures too. The House of Representatives is an inherently populist institution—indeed, it is the most plausible and legitimate outlet for populist energies in our national government. "Who are to be the electors of the federal representatives?" Madison asked in Federalist 57. He answered, "Not the rich, more than the poor; not the learned, more than the ignorant; not the haughty heirs of distinguished names, more than the humble sons of obscurity and unpropitious fortune. The electors are to be the great body of the people of the United States." And "who are to be the objects of popular choice?" Here, too, the House is likely to look like the country: "Every citizen whose merit may recommend him to the esteem and confidence of his country. No qualification of wealth, of birth, of religious faith, or of civil profession is permitted to fetter the judgement or disappoint the inclination of the people." The House is thus set up to be the most fully representative of our national institutions, and the one most directly answerable to public passions and priorities. But its purpose is not simply to empower

whichever of the factions it represents that has the greatest number of adherents but to compel the representatives of those streams of American opinion and interest to deal with one another and so build some common ground among them that would not exist if not for the forms of legislative procedure. It refines the public passions that arise most intensely from the bottom up.[9]

The Senate, meanwhile, is inherently less populist and more elitist, and so represents another vital segment of American life. But that segment's interests or priorities are not intrinsically more civilized or serious; they, too, must be refined before they can be useful ingredients in a democratic deliberation. In fact, precisely because of its more elite character, the Senate is even more fettered and constrained by the forms of legislative procedure. The factions it represents must be compelled even more forcefully into negotiations. As a result of its mode of representation, in which every state has equal power, the Senate has also been crucially important to the regional balance of our national politics—and particularly in protecting the interests of rural states (which tend to be less populated and less culturally elite) from the power of more urbanized states. This has involved different sorts of issues at different times, from economic to cultural priorities, from resource-management policy to railroad regulation, but it has always been crucial to sustaining some balance and compelling consensus and accommodation in our national politics. According to Jay Cost, "By giving voice to less populous communities, the Senate forces policymakers to account for their interests, to reconcile them to those of more populated centers, and to forge compromises that are geographically broader than they would otherwise be in a purely proportional system."[10]

And for all these reasons, the Senate has imposed some supermajority requirements on itself almost from the very beginning. Such requirements, most notably the "filibuster" rules that, in our time, require sixty out of one hundred Senate votes to end debate on many

measures and move to a final vote, are not required by the Constitution; they are discretionary Senate rules. But they certainly advance the Constitution's vision of coalition-building deliberation. In most eras, such requirements have pertained in debates about rare and critical issues. But in particularly closely divided times like ours, there is a strong case for imposing them more generally (as the modern Senate does), because their effect is to restrain narrow majorities and to encourage the formation of broader coalitions. Like the Constitution as a whole, they seek to let us determine whether majorities should get their way based on a majority's size and durability, not its intensity. They force senators to pursue measures that will appeal to more than just their own party and, therefore, more than just their own insular segment of our polarized political culture.

These requirements, by slowing and complicating the work of the Senate, also restrain the House and compel the members of that more populist body to consider opposing views and build coalitions, too, since no measure can be sent to the president for signature without passing both houses. Supermajority requirements are frustrating to narrow majorities, so they are frequently criticized as undemocratic. But frustrating narrow majorities is a key feature and aim of our system of government. And measures adapted to appeal to broader coalitions are more likely to be perceived as broadly legitimate and to endure. The Senate's commitment to such practices is never more important, or more unifying, than in narrowly divided eras like our own.

This is a crucial virtue of our legislature-centered system more generally. Legislative work may not always arrive at the most rational possible policy outcomes. As Hamilton wrote in Federalist 85, "The result of the deliberations of all collective bodies must necessarily be a compound, as well of the errors and prejudices, as of the good sense and wisdom, of the individuals of whom they are composed." But the ways by which such work amasses majorities,

negotiates accommodations, and addresses objections and grievances allows for measures that are more likely to be acceptable to the larger society.[11]

One reason this can work is that the restraints on rash legislative measures, which do slow down legislative work, can create greater confidence in the outcomes of that work. "In the legislature, promptitude of decision is oftener an evil than a benefit. The differences of opinion, and the jarring of parties in that department of the government, though they may sometimes obstruct salutary plans, yet often promote deliberation and circumspection, and serve to check excesses in the majority," Hamilton wrote in Federalist 70. A second reason is that compromise actually accounts in practice for specific concerns or objections some minorities might have to the goals of the majority. And a third is simply the fact that the forms of legislative procedure are seen to restrain the various parties to a dispute, so that the outcome of the process is understood to be a function of some restraint, which tends to render it more trustworthy.[12]

This facet of representation can sometimes quiet what otherwise threaten to be irreconcilable and irrepressible divisions that could threaten our very form of government. As Walter Berns argued, by giving people a sense that they are part of an accommodation, the legislative process can succeed in "somehow persuading these partisans to give up their desire to rule the whole society in exchange for the right merely to be represented." Political scientist Philip Wallach has shown in his magisterial recent book *Why Congress*—certainly the most important treatment of this subject so far written in this century—that the national legislature has played this crucial role in many moments of intense division in our history, perhaps most notably the stretch of national exertions from World War II through the civil rights battles of the middle of the twentieth century. Many of the achievements we tend to attribute to the larger-than-life presidents of that era were actually accomplished by the decidedly

life-sized Congresses of the time and were rendered acceptable to our divided country by that fact.[13]

THE TASK OF FORGING UNITY THROUGH THE WORK OF A LEGISLATURE generally involves three elements. First, Congress must function as *an arena of contention*, where deep differences in our society can be meaningfully represented and so can confront one another directly. Second, Congress needs to function as *an arena of coalition building*, where factions divided over important questions come out of necessity to think about their priorities in terms that are more likely to be inviting and accommodational. And third, Congress can become *an arena of integration*, where coalition building melds into nation building, which is more than merely instrumental. These three elements need not always follow in this order—indeed, as a historical matter legislatures served integration before they served representation in the English political tradition, as we shall briefly see. But all three are crucial, they are much related, and they are all endangered now.

Congress functions as an arena of contention first and foremost because it not only represents contending views and interests in society but also structures their confrontations over differences— setting rules and procedures that let those struggles get somewhere. That sort of management and regulation of disputes forms, as Madison argued, "the principal task of modern legislation." Such carefully organized contention is vital to the life of a free society. The breakdown of American political culture in our time is not a function of our having forgotten how to agree but of our having forgotten how to disagree. This is true of our public culture more generally: other institutions meant to serve as arenas of formalized contention, like the university or certain facets of journalism, have also been increasingly transformed into parallel silos, where people

agree with one another about how wrong others are rather than confronting those others in ways that put their disagreements on the table and compel some resolution. In the absence of these arenas of contention, the divisions that are inherent in any diverse free society become sources of separation and detachment, rather than serving as sources of engagement. To engage is not to put differences aside. Warring parties engage one another on battlefields. But engagement does mean contending together. And Congress does have to be a place where parties to some key disputes contend with one another, and openly disagree in organized ways.[14]

Representation also points beyond the expression of differences, however. According to Philip Wallach, "Blunt majority rule is about domesticating brute political force into a somewhat gentler form; but effective representative government reveals to us which of our interests can be joined together to support shared public endeavors and which cannot." Some legislative disputes just have to be resolved by a vote that determines a winner. But most require instead the assembling of a coalition, and therefore the evolution of differing views in the direction of agreement.[15]

Such coalition building is an essential feature of Congress's work and of its capacity to forge common ground in American life. The parties to various political and policy disputes aren't necessarily looking for common ground. But because Congress is structured to make it difficult for narrow majorities to get their way, they often have to reach out beyond their own supporters to get anything done. The process of building a coalition can then moderate their most extreme demands and make them more likely to appeal to the common interest of the larger society than to their distinct interest and, therefore, also to seek common ground and to forge it where it did not exist before.

This tends to make partisans more tolerant, and more tolerable. The process required for getting anything accomplished in Congress

compels the various interests involved, as a matter of practical necessity at first, to present themselves not as crass partisan claimants but
as differing regarding what would be good for the whole of society.
This may begin as a partisan strategy, but it is not simply cynical. It
gradually alters not only how people speak but how they think and
so becomes not merely a concession to the reality of difference but
a means of balancing competing principles of action and actually
becoming more accommodating.[16]

This is how that process of refinement that Madison describes
actually works. The larger mass of voters doesn't have to deal with
other views and interests when it seeks to advance its own priorities,
but the representative does because of the nature of the structured
bargaining demanded by the rules of the Congress. That representative, therefore, comes to understand that getting anything his
or her voters want requires working with others who want other
things. The experience of serving as a representative, therefore,
often functions as a lesson in moderation and negotiation, as many
new members of Congress continue to learn all the time. This is
why the notion that the balance between majority will and minority
rights is achieved by empowering the deliberative (and thus deliberated) will of the majority, and not its passionate whims, is neither
naïve nor unrealistic. It is a function of the hard facts of dealing with
difference in Congress. No one who has seen a legislative bargain
take shape could deny the reality of this kind of transformation—
the way in which the structure of the institution spins disagreement
into cooperation, and sometimes even into something that certainly
feels to the people involved like camaraderie.

Such coalition building is what we often actually mean by the
term *deliberation*. On its own, deliberation can sound very high-
minded and gentle. But it means pushing through disagreement
toward negotiated outcomes, and it is key to why our politics must
have the legislative branch at its heart. Presidents can help to spur

coalition building, but they cannot take it up on their own because theirs is a unitary office. They have a different role to play.[17]

This capacity for coalition building, for unity that need not be fully harmonious, is why Congress is particularly crucial in an era of intense division like our own. A key insight underlying the structure of the Constitution is that it is possible for differing factions in a diverse society to work together without resolving their underlying disagreements—to reach a workable consensus on a particular question without reaching fundamental unanimity on a general worldview. The creation of such consensus is not purely pragmatic and calculating. It can yield real comity and fellow feeling. It does help us all feel more like part of one whole society, but it does that without requiring us to abandon our differences or surrender our distinct priorities. By structuring the incentives confronting members of Congress in a way that compels them to think about how their own goals might also serve those of others, it can gradually form the character of legislators toward taking account of others and seeking their consent.

Ultimately, this means that a properly functioning Congress is more than an arena of contention or of coalition building. In key moments, it can serve as a genuinely integrative force, bringing into being common ground where none existed before. This was plainly true of the first Congress after the adoption of the Constitution, which built real consensus about how the new system should operate. It has been true in moments of crisis, as with Congress's assertive oversight and leadership during World War II. It has been true in periods of tense social division, as with passage of the Civil Rights Acts of the 1950s and 1960s. These weren't quiet, amicable legislative eras. Congress did what it does: it fought and argued and negotiated its way toward action. But because that was how action came to happen, Congress did build greater agreement in the country.

This is, in part, the function of a practical reality: working together, even (and maybe especially) working together through a tense and challenging negotiating process, helps people understand one another better, take one another more seriously, and trust and respect one another a little more. The requirement to build consensus before acting can also change people's perception of the society in which they live. "In a world with consensus requirements," legal scholar John McGinnis has argued, "citizens are more likely to identify with the polity as a whole instead of seeing themselves as part of an embattled minority waiting for its turn to rule. With more compromise, we would see each other less as targets or threats and more as partners in a common civic enterprise." Some Americans now talk a lot about "diversity and inclusion," but ironically, such talk is often divisive and domineering. The process of legislative accommodation is what genuine diversity and inclusion can look like.[18]

By enabling this kind of forging of common ground in Congress itself, the structure of the institution can also help the larger society develop a common identity and a sense of engagement in a common purpose. This is an underappreciated facet of the history of legislatures in our political tradition. As the great British historian Alfred Frederick Pollard showed, this integrative function of the British Parliament actually preceded its representative function:

> The great service which parliaments rendered in the middle ages was not, in fact, to make England a constitutional state, but to foster its growth into a national state based on something broader and deeper than monarchical centralization, to make national unity a thing of the spirit rather than a territorial expression or a mechanical matter of administration, to evoke a common political consciousness at Westminster and then to propagate it in the constituencies. The value of parliaments consisted not so much in what members brought with them as what they took away.[19]

It was less that members were representative of public preferences (which in medieval Britain, they really were not) than that they were constitutive of a national identity. In the United States, representation was a priority from the beginning, even if it was not fully realized in eras of strictly limited suffrage. But this capacity for integration through legislative bargaining, the sense that the new nation was forged by the work of its legislative institution, was nonetheless also very real. The two Continental Congresses and the Confederation Congress that preceded the Constitution were practically the only national institutions (aside from the army) in the revolutionary and early republic years, and they began to cement a kind of national identity and build public support for various national measures.

Under the constitutional system, there came to be more national institutions, and the presidency, in particular, has played an important part in creating a firmer national consciousness, as we shall see. But the Congress remained crucial to the creation of common ground in areas of division and tension, and to the working out of differences in ways that have made greater unity possible in practice at key points in American life.

Thus, the case for the centrality of Congress is rooted not just in its democratic legitimacy but also in its capacity to foster unity. Congress is the only one of our national governing institutions that operates by accommodation and bargaining, and if we want our politics to help us resolve differences through negotiated compromises, then we will need Congress to be functional.

It is crucial to see, moreover, that the framers' concern about excessive legislative strength and their desire to enable Congress to facilitate a politics of competition, negotiation, and productive tension are not at odds. Both point in the same direction: toward a Congress characterized by mechanisms of restraint and consensus, which require more than narrow majorities to move legislation. Multiple veto points, supermajority requirements, bicameralism, and an

assortment of structural restraints more burdensome than simple majority rule are what keep Congress from becoming intolerably overbearing, and they are also what ultimately compel accommodation and bargaining. They are what can make the US Congress an arena for contention, coalition building, and national integration.

AND YET, IT IS HARD TO DENY THAT TODAY'S CONGRESS STRUGGLES TO BE any of those things, and even to mobilize the ambition to do its most basic work. The framers' concern that the legislative branch would be too strong is not a worry anyone would have about the twenty-first-century Congress. Their hopes that it might foster unity do not usually apply to the contemporary Congress either. Congress is broken. That is one thing Americans do seem to agree about. Yet it is only because we have seen what the Constitution assumes the national legislature could be that we can really grasp how exactly it is failing now and what might be done about it.

On the surface, Congress appears to be debilitated by partisan animosity and by the bitter culture wars that bedevil our society. Members do still sometimes work together across party lines, but all too rarely. And they generally do so either regarding issues of low salience in the public arena or regarding problems that have become so urgent that failing to deal with them by a certain date will lead to calamity, like raising the debt limit before a federal default. Congress has responded reasonably well to genuine national emergencies in this century, too, as when the financial crisis of 2008 or the COVID-19 pandemic required massive policy action. But the everyday work of governance that is neither an emergency nor so mundane as to slip under the radar rarely gets done. The government's core fiscal health, the need to modernize our entitlement system, the imperative to realign our immigration policies with public views

and national needs, and similar challenges are put to the side and left unaddressed year after year. And Congress's regular order—the committee work, budgeting, oversight, and routine policy negotiations that ought to be the bread-and-butter of a legislature—has become deformed nearly out of existence. When legislation does advance, it is often by going around these structured processes, either through the work of ad hoc groups of members of both parties (especially in the Senate) or, more often, through leadership negotiations that do not allow most members to play any meaningful role.[20]

The result is a Congress that looks dysfunctional from every angle. But it is worth asking just precisely what function it is failing to perform. While the past decade and more has seen the emergence of a vibrant community of reformers who agree about the need to improve our national legislature, they are actually divided over the question of just what Congress is failing to do.

The most common answer, and perhaps the most intuitive one, is that Congress is failing to pass significant legislation that takes on the country's most important challenges, even when the party in power has an agenda in mind for doing that. Simply put, Congress isn't passing the bills I think are essential. This is surely true, whichever party you support and whatever legislation you would like to see enacted. And it is a view that leads some reformers (particularly in the progressive wing of our politics) to argue that it is simply too difficult for majority parties to advance legislation in Congress, so that reforms should better empower even narrow partisan majorities—which are, after all, the only kind we seem to have now—to act on their own. That could mean, for instance, eliminating the filibuster in the Senate, consolidating more of Congress's work into partisan omnibus legislation, and reducing the power of committees and of intraparty factions that now slow the institution's work. These reformers would like to move the institution in the direction of a Westminster parliament, where

the ruling coalition can act essentially unobstructed as long as it retains its majority, and where, crucially, legislative functions are largely subordinated to the executive functions of government, and efficient policy action tends to be prioritized above accommodation and negotiation.

That emphasis hearkens back to the progressive critique of American constitutionalism that we began to trace in our consideration of federalism. Progressive reformers have always been deeply impatient with Congress and have tended to reject the theory of political life implicit in the design of the institution. Skeptical of the potential for governing by negotiated accommodation, they have sought ways to empower both bare-majority will and expert knowledge and have assumed the two would point in the same direction. This has also led many progressives to prioritize executive action and to want Congress to respond to presidential initiative, not only because the president is a more effective actor but also because the national electorate that selects the chief executive renders the holder of that office more legitimate. These progressive diagnoses and prescriptions are very widespread in the academy and the political system. Their essence is nicely captured in the title (and substance) of a recent book by political scientists William Howell and Terry Moe, *Relic: How Our Constitution Undermines Effective Government and Why We Need a More Powerful Presidency.*[21]

This view implicitly assumes that divisions in the American body politic are not inherent to a free society but are functions of some people choosing to pursue their private advantage at the expense of the public good—so that unity is the natural state of our society but various "special interests" insist on pulling the country apart. What we need from politics is therefore a consolidated voice of the public that will speak up for the whole. Special interests are inherently most at home in Congress, given its sprawling multiplicity, so it is necessary to subject Congress to more consolidated leadership,

meaning stronger party leadership but also especially presidential leadership.

Political scientist Daniel Stid has dubbed this approach to Congress "Wilsonian," after Woodrow Wilson, who was not only a progressive president himself but prior to that was a leading progressive political scientist and scholar of American government. Wilson argued that the sheer plurality of the national legislature, coupled with structural divisions of power and restraints on action embedded in its design, made Congress ineffective and irresponsible. "The more power is divided, the more irresponsible it becomes," he famously wrote in his 1885 book *Congressional Government*. Power must instead be concentrated. And the notion that negotiation between factions would best serve the public, or is the purpose of politics, comes to seem backward and naïve when one party represents special interests and the other represents the national interest.[22]

It is hard to imagine a view more at odds with the basic assumptions of the framers of the Constitution. The Wilsonian vision contrasts sharply and openly with the Madisonian vision that underlies the architecture of our system. It ultimately rejects the legitimacy of the differences that divide our society and somehow assumes that if power were better concentrated, it would fall into the hands of the party that would make better use of it. It is, thus, both more democratic and more elitist—and in both respects, less republican—than the framers' view. But its dispute with Madison's political vision runs to the core of the nature of the free society. Madison assumed that our divisions and differences are, in fact, not only legitimate but unavoidable. Their existence is a function of our freedom and diversity, not of uniquely selfish interests that could be eradicated by sufficiently powerful and well-intentioned leaders. But those divisions and differences need not result in paralyzing acrimony. They can be mitigated, channeled, negotiated, and accommodated—and that can happen in Congress, above all.

That Madisonian view would suggest a very different answer to the question of what Congress is failing to do today. It is not failing to pass narrowly partisan legislation; it was never intended to pass narrowly partisan legislation and, indeed, is intended to resist doing so. Rather, Congress is failing to facilitate cross-partisan bargaining and accommodation. It is failing to mitigate the bitter partisanship of our political culture and is, instead, making it worse.

This failure also results in a shortage of substantive legislation and an inability to take up the nation's most significant challenges, so that the Wilsonian and Madisonian diagnoses sometimes begin from the same sorts of complaints. But they ultimately point in very different directions, because they are rooted in different understandings of the purpose of our system of government, if not the nature of political life.

The Madisonian view presumes that what we lack most is not precisely the right technical solution to this or that public problem but a practical spirit of cohesion that could allow Americans to see themselves as parts of one whole society, and so to trust one another a little more, to accommodate one another a little more, and to pursue public policy that would be viewed as legitimate and adequate by more of us. This view prioritizes greater cohesion over more efficient policy action, and it has lower expectations than the Wilsonian view of our system's capacity for technical prowess but higher expectations of the potential of our politics to bring Americans together. It looks to enable Americans to act together even when they don't think alike, which it takes to be the most difficult of all the challenges confronting our politics.

This is why the framers' approach to political life turns out to be more persuasive than the rival Wilsonian approach that now often dominates our politics—not because it is older or because it was James Madison's view, but because it offers a more plausible explanation of the problems with our politics and a more plausible set

of solutions. The Wilsonian approach to Congress diminishes the unifying potential of the institution and would have us deform the national legislature in the image of our worst contemporary vices. It offers no way to ease the poisonous polarization of our time and, indeed, proposes measures that would intensify it. By submerging institutional ambition beneath ideological ambition, it would only further elevate the presidency over Congress and party leaders over any broad-based process of legislative accommodation. By empowering narrow majorities to act more easily and aggressively, it would raise the stakes of our close elections, and so, the temperature of our already overheated politics. And by doing that now, in an era of two minority parties when neither Republicans nor Democrats seem able to hold power for long, it would condemn us to an endless partisan ping-pong match in Congress, as each new majority undoes the last one's achievements, and then jams through its own partisan measures for the other party to undo as soon as it returns to the majority— much as presidents now do on the regulatory front (thanks to similarly Wilsonian assumptions, as we shall see). Finally, by removing the restraints on action that, even today, still compel what little cross-partisan bargaining does happen in Congress, it would leave us with effectively none. This is not because the progressive agenda for reforming the legislative branch is somehow ill-intentioned but because it misapprehends the purpose of Congress and the dire necessity of serving that purpose in our day. It takes the structure of the institution to be the problem rather than the solution.

Seeing this can help us clarify the core question confronting reformers of Congress today. The problem they face is a function of two factors: On the one hand, the constitutional design of the Congress requires significant cross-partisan accommodation in order to advance significant legislative work. On the other hand, the political culture of our time makes such cross-partisan accommodation very hard to achieve. The result is that Congress isn't legislating much,

and almost everyone agrees that needs to change. But the question for reformers of Congress is whether they want to promote changes that would make cross-partisan accommodation *less necessary* or ones that make such accommodation *more likely*. Today's progressive reformers want to make it less necessary and so better enable Congress to enact significant legislation in the absence of bargaining and accommodation. But as we have seen, Congress is a unique and essential arena for constructive contention, meaningful coalition building, and the forging of national cohesion. To have Congress give up on these aims is to give up on them altogether, since there is no other institution in our national politics that could advance them. So not only for the sake of Congress itself but also for the sake of our political culture more generally, it is crucial to pursue reforms that would make genuine, accommodative, coalition-broadening legislative work more achievable, more appealing to members, more likely to happen, and more common.

A healthier Congress is a necessary precondition for a healthier, less poisonous, and more constructive American political life, provided that our definition of health emphasizes the institution's role in forging cohesion—or in other words, provided that we understand the purpose of Congress roughly as the framers of the Constitution did. We need not a Wilsonian but a Madisonian approach to the national legislature.

Such an approach would begin by viewing Congress as an institution designed to facilitate accommodation across lines of faction and party in a divided polity and to compel its members to form the habits required to resist the intense polarization of this moment. The members who are most conspicuously failing to be formed for such resistance to polarization now are those most adamantly refusing to be formed by Congress at all—to be molded into legislators and representatives. Instead, they choose to remain unformed members of the public, merely using Congress as a platform upon which they

can stand and essentially perform a version of what would happen in a mob. That failure of member formation is the place to begin thinking about how to change Congress. The question reformers need to answer is how traditional legislative work and the disposition it involves could be made more appealing to members.

One reason Congress now fails to mold its members into legislators is that the institution is already too centralized in the hands of party leaders, so that many backbenchers have no substantive legislative work toward which they might channel their ambitions. That centralization is the result of decades of institutional change driven in important respects by the Wilsonian case for a more partisan Congress. That case first appealed to progressive Democrats, beginning in the 1970s, and was ultimately also embraced by conservative Republicans, starting in the 1990s. The result has been a Congress increasingly dominated by party leaders, which has increasingly pushed to the margins the sort of traditional legislative work that has helped form new members into legislators in the past.[23]

Another reason for that failure of member formation is that the electoral incentives members of Congress confront move them to perceive the voters in their party primaries, rather than their constituents more generally, as their key audience. And a third reason is that the modern media environment, including social media, encourages members to understand themselves as performers and not legislators—as tribunes for the grievances of their voters rather than as negotiators on those voters' behalf. This leads many members, like many of their constituents, to confuse political expression with political action.

All of that is the result of a variety of factors driving the evolution of our political culture, but a particularly significant factor in the case of Congress is the simple fact of our closely contested politics. Polarization is not new, but a genuinely fifty-fifty politics, in which either of our major parties could win control of Congress in the next

election, has not been the norm until the last three decades or so. A minority party that believes it will win control in the next election is unlikely to seek to cooperate with the majority. A majority that fears it may lose control is likely to be in a hurry to press its own priorities and uninterested in giving the minority any legislative victories to tout. Each wants to highlight its differences from the other and, as political scientist Frances Lee has argued, "cooperating across party lines to legislate bipartisan policy is not an effective way to amplify such differences." Rather, as Lee shows, members who always believe the majority could change hands in the next election are always inclined to hold back from dealing with the other party. The long stretch of extremely close elections we have experienced since the 1990s has, thus, made cross-partisan cooperation much less likely and has encouraged members of Congress to think of themselves in partisan terms far more than in institutional terms.[24]

The radical transparency to which Congress has subjected itself, with cameras in every deliberative space, has interacted with this new environment in ways that have made all these problems worse. Some transparency is vital, but it must also have its limits if the institution is to enable negotiation. There is really no such thing as negotiating in public, and when there are no private spaces in which members can engage with one another, Congress's work ends up getting done behind the doors of the leadership offices (which are almost the only places to work privately) in ways that exclude too many members.[25]

These related dysfunctions—and the resulting failure to form members of Congress into legislators—then throw the broader constitutional system out of balance, because they not only mean that cross-partisan negotiation is too rare but also result in a Congress that has lost much of its ambition to dominate the national government. Congress does not want to take up the most difficult public questions, because members feel safer letting those be

decided by the other two branches while they act as pundits on the sidelines. Congress is weak, simply put, because its members want it to be weak. And that weakness invites aggression and hyperactivity by both presidents and courts. Many of the most contentious and complicated cases before the Supreme Court arise because Congress has legislated too vaguely or has delegated its authority to the executive branch in constitutionally dubious ways. A lot of executive overreach is, ultimately, a function of legislative underreach.

The result is a sicker and more divided political culture: when Congress breaks down and the presidency, the bureaucracy, and the courts take over, our implicit model of political action and social change—the civic blueprint in our heads—gradually transforms into a less accommodational and more imperious framework and leaves us more inclined to think of politics in winner-take-all terms and less inclined to seek compromise. That attitude then seeps back into Congress as well, completing a vicious cycle that our constitutional system now struggles in vain to break.

Congress's willful weakness and the breakdown of cross-partisan deal making are, therefore, two sides of the same coin. Without an assertive legislature, jealous of its prerogatives, our system unavoidably falls into dysfunction. And without a functional arena for negotiation, our national politics tends to overflow with bitter bile. Both problems call for the same sorts of structural reforms, which might help invest the ambitions of members in the strength of the institution and do so by creating incentives for them to engage in traditional legislative work—incentives, that is, to let the institution change them into agents of accommodation.

What might such reforms look like? Some would have to involve changing the electoral incentives members confront, as these are unavoidably powerful motivators. Changing such incentives and, especially, rethinking the primary system, would involve electoral

reforms more than reform of Congress and so is a subject we will take up in chapter 8.

Within Congress, reforms that might make legislative work more appealing would require some concerted decentralization, pulling power back from party leaders but providing it not so much to individual members as to groups of members looking to both advance shared priorities and negotiate differences. Such groups compose the middle layer of the Congress and consist especially of intraparty factions and congressional committees.

Intraparty factions have a bad reputation in our time. They're taken to be agents of chaos and dysfunction, undermining the ability of party leaders in both houses to exercise control efficiently. But as Daniel DiSalvo has argued, these factions are actually a vital source of energy and creativity. And crucially, they can create space for bargaining across party lines by enabling within our two-party system the kind of multipolarity that James Madison thought essential to sustaining a free society. Steven Teles and Robert Saldin have put this point well: "Polarization is commonly understood as a dynamic in which the two parties move further apart. However, another important feature of polarization is increasing homogeneity within each party's cohort of elected officials. This pattern stifles demand for the kind of intra-party factions that used to provide necessary outlets for the much more varied preferences of elected politicians. Understanding the last two decades through this lens helps explain why there has been such a decline in cross-party lawmaking."[26]

Encouraging intraparty factions would require party organizing efforts well beyond Congress (which, again, is a subject to be taken up in chapter 8), but there are some ways to create space for them within the institution if rank-and-file members insist on it and if they approach party leaders with specific demands for a greater role for these semiformal caucuses. The approach of some Republicans to their party's 2023 leadership struggles in the House

of Representatives—including a demand for seats on the powerful House Rules Committee for members of the Freedom Caucus faction—offered an example of how this can work and why it can matter. More internal diversity within the parties would make more cross-partisan bargaining possible.

But reempowering the congressional committees is truly at the heart of how reformers could open some space for negotiated legislation. Critics of strong party leaders in both houses often seek to empower individual members and turn the floor of each chamber into more of an open venue for proposals and amendments. But individual members are more easily overpowered by party leaders, and the House and Senate floors are essentially television studios. Real decentralization would require giving operational power to the committees, which are organized around substantive policy domains and where members can work out differences in smaller groups and more focused ways across party lines. In a Congress tightly run by party leaders, the work of the committees barely matters. And since committee work is the only real legislative work that most members do, the majority of members (especially in the House of Representatives) are left feeling as though they have no role in advancing serious legislative efforts. Helping the committees matter more is crucial to changing how members think about the nature and purpose of the institution and about their own ambitions and responsibilities.

For instance, the rules of both houses could be reformed to give each authorizing committee control over some modest portion of time on the floor, allowing legislation that has made it through the committee (ideally with at least one vote from a member of the minority party) to be considered by the entire chamber, even if it is not a leadership priority. If members had the sense that their committees were firing with real bullets, they would take that work more seriously and help their voters do the same. Members of committees

could also be permitted to elect their own chairs rather than having them chosen by steering committees controlled by party leaders. That would create incentives for ambitious members to devote themselves to substantive committee work that could win the support of their colleagues, rather than only to the agendas of party leaders.

Reformers could also more aggressively empower the committees by eliminating the long-standing boundary between authorization and appropriation in Congress. Authorizing bills create or alter laws or programs, while appropriating bills devote specific sums of federal money to particular ends. Since setting spending levels is much of what Congress does in most years, the work of the authorizers ends up being far less significant. Allowing the committees that write policy to also propose the spending required to implement it would give members who aren't now appropriators a reason to take their committee work more seriously. Congress worked this way from the late 1870s until 1921, and while there are cautionary lessons to learn from that period of decentralized appropriations, there are strong reasons to embrace that approach again.[27]

Facilitating cross-partisan negotiating in congressional committees would also require more private work sessions, in which there are no television cameras. Real bargaining and accommodation simply cannot happen in public, as negotiators fear being seen to make concessions before they can point to what they gain in return. The Constitution actually owes its origins to its framers' understanding of that fact, as the Philadelphia Convention was held behind closed doors for just this reason. "Had the deliberations been open," Alexander Hamilton argued in 1792, "the clamours of faction would have prevented any satisfactory result." The point was not to keep out the public's interests and views but to provide a protected arena to work out deals. Decades later, James Madison told the historian Jared Sparks that he thought "no Constitution would ever have been

adopted by the Convention if the debates had been public." Congress needs to recognize the same reality. Transparency matters. Without it, institutions that serve a public purpose can easily become debased and unaccountable. But every good thing is a matter of degree, and political reformers have treated transparency as a benefit with no costs, when in fact it can have enormous costs that have to be accounted for. In this case, the price can be measured in a loss of bargaining spaces, and the result of ignoring it is a Congress that increasingly has the appearance of a show. Members should consider creating more spaces for substantive committee work that is not televised or live-streamed. Even if formal hearings (let alone floor action) continue to be televised, it should be possible to build out other formats of committee work, like more private working sessions, that can enable members to actually engage with one another and with the substantive policy challenges they confront.[28]

Reform-minded members could also demand a rethinking of the congressional budget process. Created in the mid-1970s to serve a legislature facing very different challenges than today's, the budget process is now at the heart of Congress's dysfunction. It encourages symbolic battles and vague sloganeering rather than practical negotiations and concrete measures. And its dysfunction empowers party leaders to produce massive legislative packages without the involvement of most members, and so excludes almost everyone in Congress from any meaningful negotiating experience. Eliminating the budget committees and breaking up that consolidated process into more and smaller portions, to be accomplished by the work of Congress's substantive authorizing committees in an ongoing way, would depolarize spending debates a little and help committee work matter more.

One further reform could help facilitate the others. Members of Congress should take up a bit of constitutional maintenance and modestly increase the size of the House of Representatives. When

the Constitution was first ratified, the House had sixty-five members, each of whom represented approximately thirty thousand Americans. As the nation grew, the House also did at first, expanding after every decennial census throughout the nineteenth century. It reached its current size in 1911, when each of its 435 members represented about 210,000 people. Under a law enacted in 1929, the House has not increased in size since then, even though the population of the nation has more than tripled, so that each member now represents about 745,000 Americans. An increase in the size of the House could improve its capacity to represent the American public, though of course, any such increase would need to consider that the House is intended to function as a venue for face-to-face bargaining, so it can only grow so large. A group of political scientists (including myself) convened by the American Academy of Arts and Sciences recently proposed expanding the House by 150 members—which is how much larger it would have been today if the formula used for its growth until the 1920 census had continued to be used. Such a change would be a matter of simple legislation, not a constitutional amendment. It would not only bring the House better into line with the expectations of the framers of the Constitution but would also modestly improve representation, increase the likelihood of more varied intraparty factions, and serve as a shot in the arm to spur other needed reforms.[29]

These are just a few possible measures and are only briefly sketched out to suggest the general direction that reforms of Congress should take. Crucially, they are Madisonian reforms, in that they recognize that institutional structure creates political culture, they take incentives seriously, and they are intended to encourage members of Congress to be more thoroughly molded by the roles they have. Discrete, even dull, institutional adjustments may seem too small a response to what is plainly a gargantuan cultural breakdown. But the entire framework of our Constitution is premised on

the view that structures and incentives built to interact in realistic, healthy ways with human nature and the instincts of our society can facilitate a healthier political culture. Political reformers generally cannot transform culture directly, so they should look for the intersection of what is achievable and what is required. What they will find at that intersection will often be an opportunity to alter rules and processes and, therefore, habits and assumptions and, ultimately, ways of acting toward and with one another. So while these are modest proposals, they are built on the premise that structural subtleties can make a mighty difference. And they all gesture toward the crucial fact that Congress's dysfunction is not an irremediable reality. It could be corrected, particularly by members of Congress themselves, if they were more aware that they possess the power to reform the institution and were better informed about what its renewal would need to involve.

THE RENEWAL OF CONGRESS MUST AIM TO RECOVER THE INSTITUTION'S capacity to forge common ground and govern legitimately and effectively. It must make cross-partisan bargaining more likely, rather than making it less necessary. And it should make legislative work seem like a better use of time than political performance art. Members of Congress are intelligent, ambitious men and women, and at the moment, they have every incentive to channel their ambitions against Congress's constitutional purpose and not toward it. They need better reasons to identify their own best interests with those of the institution and its success and significance with theirs. "The interest of the man must be connected with the constitutional rights of the place," as Madison put it.[30]

The general case for thinking this way must precede any particular reform measures, because reforms of the Congress can only

happen if the institution's members want them. The first question that stands in the way of revitalizing Congress is not so much "how?" as "why?" That more fundamental question can only be answered by recurring to the logic of the Constitution and illuminating its relevance to our contemporary circumstances.

This is a tall order. It will take time and perseverance. But revitalizing Congress in accordance with the framers' understanding of its purpose must be the single most important goal of any champion of the American constitutional order today. Our society's capacity for unity depends on it. While the other branches of our national government confront their own distinct challenges, as we shall now see, their health also decisively depends on a healthier first branch.

Chapter 6

THE PRESIDENCY

THE AMERICAN PRESIDENCY WAS THE BOLDEST AND MOST ORIGI-
nal of the framers' institutional innovations. There had never
been anything quite like it. The Congress and the courts were given
some novel roles by the Constitution, but structurally they were a
legislature and a judiciary—familiar forms in the Anglo-American
political tradition. Giving form to a republican national executive
posed a different kind of challenge, and the available models mostly
offered examples of what not to do. The need for energy and dispatch somehow had to be balanced with the need for accountability
to the people; the need for a head of state had to be married to the
need for a chief administrator; the need to give some direction to
our frenetic politics had to be set against the need to reflect the will
of the public; and all of that had to be accomplished without threatening the rights and freedoms of the citizenry.

To achieve all this, the framers settled on a unitary office: one
person would be charged with all executive power at the national
level. But they defined the contours of that office fairly vaguely
and allowed it to be shaped to a degree by the large personalities

that would inevitably come to occupy it. As a unitary institution, the presidency cannot play the same role as Congress in advancing national cohesion. It is not a venue for accommodation and bargaining but a locus of action, both to execute the laws and to respond to demanding exigencies on behalf of the nation. Yet in both respects, and along with his other essential duties, the president does have an important role to play in making greater national unity possible. Stability and steadiness in administering the government are particularly critical and were exceptionally prominent in the framers' aims for the office. Steady administration can help secure both an orderly national life and public confidence in the system as a foundation for cohesion. Securing such stability in an unstable world requires particular virtues of the republican executive—personal character is more important in the presidency than in any other constitutional office.

We have tended to forget all this with time, however. The presidency quickly grew in stature in our politics, becoming a focal point for partisan division and conflict. As our expectations of the national government changed, our demands of the president came to vastly exceed the constitutional reach of the office. We now often treat the chief executive as a tribune of the people and the administrative apparatus beneath him as a substitute legislature. This has undermined effective administration, but it has especially undermined unity and cohesion in American life. Reformers looking to make modern presidents both more effective and more unifying would have to start by recognizing the vital importance of stability in the politics of a dynamic society.

ON JUNE 1, 1787, THE SEVENTH WORKING DAY OF THE PHILADELPHIA Convention, the delegates took up the question of a national

executive, and Pennsylvania delegate James Wilson quickly put his finger on the nature of the challenge they confronted. The extent of the United States and the likely complexity of the national government's work would require a presidency invested "with the vigour of monarchy," Wilson said. Yet the manners and principles of the people of the United States demanded that the presidency be "purely republican." Monarchic vigor and republican mores would seem to pull in opposite directions, and finding a point of balance between them was a task so challenging that American constitution makers up to that point had mostly avoided it.[1]

The national government under the Articles of Confederation had no executive at all, instead assigning a set of executive powers to the Congress along with its traditional legislative role. This arrangement had plainly failed, and the delegates in Philadelphia were broadly in agreement that they should not repeat the mistake of assigning executive powers to the legislature. Their work on this subject was launched by a resolution (taken up that same day, June 1) that called for a national executive who "ought to enjoy the Executive rights vested in Congress by the Confederation." The thirteen states had governors, but their offices (with the partial exception of New York's) were weak and ineffective. Having fought a revolution against the usurpations of a king, the Americans had not been inclined early on to give their governors much power. But many of the delegates in Philadelphia arrived with the conviction that this, too, was a mistake that should not be repeated at the national level. The delegates had some significant executive experience between them. As Joseph Bessette and Gary Schmitt have noted, of the fifty-five men who participated in the convention, "more than three-fifths had significant civilian executive experience before arriving in Philadelphia. . . . Eight had served or were serving as governor, and more than a fourth had served on their state's committee of safety, which wielded executive power before the new constitutions were enacted."[2]

But agreeing that the new national government needed a relatively strong executive did not mean they agreed about how strong the president should be or how that could be achieved. Charles Pinckney spoke for many of his fellow delegates when he said that he "was for a vigorous Executive but was afraid the Executive powers of the existing Congress might extend to peace and war etc., which would render the Executive a monarchy, and of the worst kind, to wit an elective one." An elective monarch would not make for a vigorous republican executive. But what would?[3]

In time, the delegates came to agree that, at the very least, the executive power needed to be vested in one individual, not a council. Congress had to be plural in order to be representative. But the president had to be singular in order to be capable of decision and action. This was, in part, because exercising executive power required a particularly high degree of accountability. As Alexander Hamilton wrote in Federalist 76, "The sole and undivided responsibility of one man, will naturally beget a livelier sense of duty, and a more exact obligation to reputation." But it also had to do with the particular demands that the Constitution would make of the national executive. "Decision, activity, secrecy, and dispatch will generally characterize the proceedings of one man in a much more eminent degree than the proceedings of any greater number; and in proportion as the number is increased, these qualities will be diminished," Hamilton concluded in Federalist 70.[4]

As those demands took shape in the course of the convention, the office of the presidency did too. It is, in one sense, a constrained office, since the president is charged with acting within the legal frameworks established by Congress and must, as the Constitution puts it, "take Care that the Laws be faithfully executed," whether or not those laws are to his liking. The document grants the chief executive some distinct authorities: He is the commander in chief of the military and the superior of the principal officers of each of the

executive departments. With the Senate's consent, he can appoint executive officials, judges, and ambassadors and can make treaties with foreign nations. He can propose legislation to Congress and can veto congressional measures (though Congress can override that veto with supermajorities in both houses).

And yet, despite the constraints of the office, the relative breadth of the president's powers is also a source of a great deal of independence and flexibility for him. Article II, which defines the office, begins with this general assertion: "The executive Power shall be vested in a President of the United States of America." That language might be usefully contrasted with the opening sentence of Article I: "All legislative Powers *herein granted* shall be vested in a Congress of the United States" (emphasis added). Because Article I defines the scope of federal power in the course of defining the powers of Congress, it was necessary to constrain it to only those powers specifically listed in the Constitution's text. That the executive power is not similarly circumscribed hints at the sort of freedom of action that is essential to the president's deployment of his powers.

Indeed, *action* more generally is the essence of the presidency. It is an office built for action and rendered in the present tense. Where the Congress constructs forward-looking statutory frameworks and the courts review past behavior in light of them, the president acts in the present, contending with pressures and events on behalf of the nation as they arise. This imposes heavy obligations on the chief executive. The Constitution and its amendments use the terms *duty* or *duties* (outside the realm of taxation) eleven separate times, all in relation to the executive branch. The document particularly uses the phrase *powers and duties* to describe the executive and repeatedly refers to the presidency as an *office*—which we might define as a patchwork of powers and duties. Hamilton, in Federalist 72, offers an overview of the key elements of that office: "The actual conduct of foreign negotiations, the preparatory plans of finance, the

application and disbursement of the public moneys in conformity to the general appropriations of the legislature, the arrangement of the army and navy, the directions of the operations of war, these, and other matters of a like nature, constitute what seems to be most properly understood by the administration of government."[5]

A lot of these powers and duties of the president have to do with the exercise of judgment under pressure, in response to real-world contingencies. This is part of what makes executive action fundamentally different from legislative deliberation, and it is why the president, for all that he does execute the laws Congress creates, is left independent of Congress in some important respects.

This was a point of some dispute at the Philadelphia Convention and has been ever since. Roger Sherman, a delegate from Connecticut, said at the convention that he "considered the Executive magistracy as nothing more than an institution for carrying the will of the Legislature into effect." But this was far from the dominant view in Philadelphia. Even George Mason of Virginia, who worried intensely about the dangers of presidential power (and ultimately refused to support the Constitution), told the delegates he was staunchly opposed to "making the Executive the mere creature of the Legislature," as that would be "a violation of the fundamental principle of good Government." This was not because the president should ever stand above the law, but because the legislature and the law are not the same. "It is one thing to be subordinate to the laws," Hamilton wrote in Federalist 71, "and another to be dependent on the legislative body." And if the legislature and the law are not the same, then certainly the legislature and the public are not. Hamilton continued, "However inclined we might be to insist upon an unbounded complaisance in the Executive to the inclinations of the people, we can with no propriety contend for a like complaisance to the humors of the legislature. The latter may sometimes stand in opposition to the former, and at other times the people may be

entirely neutral. In either supposition, it is certainly desirable that the Executive should be in a situation to dare to act his own opinion with vigor and decision." Note the move that Hamilton makes in this brief paragraph, from an openness to the notion that the president should seek to follow the public, if not the legislature, to an insistence that he must have the room and the daring to act on his own views.[6]

Terms like *vigor and decision* arise repeatedly in the framers' descriptions of the president's role. They considered the strength of the executive crucial to the success of the regime. Hamilton was particularly insistent on this point. "A feeble Executive implies a feeble execution of the government," he wrote. "A feeble execution is but another phrase for a bad execution; and a government ill executed, whatever it may be in theory, must be, in practice, a bad government." To be strong instead of feeble, the executive requires some room to act. A degree of independence is essential to the office, because the republic requires the president to be energetic and always in motion. The structure of the executive, Hamilton said in Federalist 77, "combines, as far as republican principles will admit, all the requisites to energy." Such energy is a foundational executive trait: "Energy in the Executive is a leading character in the definition of good government. It is essential to the protection of the community against foreign attacks; it is not less essential to the steady administration of the laws; to the protection of property against those irregular and high-handed combinations which sometimes interrupt the ordinary course of justice; to the security of liberty against the enterprises and assaults of ambition, of faction, and of anarchy." This kind of energetic executive could hardly be a mere supplicant of Congress because, as all of Hamilton's examples in the above quote suggest, he is called on to act in the world and so must have the space to make practical decisions about practical necessities within the framework of the laws.[7]

This need for space for the executive to act was not a choice the convention made but an inescapable fact of the situation of the republican executive and of the relation between his work and that of the legislature. The executive is subordinate to the law, but the law can never be specific enough to cover every possible eventuality. The infinite complexity and unpredictability of the real world will always create situations the legislator could not have envisioned. The executive must act in these situations and must have the room to make reasonable and prudential judgments about how to act. His actions may later be deemed to have been inappropriate by the courts or may result in some legislative response to prevent similar actions in the future. They may even get him impeached. But in the moment of decision, there are bound to be times when the written law just does not adequately resolve a question, and the president must call on his judgment. That means the presidency should not be structured to require pure, unthinking execution but must offer its occupant some room in the joints. The office, thus, exists in an intentionally uneasy relationship to the republican legislature. It is, as Harvey Mansfield has argued, "juxtaposed to the legislative power, in the ambivalence we recognize: now subordinate, now independent. In the deliberate construction of this ambivalence may be found the modern doctrine of executive power."[8]

This ambivalence can be dangerous, of course, so the president must somehow be restrained, even as he is granted room to act. The inherent limits of executive power, even given the partial mixing of powers envisioned by the Constitution, do provide some protection. "The magistrate in whom the whole executive power resides cannot of himself make a law, though he can put a negative on every law; nor administer justice in person, though he has the appointment of those who do administer it," Madison wrote. He is given significant but curtailed powers. But the need to keep him simultaneously subject to the laws, yet independent of Congress, also called for a

more sophisticated mechanism of simultaneous empowerment and restraint—an ambivalent mode of election designed to populate an ambivalent office.[9]

In the case of the legislature, election offered a way to fill the body with members who would be both representative of the people and elevated above the people to refine their passions and priorities. Congressional elections ask citizens who should speak for them in the deliberative work of self-government. But the president, being a single individual, cannot be representative, and most of the framers showed no real interest in making him representative. In his case, the purpose of the mode of selection they designed was precisely to achieve the precarious ambivalence required by the modern doctrine of executive power. That mode of selection had to, first of all, choose a capable person for what would be a very challenging job. But it also had to hold that person accountable while providing him with legitimacy rooted in the will of the voting public and not of the legislature. The delegates in Philadelphia considered empowering Congress to choose the president but decided this would make him too dependent on the first branch. They considered allowing the public to elect the chief executive directly but decided this would only result in demagogues being elected. The small states also worried that direct election would empower those candidates who were most popular in larger states; the larger states thought giving the Senate any role in choosing presidents would unfairly disadvantage them.[10]

In the end, after devoting some portion of twenty-one days and more than thirty separate votes to the subject, the convention determined that some middle institution was required and created the most peculiar of all the institutions of our system: the Electoral College. The voting public in each state would select a number of electors equal to that state's congressional delegation, and those electors would then choose the president. That middle layer, the framers

imagined, would allow for some distance from public passions and even some elite deliberation, but the entire process would still be rooted in a public vote. The system would, thus, be more likely to choose a person of good character and qualifications but also one with some degree of public support across a range of states.

Alexander Hamilton was surely bluffing a bit when he wrote, in Federalist 68, that "the mode of appointment of the Chief Magistrate of the United States is almost the only part of the system, of any consequence, which has escaped without severe censure, or which has received the slightest mark of approbation from its opponents." But the case he makes for the Electoral College is essentially the one that won the day at the convention. "It unites in an eminent degree all the advantages, the union of which was to be wished for," he wrote.

> It was desirable that the sense of the people should operate in the choice of the person to whom so important a trust was to be confided. This end will be answered by committing the right of making it, not to any preestablished body, but to men chosen by the people for the special purpose, and at the particular conjuncture.

> It was equally desirable, that the immediate election should be made by men most capable of analyzing the qualities adapted to the station, and acting under circumstances favorable to deliberation, and to a judicious combination of all the reasons and inducements which were proper to govern their choice. A small number of persons, selected by their fellow-citizens from the general mass, will be most likely to possess the information and discernment requisite to such complicated investigations.[11]

But this vision was never truly realized. Almost from the very beginning, the Electoral College came to operate as a kind of mediated public election rather than a venue for deliberation. The electors in

each state did not really deliberate, and they soon came to be chosen based on a commitment to vote for a particular candidate so that their election was a vote of the public, channeled through the formula for representing the state populations in Congress, rather than a way of empowering an elite body to choose. As we shall see in chapter 8, the American party system came to play something of the role originally envisioned for the Electoral College, the role of empowering some elite deliberation to play a part in the selection of the president, because the Electoral College itself never did play that role.

Although this mode of election is more direct than was intended, as we have seen in a variety of ways, it does actually offer crucial protections against the risks of factional polarization and demagoguery that worried the framers. The structure of the system compels candidates to appeal to regions of the country that are politically competitive and, therefore, to the persuadable center of the electorate. It prevents the parties from appealing only to their most devoted voters (as they would in a direct popular vote) and, therefore, mitigates the tendency of presidential elections to worsen partisan polarization. And the nature of the vote—which involves creating an electorate around the need to fill a particular office with a particular person—moves voters to consider the distinct qualifications required for the office, even (if to a lesser degree) in starkly partisan times. This is hardly a foolproof mechanism, of course; demagogues have certainly been elected president a few times. But on the whole, it has worked remarkably well.

The Electoral College is plausibly accused of being a suboptimal mechanism of representation, but the presidency is an administrative office and not a representative one, and the Electoral College was intended to be a mechanism of selection and accountability, not of representation. The purpose of electing presidents is to choose capable people for the job and (especially by holding out the possibility

of reelection) to hold them to account. The Congress is meant to be full of representative men and women; the president is intended to be an exceptional person.

To say that the presidency is an administrative more than a representative office is not to diminish its significance or stature, however. On the contrary, the framers considered administration to be utterly crucial work and the essence of appropriate strength in government. "The true test of a good government," Hamilton wrote in Federalist 68, "is its aptitude and tendency to produce a good administration." Their understanding of the value of administration focused especially on its capacity to yield stability and steadiness—crucial executive virtues, which along with their importance in facilitating effective government, are also the chief contributions of the American president to the cause of national unity.

THE PECULIAR EMPHASIS ON ADMINISTRATION IN THE THINKING OF THE founding generation was very much a function of the revolutionary and early republican experience. In a short span of years, Americans had seen both abuses of administrative authority and failures of administrative prowess. The British had shown them what excessive executive power could look like. As James Q. Wilson put it, "Except for the issue of taxation, which raised for the colonists major questions of representation, almost all of their complaints [against the British] involved the abuse of administrative powers." This led them, as noted above, to establish relatively weak executive offices in the state governments. But that quickly produced disastrous failures of administration, and it was the lessons of these failures that really pointed toward the shape of the presidency.[12]

The foremost lesson, and the one most relevant to the capacity of the constitutional executive to engender greater national unity

as well, was that weak administration leads to dangerous instability. This danger was a primary motive for pursuing a new constitution, especially for James Madison. In his outline of the "Vices of the Political System of the United States," produced in preparation for the convention, Madison sketched the ways that the mutability of the laws of the states and the absence of consistent enforcement and governance created not only uncertainty and chaos but also injustice. In the wake of the convention, Madison knew that the case for stable governance would be crucial to persuading the public to support the Constitution. "The sober people of America are weary of the fluctuating policy which has directed the public councils," he wrote in Federalist 44. Constant turmoil is a threat to the very future of the regime because it undermines the public's sense that their government is just and fair. In Federalist 10, Madison said it this way: "Complaints are everywhere heard from our most considerate and virtuous citizens, equally the friends of public and private faith, and of public and personal liberty, that our governments are too unstable, that the public good is disregarded in the conflicts of rival parties, and that measures are too often decided, not according to the rules of justice and the rights of the minor party, but by the superior force of an interested and overbearing majority."

This could easily pose a grave danger to the regime, as any student of the history of republics knows. "The instability, injustice, and confusion, introduced into the public councils have, in truth, been the mortal diseases under which popular governments have every where perished," Madison wrote. And this danger was already evident in America. The growing worry about the durability of the union and the loss of public trust in government in the United States in his time, he argued, "must be chiefly, if not wholly, effects of the unsteadiness and injustice with which a factious spirit has tainted our public administrations."[13]

Madison went out of his way to link this concern to Hamilton's emphasis on energy, and yet also to distinguish those two priorities in a way that clarifies both. In Federalist 37, he wrote:

> Energy in government is essential to that security against external and internal danger, and to that prompt and salutary execution of the laws which enter into the very definition of good government. Stability in government is essential to national character and to the advantages annexed to it, as well as to that repose and confidence in the minds of the people, which are among the chief blessings of civil society. An irregular and mutable legislation is not more an evil in itself than it is odious to the people; and it may be pronounced with assurance that the people of this country, enlightened as they are with regard to the nature, and interested, as the great body of them are, in the effects of good government, will never be satisfied till some remedy be applied to the vicissitudes and uncertainties which characterize the State administrations.[14]

Here we find, outlined with Madison's characteristic clarity, the distinction between the executive's (and the government's) vital role in keeping the country safe from foreign and domestic enemies and its essential part in keeping the country unified and peaceful. Hamilton embraced this view as well, and both of them, along with other key framers of the Constitution, came to emphasize stability and consistency in administration as key features of the kind of government they were looking to establish—precisely because of the necessity of stability as a precondition for greater national cohesion.

"Steady administration," in Hamilton's words, thus forms the president's distinct and crucial contribution to the unity of our society. This is not what we naturally think of when we seek for the unifying potential of the executive today. The unitary character of the office suggests that the president might unify Americans by serving

as a kind of emblem of the nation—a figurehead that all can look to as their leader, and truly, one drawn out of many. There have certainly been times, especially in moments of national emergency, when presidential rhetoric and leadership have brought Americans together in this way. But at least since George Washington left office, the American presidency and the struggle to select its occupant has far more often been a source of intense division in our politics, and the president has been a focal point for polarized partisan emotions. It is not the president's person or his electoral mandate that has enabled our chief executives to unify the public but rather the president's work—the work of administration, when it is pursued with stability in mind.

In Federalist 72, Hamilton makes it clear that stability of administration is a vital function of the president, in particular, but also a real challenge in a system where presidents are elected, even indirectly. There is, he says, an "intimate connection between the duration of the executive magistrate in office and the stability of the system of administration." After all, he continues, "to reverse and undo what has been done by a predecessor, is very often considered by a successor as the best proof he can give of his own capacity and desert; and in addition to this propensity, where the alteration has been the result of public choice, the person substituted is warranted in supposing that the dismission of his predecessor has proceeded from a dislike to his measures; and that the less he resembles him, the more he will recommend himself to the favor of his constituents."

This might tend to cause every new president to begin by undoing his predecessor's work, and that, Hamilton argues, "could not fail to occasion a disgraceful and ruinous mutability in the administration of the government." One way to deal with that risk is to allow presidents to run for reelection, which gives them an interest in more durable modes of administration. But another is to invest the chief executive with a sense of his office as extending beyond

his own time and help him grasp the importance of stable, durable administration.[15]

This is not to say that the president should be a neutral administrator. Steadiness is not stasis, and steady administration involves a mix of firm direction and stability. The president was clearly intended, in part, to be a kind of first mover in our politics and to set the general direction of the national government by setting some priorities, even if it was left to Congress to determine just how (and how far) those priorities would be taken up. But a steady administrator would avoid sharp turns and hard stops and, even in changing direction, would seek some continuity and some smoothing of transitions.

This was also how the president was expected to use some of his distinct powers in relation to Congress. The veto, for instance, was a means not only to allow the president's will and agenda to play a part in setting the direction of legislation but also a way to restrain the mutability of the laws. As Hamilton wrote in Federalist 73:

> It may perhaps be said that the power of preventing bad laws includes that of preventing good ones; and may be used to the one purpose as well as to the other. But this objection will have little weight with those who can properly estimate the mischiefs of that inconstancy and mutability in the laws, which form the greatest blemish in the character and genius of our governments. They will consider every institution calculated to restrain the excess of law-making, and to keep things in the same state in which they happen to be at any given period, as much more likely to do good than harm; because it is favorable to greater stability in the system of legislation.[16]

But it is through the work of administration itself that the president has the greatest opportunity to facilitate stability, and a lot depends on his ability to do so. Basic social peace requires a stable backdrop

for public life, and conditions of instability and uncertainty can easily make it impossible for people to build flourishing lives.

In Federalist 62, Madison lays out, in its fullest form, his case for the importance of stability in holding together a republican regime. Too much unpredictability in government threatens the country's security because it "forfeits the respect and confidence of other nations, and all the advantages connected with national character." More importantly, unsteadiness in government makes it impossible for anyone to be a faithful, law-abiding citizen. "Law is defined to be a rule of action; but how can that be a rule, which is little known, and less fixed?" And unsteady administration also tends to benefit those with the resources to keep up with new laws and rules at the expense of everyone else: "Every new regulation concerning commerce or revenue, or in any way affecting the value of the different species of property, presents a new harvest to those who watch the change, and can trace its consequences; a harvest, reared not by themselves, but by the toils and cares of the great body of their fellow-citizens."

Precarious and changeable laws and regulations also undermine people's incentive to invest in their society's future. "What prudent merchant will hazard his fortunes in any new branch of commerce when he knows not but that his plans may be rendered unlawful before they can be executed?" Madison asks. "What farmer or manufacturer will lay himself out for the encouragement given to any particular cultivation or establishment, when he can have no assurance that his preparatory labors and advances will not render him a victim to an inconstant government?"[17]

These arguments do not apply exclusively to the executive, of course. They are crucial with respect to Congress, too, and for Madison, they were particularly relevant to the role of the Senate. But it is the president, because of his capacity for unitary action and direction, who bears the greatest responsibility to act with steadiness

and with stability. The election of a chief executive alters the entire executive branch all at once, and the occupant of the office has an obligation to reduce the potential for instability inherent in that fact. Some continuity in administration can reduce the stakes of presidential elections and, therefore, their divisiveness and the temperature of our politics. Our system is intended to change only at the speed of Congress, which is a very slow speed. The sense that an election could mean a sudden and sharp change of direction inevitably invites intense and bitter partisan divisions.

More generally, it is ultimately the steadiness of administration that determines its quality, and its quality that, in turn, determines the fate of the government and even the public's attachment to it. It may seem strange that the quality of administration should be so significant, but the framers clearly thought it was. "I believe it may be laid down as a general rule that [public] confidence in and obedience to a government will commonly be proportioned to the goodness or badness of its administration," Hamilton wrote in Federalist 27. Madison could hardly agree more: "No government, any more than an individual, will long be respected without being truly respectable," he writes, "nor be truly respectable, without possessing a certain portion of order and stability."[18]

Representation is a vital source of legitimacy for a republican government, as we have seen, but good administration is a vital source of confidence in such a government. Just as the president would have nothing to administer if Congress did not first render the public's will into an ordered framework for governing, so Congress's legislation would achieve nothing without effective administration to put it into action. As Harvey Flaumenhaft said, "Popular representation avails little without efficacious administration. Although the beginning and the end of good government is the people, between the source and the outcome operates that organization of means which is administration."[19]

Confidence in government is, in turn, essential to the public's unity around it. The sheer incompetence of American government under the Articles of Confederation was a threat to the durability of the union, and a well-working government would be essential to holding the country together. This was a crucial point of agreement between the friends and critics of the Constitution. The great federalist James Wilson, who was a delegate from Pennsylvania at the convention, argued to his fellow delegates that "no government could long subsist without the confidence of the people. In a republican government this confidence was peculiarly essential." The antifederalist writer who used the pen name "Federal Farmer" similarly argued that "the great object of a free people must be so to form their government and laws, and so to administer them, as to create a confidence in, and a respect for the laws; and thereby induce the sensible and virtuous part of the community to declare in favor of the laws, and to support them without an expensive military force." That generation of Americans understood, based on their own experience, that a collapse of faith in government can lead to a collapse of public order, and of unity and camaraderie among the people.[20]

Steady administration is thus a vital ingredient in a successful and durable republican regime and is especially vital for the unity of society. It is the president's particular contribution, and it requires presidents to be distinctly self-restrained, deliberate, and intentional about how they use their office and how they regard its unique mix of powers and duties. The office, in this sense, does not do the work on its own. The president as an individual, as a human being chosen to lead, must take upon his own shoulders an extraordinary burden of responsibility—a kind of aristocratic burden to sustain the preconditions for republicanism. This paradox is inherent in the structure of the office. Just as the Constitution seeks to sustain a productive tension between majority will and minority rights, so it also sustains a productive tension between democratic liberty and

aristocratic grandeur. It is a democratic system, built around various instruments of public empowerment and accountability. But it also makes room for an executive who is expected to sometimes be a statesman—a person of broad perspective and real magnanimity.

Such elevated leadership is not always forthcoming, of course. The Constitution does not rest on the presumption that all our presidents will be great men and women. "Enlightened statesmen will not always be at the helm," as Madison notes. But occasionally, and especially in times of great national need, they may be, and we should want to maximize the likelihood that they will be.[21]

To maximize that likelihood, we must keep in mind what kind of greatness and what kind of everyday duty is demanded of the republican executive. His role is not to be a tribune of the people or a visionary tyrant but to engender stability and steadiness in a republican polity that always threatens to burst at the seams. Confusion over this purpose and over the kind of excellence we should expect from our presidents has done much to undermine the presidency in our time and, therefore, to diminish our society's capacity for unity.

THE TROUBLE IS ROOTED IN THE SAME PROGRESSIVE CHALLENGE TO THE political anthropology of the Constitution that we have been tracing now for several chapters. That challenge began with a concern that the American system was just too restrained and divided to meet the needs of a modern society. In one sense, this progressive worry about the incoherence of American government would seem to be related to the framers' worry about instability and unsteadiness. "At present," Woodrow Wilson wrote in 1885, "the federal government lacks strength because its powers are divided, lacks promptness because its authorities are multiplied, lacks wieldiness because its processes are roundabout, lacks efficiency because its responsibility

is indistinct and its action without competent direction." What was needed was a strong guiding hand at the center. Wilson, at first, thought such a strong hand might emerge in Congress, in the form of a majority party leader who could function like a kind of American prime minister. But over time, he and other progressives came to conclude that this hand should be the president's, since he is the one public official accountable to a single national electorate.[22]

As it developed, this Wilsonian critique essentially substituted administration for deliberation, and in the process, it misplaced the locus of representation and rejected the premise of the framers' republicanism. It repudiated the means of the Constitution because it first dismissed its ends and ignored the need to forge common ground and build national unity through common action across lines of difference. Wilson's core critique of Congress—that it was not well ordered to enable energetic and accountable policy action—and his preference for the Westminster model clarified his approach to the presidency too. In effect, he hoped to pursue legislative ends through administrative means, as the latter were plainly more energetic and assertive.

What Wilson meant by the unwieldiness and unsteadiness of the federal government was not that policy would swing too quickly and sharply from one direction to another—which was what Madison had in mind by instability—but rather that policymaking was slow and incremental and proceeded through negotiated half measures that did not answer to any one clear vision. In other words, Madison's solution was Wilson's problem.

This was, in part, because Wilson rejected a key premise of Madison's case for the separation of powers. In Wilson's view, the separation of powers was merely a set of checks and balances—a way of restraining everyone. This was certainly part of the framers' conception. But Madison also thought that the powers being kept separate by institutional design were actually inherently separate in

themselves, so that mixing them too much would mean corrupting them and, ultimately, that "the accumulation of all powers, legislative, executive, and judiciary, in the same hands, whether of one, a few, or many, and whether hereditary, self-appointed, or elective, may justly be pronounced the very definition of tyranny." Wilson disagreed. He found Madison's approach too "Newtonian," as he put it. It treated government like a machine with distinct parts. But in fact, in Wilson's words, "government is not a machine but a living thing. It falls, not under the theory of the universe but the theory of organic life. It is accountable to Darwin, not to Newton." This meant that separating powers made no sense: "No living thing can have its organs offset against each other as checks and live. On the contrary, its life is dependent upon their quick cooperation, their ready response to the commands of instinct or intelligence, their amicable community of purpose." Wilson, thus, gave voice to the appeal of various kinds of integralism, an appeal that has always been at the heart of the deepest critiques of the American constitutional vision. The framers treated the constitutional system as an instrument, but Wilson wanted to treat it as an organism, and this meant that it required a singular, integrated direction and could only function if its different limbs and organs worked as one and were jointly directed.[23]

Such direction almost had to come from the executive, because the executive is one and not many and because he has a national constituency and is accountable to the whole of the nation. This also makes the president best positioned to discern the public's priorities and to represent the people's will, as well as to lead the public—to inform, to persuade, and to move a national audience.

These were Hamilton's reasons for wanting the executive to be unitary. But for Wilson, because he did not recognize the legitimacy or the inevitability of the multiplicity of interests and views in society, the desire for energy and dispatch applied to all of government,

not just to the deployment of powers that are distinctly executive. He worried far more about inefficiency and inaction than about recklessness and injustice. And he was not concerned about disunity in the broader public but, rather, about the fractiousness of Congress, which results in a failure to express and embody in government action the underlying unity of public desires. Wilson acknowledged that what he meant by public desires was the will of the majority, but he took this to be a legitimate and democratic understanding. He, therefore, ultimately argued for a politics organized by "responsible parties," which represent substantive differences of policy views and a mode of government that (as in European parliamentary democracies) allows the majority party to effectively and efficiently deploy the power of the state while it is in power. The president is the leader of his party and, therefore, in effect, the leader of the government as well.

This view, which Wilson would describe as a case for steadier government, is actually subject to all the concerns expressed by the framers about unsteady government. It would mean that transfers of power from one party to another at election time would result in stark and sudden changes in policy direction and would, therefore, heighten the stakes of our elections—and especially our presidential elections—and raise the temperature of our partisan politics. And it would mean that prominent and divisive policy questions were resolved decisively in favor of one side or another rather than through negotiated settlements that allowed all sides to accept the outcome and permit it to endure. It would undermine the stability of our national life and intensify the divisions in our politics.

IN FACT, IT HAS. OBVIOUSLY, MODERN PROGRESSIVISM IS NOT SIMPLY applied Wilsonianism, and the development of the so-called

administrative state over the past century was also, by no means, purely a progressive project. But that development has, nonetheless, been deeply informed by the logic of Wilson's critique of the separation of powers and by the appeal of pursuing legislative aims by administrative means.

The growth of administrative agencies began as an effort to regulate the increasingly complex industrial economy in the late nineteenth century and was, at first, driven by Congress, largely in an effort to contain presidential power rather than inflate it. Until the 1880s, Congress had exercised its power to regulate interstate commerce directly, through legislative action. But with the creation of the Interstate Commerce Commission (ICC) in 1887, it began gradually to delegate that work. The ICC was designed as a bipartisan commission, with seven members, to facilitate negotiation between shippers and the railroad companies over carriage rates. Over the subsequent several decades, similar bodies were created to perform similar functions, as well as more active regulation in other sectors: power, water, communications, commodity markets, and more. Congress took this route because it did not want to delegate these regulatory powers to the president or to overburden the courts with them, but also did not want to (or believe it could) exercise them on its own in individual instances. Legislators also had a more forthrightly constitutional purpose: growing partisanship and patronage in the nineteenth century had made the presidency less of a force for stability and meant that the direction of administration was more likely to change abruptly with election results. More independent administrators (along with greater protections for civil servants) were viewed by some in Congress as more likely to sustain a steady administrative direction across presidential administrations. So these commissions were given a peculiar independence: the president could not instruct them to make certain decisions and could only fire their commissioners for cause, unlike most executive

branch officials. And yet, they were executive agencies, carrying out the laws.[24]

Over the first third of the twentieth century, such agencies gradually took on more regulatory authority, and the federal courts gradually loosened their objections to Congress delegating its legislative powers to these essentially (and increasingly) executive bodies. Provided the delegation was specific enough to guide executive action, the courts concluded, it could be constitutionally tolerable. This enabled the power of the agencies to grow, and eventually, Congress moved to formalize their role through the Administrative Procedure Act (APA) of 1946. The APA recognized that regulatory action by executive agencies was unavoidable but required that such action be grounded in statutes passed by Congress and that it provide the public with notice of proposed actions and consider public comments before finalizing those actions to give affected citizens some say in the process.

By then, administrative agencies (particularly those created in the New Deal era) were regulating economic activity in minute detail across vast sectors of American life—setting prices and requiring particular provisions of service in transportation, energy, and other markets. Some of the most ambitious and intrusive of these efforts were rolled back in a deregulatory effort that spanned Democratic and Republican presidencies in the 1970s and 1980s, but the volume and density of rules only continued to grow, and in recent decades, such regulation has increasingly taken on the form of general rules (resembling legislation) rather than case-specific determinations. In our time, the term *administrative state* describes more than four hundred agencies, some relatively independent and some subject to more direct presidential control, that employ more than two million officials and issue thousands of binding rules every year.

The scope and quantity of federal regulations easily dwarf those of legislation passed by Congress, and an enormous amount of what

is effectively lawmaking now takes the form of such administrative (and, therefore, technically executive) action. As Chief Justice John Roberts stated in a 2013 Supreme Court opinion, "The Framers could hardly have envisioned today's vast and varied federal bureaucracy and the authority administrative agencies now hold over our economic, social, and political activities." This mode of governing is, in essence, what Woodrow Wilson was looking for: decisions that are legislative in character—in that they create binding rules intended to achieve public aims—but are pursued by administrative means and, therefore, are not channeled through the slow and arduous accommodative mechanisms of the Congress. Administrative agencies often negotiate with relevant interests around such rules, and they are required to invite and consider comments from the general public, but they are not constituted by representatives of the public and their work is not the product of negotiation among factions of such representatives. That some are pursued by so-called independent agencies only makes them less accountable, not more, since those amount to executive actions not subject to the modes of accountability that apply to the president. As Judge Neomi Rao of the US Court of Appeals for the DC Circuit has put it, "Founding era political theory and the Framers connected the collective and representative legislature with certain fundamental features of a legitimate government. Lawmaking by the executive shares none of the features of a collective and representative legislature."[25]

The modern administrative state appeals to many political activists precisely because it diminishes the need for bargaining and compromise. Congress exists to negotiate in order to resolve disputes. The president exists to act prudentially in response to circumstances within the frameworks Congress creates. Judges exist to assess the uses of power in the system and vindicate the rules of the constitutional order. But now too many people on all sides of our politics want to do something none of these institutions exist to

do: to advance a policy agenda without bargaining with opponents, without prioritizing prudence, and without regard for the constitutional order. In the case of executive action, this leads, in particular, to the adoption of essentially legislative measures that are too partisan to have garnered enough support to make it through Congress and that advance instead thanks to a kind of loophole through the constitutional arrangements intended to prevent rash partisan mistakes.[26]

Some administrative expertise is undoubtedly necessary given the complexity of our society's expectations of its national government. The president's work must be informed and supported by a significant administrative apparatus. But that apparatus must be rooted in a clear distinction between legislative and executive functions and so must exist in support of the president's work and not in lieu of Congress. The administrative state blurs that distinction and, therefore, lacks a natural home in the framework of the constitutional system. It is in tension with that system's means and ends—including the aim of promoting social peace and national cohesion. As we saw in chapter 5, this often happens with Congress's approval and sanction. Members now want to delegate legislative power to administrative agencies, both to avoid having to make difficult choices and to enable their desired agenda to be pursued more aggressively and without the need to compromise with political opponents.[27]

As a result, we often treat legislative and administrative action as interchangeable. When Congress declines (or fails) to act on immigration reform, student-loan relief, health policy, or any number of other domains, the president steps in. In 2011, President Barack Obama made this point explicit in remarks to an audience in Colorado: "But listen, we're not going to wait, though. We're not waiting for Congress. Last month, when I addressed a joint session of Congress about our jobs crisis, I said I intend to do everything in my power right now to act on behalf of the American people—with or

without Congress. We can't wait for Congress to do its job. So where they won't act, I will."[28]

Few modern presidents have been quite so brazen in declaring their willingness to take essentially legislative actions, but all have taken such actions, and all have used their administrative powers in ways that have undermined rather than served steady administration. Recent presidents have also gradually recognized that they can exercise enormous power by selectively refraining from acting when the law requires them to act—granting enforcement waivers in different areas, not prosecuting in certain circumstances, not enforcing immigration laws in some situations, forgiving some student loans. They can thereby make policy by inaction, using a broad legislative mandate as merely a canvas for governing by administrative will. Such willful inaction is constitutionally dubious, whether it is technically legal or not. The president takes an oath to faithfully execute an office charged with carrying out the laws, and both the use of administrative power in legislative domains and the withholding of executive action in executive domains are derelictions of that obligation.

Today, just as the framers feared, a change of the party in power means a sudden change of direction in many policy domains, as a new president begins his term by undoing his predecessor's key actions. This renders our politics more divided and heated and puts power in the hands of the most partisan activist fringe of the president's party, which could not nearly so easily dominate legislative work. It, therefore, undermines not only the legislature but the executive, too, making it far more difficult for the president to provide the kind of background stability that our system expects of him.

BUT IT IS NOT ONLY IN THE REALM OF FORMAL ADMINISTRATION THAT the modern presidency has been deformed by the Wilsonian vision

of the constitutional order. The president's role in relation to the public, and so the chief executive's place in our political culture, has changed dramatically as well. Woodrow Wilson's vision of the presidency was rooted in its capacity for statesmanlike leadership of public opinion and in the chief executive's national constituency, which certainly are part of the president's role. But in Wilson's view, the president needed to draw on those to make himself society's chief policy advocate and to single-handedly set the direction of the federal government. The Constitution expects the president's policy rhetoric to be directed to Congress, not to the public. But Wilson argued that this could no longer suffice. As Jeffrey Tulis noted in his important 1987 book *The Rhetorical Presidency,* "Since the presidencies of Theodore Roosevelt and Woodrow Wilson, popular or mass rhetoric has become a principal tool of presidential governance [so that] the doctrine that a president ought to be a popular leader has become an unquestioned premise of our political culture. . . . And for many, this presidential 'function' is not one duty among many, but rather the heart of the presidency—an essential task."[29]

This understanding of the presidency evinces an essentially expressive ideal of politics, and it, too, is rooted in a misunderstanding of the nature of representation in the American system. It assumes that the president must be the most representative figure in our government because he is the only one empowered by a national electorate and able to speak with one voice on its behalf. And by speaking in one voice for the nation, he can unite the nation, because his vantage point enables him to see its unity and common purpose as no one else could. As Wilson put it, the chief executive could be "a man in whose ears the voices of the nation do not sound like accidental and discordant notes that come from the voice of a mob, but concurrent and concordant like the united voices of a chorus, whose many meanings, spoken by melodious tongues, unite in his understanding in a single meaning and reveal to him a single

vision, so that he can speak what no man else knows, the common meaning of the common voice."[30]

But what if Wilson was wrong to imagine that such a common voice is there to be heard by our presidents? What if our unity is in need of formation, not detection and expression? Where can it be formed? Only where our plurality is represented and its factions can encounter and deal with one another—that is, only in Congress. The president's role is enormously important, but it is distinctly executive. If the differences that define and divide us are real, then the president's administrative office cannot be ultimately representative, and it can be persuasive only to a limited degree. The rhetorical presidency is set up to fail to deliver on its promises, since it is not capable of playing the role that the Wilsonian view would assign to it.

These failures, however, have often only moved modern presidents to double down on the rhetorical facets of their office: rather than operate as insiders, administering the government, they have sought to lead as outsiders speaking at and to the government. Unable to speak on behalf of a unified public in our divided time, they have settled for speaking for their particular partisans, thereby using their office to intensify our divisions.

This has only become easier and more attractive in the age of social media, in which we incline to replace arenas of engagement and contention with echo chambers that reward performative, partisan virtue signaling. Such theatrics have proven irresistible to recent presidents. This has been true of none of them more than of Donald Trump, whose practical conception of executive leadership was formed not through experience working in our constitutional system but through a lifetime of cultural performance art. As Mikael Good and Philip Wallach wrote:

A seasoned entertainer, Trump unified his supporters by giving vent to their emotions. Employing cadences borrowed from stand-up

comics and radio shock jocks, Trump transformed populist rage into a positive emotion: gleeful shared mockery of the politicians and elites who had betrayed the true Americans. This was, in the loosest sense, a Wilsonian act of "interpretation," channeling and guiding a well of anger and alienation held in common (at least on an affective level) by many different Americans. If it is not possible for one man to meaningfully represent the political interests of the whole people, Trump did at least manage to stir up the nebulous emotion of his base such that it became a political phenomenon with genuine unifying force. But rather than translating people's grievances into action, Trump's performances were offered as their own reward.[31]

This is the almost inevitable trap of the rhetorical presidency that Wilson proposed—treating the office as a stage for mass performance tempts its occupant to abandon the office's constitutional purpose altogether. And in the process, the president also surrenders his capacity for unifying action aimed at securing the steadiness and stability of the American regime. The American presidency is now likely the single most divisive facet of our politics—an incessant and inexhaustible fountain of tribalism and disunity.

CHANGING THAT WOULD HAVE TO INVOLVE RECOVERING SOMETHING OF the office's original function and structure and the vision underlying it. There is no avoiding the fact that this would first require a revitalization of Congress.

The presidency (like the judiciary) has become overgrown and inflamed, in large part, because Congress has left a dangerous vacuum at the heart of our system of government, and a restoration of the second branch to its proper proportions could only follow a

restoration of the first. The president has an important role in setting the agenda of the federal government, raising some key questions to particular prominence, and pressing Congress to take them up. But taking them up has to mean more than talking about them on the internet and more then pressing the president for administrative action. It has to mean negotiating toward detailed, durable legislation that then assigns to the executive and his agents discrete administrative tasks and not general legislative ones.

But although only Congress could uproot our deepest constitutional dysfunctions, some reforms of the presidency could advance that goal or increase the likelihood of reforms of Congress. The extra-constitutional character of "independent" administrative agencies has to be dealt with, for one thing. From the National Labor Relations Board and the Consumer Product Safety Commission to the Securities and Exchange Commission, the Federal Communications Commission, the Federal Deposit Insurance Corporation, and the rest of the dozen or so commissions that regulate the national economy, these agencies are considered independent because there is a limit on the president's ability to remove their leaders. But as a practical matter, they are also generally independent of the review and coordination process by which the president and his senior appointees oversee the regulatory function of the executive branch. Bringing these agencies under the umbrella of presidential review and control would be a step toward bringing them more generally into the fold of the constitutional system, which has only three branches of government and no fourth superbranch of regulators. The president could launch that reform with the powers already available to him.

A further step in that direction would need to involve restraints on the essentially legislative and judicial powers now frequently exercised by regulatory agencies. In the absence of legislation mandating such changes, such a reform would need to be a presidential

initiative to require agency regulatory processes to more clearly demonstrate a statutory foundation for every major administrative action and to justify the distinctly executive character of every such action. At the Philadelphia Convention, James Madison proposed that language along these lines be included in the text of the Constitution. He suggested that after the language establishing a national executive, "there be inserted the words following viz. 'with power to carry into effect the national laws, to appoint to offices in cases not otherwise provided for, and to execute such other powers not Legislative nor Judiciary in their nature, as may from time to time be delegated by the national Legislature.'"

In his notes on the convention, Madison comments that "the words 'not legislative nor judiciary in their nature' were added to the proposed amendment in consequence of a suggestion by General Pinckney that improper powers might otherwise be delegated." This language was not ultimately adopted into the Constitution, but presidents in our day would be wise to behave as though it was.[32] This points to the broader character of the kinds of reforms of the presidency that now seem called for. Generally speaking, they are not technical structural reforms like those that would be helpful in Congress but, rather, forms of restraint and self-conscious circumspection by our presidents. This is a function of the nature of the office. The presidency, more than any other institution in our system, depends on its occupant possessing a particular sort of character. The president has a lot of leeway to make judgments and pursue courses of action. These can sometimes be reversed in retrospect by the judiciary, as we shall see. But they can rarely be restrained in real time or proscribed in advance. The scope of presidential power is intentionally vague and flexible, and this imposes unique burdens of responsibility on the chief executive.

This demands that American voters seek out for the presidency people who are uniquely responsible—which has not always been

our priority as citizens voting for that office in recent years, to put it mildly. But it also demands that presidents be formed by their office, just as legislators and judges must be by theirs, and that they be formed in particular for restraint and self-control and for the sort of temperamental moderation that is the essence of the statesman's character. They need to show such restraint in their deployment of regulatory power; presidents need to be comfortable saying that they lack the authority to do what some of their partisans and allies want them to do. There is strength in such assertions of responsible restraint that contemporary presidents have failed to grasp. They can be persuasive arguments for congressional action, and they can also help legitimate and reinforce those executive actions that an otherwise restrained president does take. By clearly defining the scope of his power, the chief executive improves his effectiveness in using that power.

The same restraint is called for in the use of the presidency as a stage for political rhetoric—a "bully pulpit" as Theodore Roosevelt famously called it. This would be even harder for contemporary chief executives, as the power of the presidency as a platform for political expression is now, perhaps, its chief appeal for them. The president certainly does have a role to play as a leader of our national political culture and a figure with unique persuasive tools at his disposal. But persuasion is not the core duty or power of the presidency, and rhetorical performance is not one of those powers that are "in their nature executive," as Madison put it. The presidency must be directed to action more than to speech, and the emphasis on political performance unquestionably undermines the capacity of the president to take up the core work of the office, because it renders the chief executive into merely another partisan voice in the divisive cacophony of our political culture.[33]

This cannot be addressed by the president merely trying to be a voice for unity—as to one extent or another, every recent president

has tried to be. Unity, as we have been discovering, is not a rhetorical style or an intellectual condition but a mode of action. It consists not of thinking alike or speaking alike but of acting together. There are, of course, unique moments of national crisis or triumph when presidential rhetoric can serve as a foundation for genuine unity. We all can think of such times, especially in war. But those examples do not merely involve rhetoric either. We remember the words of our presidents because they articulated the foundations for actions taken in the name of the larger society—and generally with the support of Congress. Presidential rhetoric can validate and elevate such unifying action, but it cannot substitute for it.

Our presidents have increasingly forgotten that. To remind themselves of it, they should pull back their rhetoric and reground their self-understanding in the character of the executive's work. They should return, for instance, to delivering their annual reports on the state of the union (which are mandated by the Constitution) in writing, as presidents did throughout the nineteenth century, rather than through the increasingly ridiculous and pompous televised formal speeches that have been the norm since Woodrow Wilson's presidency. They should self-consciously fade just a little into the background of our national life—not because the presidency is not a uniquely prominent national office but because, in our particular time, its prominence has become outrageously exaggerated in ways that have deformed American government.

That deformation has particularly undermined our society's capacity for unity. To restore the real strengths of their office, presidents should, therefore, consider the distinct role they have in facilitating unity. That should lead them to focus on steadiness and stability, both in how they use their formal powers and how they talk about them.

Such reflection should also shape how American presidents approach the other branches of our government. The problem to be

addressed—the growing disunity of our society, and the apparent inability of our constitutional system to ameliorate disunity as it was designed to do—requires more than changes in the behavior of one public official. They require a concerted project of rediscovery and renewal, reaching to the roots and purposes of our institutions and restoring some crucial but diminished capacities. Congress and the president must engage in that work in the coming years, and there is a role for the courts in it as well.

Chapter 7

THE COURTS

THE JUDICIAL POWER CREATED BY THE CONSTITUTION EXHIBITS A
paradoxical mix of weakness and strength. The federal judiciary
has relatively few formal tools at its disposal for engaging in the
interbranch struggles envisioned by the framers, but the courts are
empowered by an aura of authority that generates enormous deference from others in the system. The framers emphasized the need
for independent judges, but the Constitution did not fully delineate
the distinct role of federal courts. The most significant power of
the courts—the power to nullify legislative and executive actions
that judges deem to violate the text of the Constitution—actually
appears nowhere in that text and had to be construed from the general character of the judicial power.

The potential of the federal courts, armed with this power of
judicial review, to transform American political life emerged only
gradually as judges began to exercise that power, not only to police
the boundaries of interbranch conflict but also to conjure novel individual rights that constrained the scope of government action. At
first, the courts used that approach to thwart progressive ambitions

in the economic domain. But with time, the judiciary came to be an enabler of progressive constitutional transformation in the social arena. The conservative response to this evolution led to the emergence of the doctrine of originalism, with its emphasis on judicial restraint, which has become the dominant intellectual framework for debates about the role of the courts in our time. Such debates now increasingly look beyond the question of restraint regarding judge-made rights and toward more of an emphasis on constitutional structure and function.

For that reason, it's critical to grasp the role of the courts in enabling greater national cohesion. Their potential to unify us is not rooted where we might expect; it is not so much a function of their capacity to settle disputes as of their power to keep our system of government true to itself. The federal judiciary can preserve the bargains that Congress and the Constitution have settled; it can route political conflict back to Congress or the states, at least when there is no clear constitutional text that decisively settles the matter; it can facilitate the operation of majority rule and the protection of minority rights; and it can guard key constitutional boundaries. We should look to the courts to secure these core constitutional functions, not to offer shortcuts to our preferred policy outcomes when we don't have the patience for politics.

THE NEED FOR A FEDERAL JUDICIARY WAS AMONG THE IMMEDIATE CAUSES of the process that led to the Constitutional Convention in Philadelphia. The Articles of Confederation had proven inadequate on many fronts, but it was the absence of a forum for resolving disputes between states—including trade and boundary disputes that were essentially legal in nature—that led first to a conference of delegates from Maryland and Virginia at Mount Vernon in 1785, then

to another convention in Annapolis the following year (to which five states sent delegates), and finally to the Philadelphia Convention with its constitutional ambitions. Once they resolved to rethink the articles altogether, the delegates took it for granted that they should set up a national judiciary. All the major proposals for structuring the new government envisioned a federal court, even if none of them went into much detail about its work.

This assumption of the need for a judiciary was very much a function of the experience of life under the articles and of failures of governance at the state level in the post-revolution years. It would not have been predictable a decade earlier. In the years leading up to independence, the place of courts of law in colonial governance had degraded dramatically, and the courts had come to be understood as effectively appendages of the executive branch, engaged in a variety of administrative tasks and thoroughly lacking independence from royal governors. The revolution only made things worse at first. As historian Gordon Wood wrote, "Because judges had been so much identified with the hated magisterial power, many American Revolutionaries in 1776 sought not to strengthen the judiciary but to weaken it." Governors were often stripped of the power to appoint judges, but the judiciary was made subservient to the state legislatures instead, and that subservience was, if anything, even more extreme. In the earliest years after independence, state legislatures set out to simplify and codify the immensely complex English common law, but these efforts soon produced their own complicated, incoherent, and uncoordinated legal systems, especially as the legislatures were overtaken by the kind of populist fervor that so worried the federalists in Philadelphia. As Wood noted, "Consequently, with democracy running wild, more and more American leaders began looking to the once-feared judiciary as a principal means of restraining these rampaging popular legislatures."[1]

This mix of concerns came together at the Philadelphia Convention. Part of the framers' intention in creating a federal judiciary was simply to enable newly enacted laws to gain some definition and clarity. As Alexander Hamilton wrote in Federalist 22, "A circumstance which crowns the defects of the Confederation remains yet to be mentioned, the want of a judiciary power. Laws are a dead letter without courts to expound and define their true meaning and operation." This was especially important in a new republic, where many novel laws would need to be enacted. The language of the legislature would be the crucial factor in determining the meaning of these laws, of course, but the text of the law can never be sufficiently comprehensive to address every circumstance. Just as the president must have some independence to act when the law is not detailed enough to give him guidance in particular real-world situations, so courts must sometimes be called on to resolve the meaning of the law in circumstances that were not fully anticipated by legislators. This reality is rooted in the limits of legislative language (and indeed of language itself) but is especially important when new laws come into effect. James Madison described this quandary powerfully in Federalist 37:

> All new laws, though penned with the greatest technical skill, and passed on the fullest and most mature deliberation, are considered as more or less obscure and equivocal, until their meaning be liquidated and ascertained by a series of particular discussions and adjudications. Besides the obscurity arising from the complexity of objects, and the imperfection of the human faculties, the medium through which the conceptions of men are conveyed to each other adds a fresh embarrassment. The use of words is to express ideas. Perspicuity, therefore, requires not only that the ideas should be distinctly formed, but that they should be expressed by words distinctly and exclusively appropriate to them. But no language is so copious

as to supply words and phrases for every complex idea, or so correct as not to include many equivocally denoting different ideas. Hence it must happen that however accurately objects may be discriminated in themselves, and however accurately the discrimination may be considered, the definition of them may be rendered inaccurate by the inaccuracy of the terms in which it is delivered. And this unavoidable inaccuracy must be greater or less, according to the complexity and novelty of the objects defined. When the Almighty himself condescends to address mankind in their own language, his meaning, luminous as it must be, is rendered dim and doubtful by the cloudy medium through which it is communicated.

This "liquidation" of the meaning of the laws happens through the practice of political life. It is advanced, in part, through executive and administrative action and, in part, through the ways in which citizens live under the law but also, in large part, through the work of the courts. When laws are unclear or when different laws contradict one another in ways that point to no obvious resolution, it is, as Hamilton stated in Federalist 78, "the province of the courts to liquidate and fix their meaning and operation."[2]

As we have seen, such judicial liquidation happens in the past tense in relation to legislation that was drafted in the future tense and administration that occurs in the present tense. This means that courts must show some deference to both legislators and administrators and must begin from how those officials have given shape to the law already. It also means that judges have a responsibility to render some coherent and steady meaning to the law after time and practice have allowed that meaning to begin congealing. The courts must make the laws both clearer and more uniform. This is especially important in a compound republic, where state and federal laws coexist and where different states legislate in the same terrain. As Hamilton put it:

If there is in each State a court of final jurisdiction, there may be as many different final determinations on the same point as there are courts. There are endless diversities in the opinions of men. We often see not only different courts but the judges of the same court differing from each other. To avoid the confusion which would unavoidably result from the contradictory decisions of a number of independent judicatories, all nations have found it necessary to establish one court paramount to the rest, possessing a general superintendence, and authorized to settle and declare in the last resort a uniform rule of civil justice.[3]

The framers therefore created a court that was to be supreme in matters that involve the purview of the federal government. It would need to settle jurisdictional disputes, resolve contradictions in the law, and protect the rights of Americans in the novel civil and (to a lesser extent) criminal circumstances created by the structure and operation of the new regime.

To clarify the purview of this court, the Constitution gives much more attention to the jurisdiction of the federal judiciary than to the nature of its work. After simply declaring that "the judicial Power of the United States, shall be vested in one supreme Court, and in such inferior Courts as the Congress may from time to time ordain and establish," and determining that judges in these courts will serve life terms during good behavior, the great bulk of Article III is devoted to defining the kinds of cases in which the federal courts would be involved. The document assumes a well-established understanding of what a judge is and what "the judicial power" involves. In Federalist 81, Hamilton insists that the Constitution does not create a new kind of judge or court at all, and that nothing about the federal courts would be all that different from the state courts or from courts long familiar to the English political tradition.[4]

But this could not be quite true. Because the role of courts was changing in America at the time of the convention and because the nature of the new federal system would require frequent resolutions of complicated jurisdictional disputes, these new federal courts would not be just like the state courts. Perhaps above all, the new system would require the courts to play an active part in the interbranch struggle for power that the Constitution rendered intentionally complicated and unsettled. Federal courts would police the structures and boundaries of the system, and this required them to be genuinely independent. Judges could not be subservient to the executive (as colonial courts had been) or to the legislature (as state courts tended to be in the early republic). And the framers' commitment to this independence was extraordinary. They provided judges not only with life tenure in good behavior but also with a guarantee that their pay could not be reduced while they were in office and a mode of appointment (in which the president nominates judges and the Senate confirms them) as removed from direct political control as possible. No state afforded its judges this degree of protection.

This shielding from the heat of democratic politics was meant to guard judges from both of the elected branches, but the framers were plainly most concerned about an overbearing Congress. As Hamilton said, "The standard of good behavior for the continuance in office of the judicial magistracy, is certainly one of the most valuable of the modern improvements in the practice of government. In a monarchy it is an excellent barrier to the despotism of the prince; in a republic it is a no less excellent barrier to the encroachments and oppressions of the representative body. And it is the best expedient which can be devised in any government, to secure a steady, upright, and impartial administration of the laws."[5]

Protecting the courts from congressional encroachment and oppression meant, in truth, protecting the courts from the public and from the power of majorities. Judges would be at the very end of

what Madison described at the convention as "the policy of refining the popular appointments by successive filtrations," further and further from the voice of the people while still ultimately accountable to them. The court would be the least democratic institution of the new regime, precisely because it was an essential guardian of the republican order.[6]

Such independence can easily become dangerous to republicanism. But the framers insisted that the courts would be in no position to abuse it, because the judiciary lacked the sorts of active powers that the other branches possessed. "The judiciary is beyond comparison the weakest of the three departments of power," Hamilton insisted.

> In a government in which they are separated from each other, the judiciary, from the nature of its functions, will always be the least dangerous to the political rights of the Constitution; because it will be least in a capacity to annoy or injure them. The Executive not only dispenses the honors, but holds the sword of the community. The legislature not only commands the purse, but prescribes the rules by which the duties and rights of every citizen are to be regulated. The judiciary, on the contrary, has no influence over either the sword or the purse; no direction either of the strength or of the wealth of the society; and can take no active resolution whatever. It may truly be said to have neither FORCE nor WILL, but merely judgment; and must ultimately depend upon the aid of the executive arm even for the efficacy of its judgments.[7]

But these protestations of helplessness and weakness were hardly persuasive to the Constitution's critics. The Supreme Court's role as guardian of the new order made the independence of the judiciary a point of great contention in the debates over ratification. The fact that essentially unaccountable judges would be empowered to

police constitutional boundaries suggested that the courts would somehow stand above the rest of the government and, indeed, the public. Hamilton almost said as much in Federalist 78:

> The complete independence of the courts of justice is peculiarly essential in a limited Constitution. By a limited Constitution, I understand one which contains certain specified exceptions to the legislative authority; such, for instance, as that it shall pass no bills of attainder, no ex-post-facto laws, and the like. Limitations of this kind can be preserved in practice no other way than through the medium of courts of justice, whose duty it must be to declare all acts contrary to the manifest tenor of the Constitution void. Without this, all the reservations of particular rights or privileges would amount to nothing.[8]

By this logic, the limits on the other branches laid out in the Constitution would have to be enforced by the Supreme Court so that the court would treat the Constitution itself as a law to be applied. But what, then, would be the limits on the court? And how would those be enforced?

These questions were raised with great vigor by the antifederalists. The pseudonymous Brutus, one of the sharpest critics of the Constitution in the state ratification debates, warned his readers that "the supreme court under this constitution would be exalted above all other power in the government, and subject to no control." The independence that judges were granted along with their power to interpret the Constitution meant that every contested question in American politics would fall to them to resolve. "I question whether the world ever saw, in any period of it, a court of justice invested with such immense powers, and yet placed in a situation so little responsible," Brutus wrote. "There is no power above them that can control their decisions, or correct their errors. There is no authority

that can remove them from office for any errors or want of capacity, or lower their salaries, and in many cases their power is superior to that of the legislature." What is more, he continued, "this court will be authorized to decide upon the meaning of the constitution, and that, not only according to the natural and obvious meaning of the words, but also according to the spirit and intention of it. In the exercise of this power they will not be subordinate to, but above the legislature." A court so powerful and independent would nullify any claims the rest of the system might make to republican accountability, especially if it could, as Hamilton plainly said, nullify the acts of the other branches and of the state governments at will if it deemed them unconstitutional.[9]

THE AUTHORITY AT ISSUE IN THESE ARGUMENTS IS WHAT HAS COME TO BE known as "judicial review"—the power of judges to nullify a statute or administrative action they take to be contrary to the Constitution. The power of judicial review was, at times, treated by both Madison and Hamilton as unavoidably implicit in the judicial power itself. Hamilton argued in Federalist 16 that courts have the power to "pronounce the resolutions of . . . a majority to be contrary to the supreme law of the land, unconstitutional, and void." Madison made a similar suggestion in Federalist 44. But the assertion of such authority was actually quite controversial and, ultimately, required a set of novel arguments—put forward especially by Hamilton in Federalist 78 through 83—that suggested a distinct role for the courts in the new system with great bearing on its potential for producing cohesion and unity.[10]

That role becomes clearer in light of what the framers decided *not* to let judges do. In the course of the convention, Madison (with James Wilson of Pennsylvania) several times proposed giving the federal

courts a role along with the president in the exercise of the veto over congressional enactments. They worried that the president alone would be too fearful of Congress to use his veto power, given that he was ultimately subject to the will of the electoral majority. An independent judiciary further removed from voters could be more reliably resistant to congressional pressure and would strengthen the president's resolve. But the idea was ultimately rejected by the convention because it would have involved judges in political decision-making. As Eldridge Gerry of Massachusetts argued, the office of the judge requires a certain distance from partisan considerations. "It was quite foreign from the nature of the office to make them judges of the policy of public measures." Rufus King made the problem even clearer: "The Judges ought to be able to expound the law as it should come before them, free from the bias of having participated in its formation." But delegates on both sides of that debate sometimes suggested that the kind of policing of constitutional boundaries that Madison and Wilson hoped to enable would, nonetheless, be made possible by judicial review, without undermining judicial independence. It wasn't necessary to involve judges in vetoing legislation, Gerry insisted, "as they will have a sufficient check against encroachments on their own department by their exposition of the laws, which involved a power of deciding on their Constitutionality." In fact, he told the delegates, "in some States the Judges had actually set aside laws as being against the Constitution," and, presumably, federal judges could do the same.[11]

As we saw in chapter 4, the convention also considered giving the federal government a veto power over state laws to protect federal prerogatives and the rights of the people. This proposal was also rejected, but it, too, led to some discussion of the power of judges to guard against state violations of the federal Constitution through the use of judicial review. At first, the delegates assumed state judges would do this. Roger Sherman of Connecticut insisted that

a federal veto over state legislation was "unnecessary, as the Courts of the States would not consider as valid any law contravening the Authority of the Union." New York's Gouverneur Morris agreed that "a law that ought to be negatived will be set aside in the Judiciary department."[12]

The Constitution did not specifically grant the federal courts the power to take such actions. And, as legal scholar Larry Kramer showed in his magisterial study of this subject, such judicial review was by no means assumed by most Americans to inhere in the power of judges. Yet the debates among the delegates in Philadelphia suggested that a significant number of them assumed that such authority would be available to federal judges. As just noted, some pointed toward this power as a convenient alternative to allowing judges to play a role in the process of enacting legislation or to giving Congress the power to stop state legislation. But others insisted that such power would be available to the federal courts by virtue of the basic character of the judicial power. This was the essence of Hamilton's answer to Brutus and the anti-federalists, which was not immediately persuasive in the course of the ratification debates but became important to the self-understanding of the federal courts over time. Hamilton insisted that there was no new authority in the Constitution that allowed judges to exercise unrestrained power. Rather, the judicial power, by definition, permitted judges to resolve contradictions between different laws, and in a case where a statute contradicts the Constitution, there was no question that the resolution should favor the higher law over the lower.[13]

This may seem like a simple point, but it is a function of an extraordinary innovation of American constitutionalism. In the British common-law tradition, with its unwritten constitution, the fundamental law that underlay the written law could only be approached implicitly and indirectly. Courts did, at times, enforce that fundamental law against acts of parliament, but these were rare,

extreme, and solemn occasions when parliament was taken to have violated a fundamental tenet of justice or the natural law. But in the American system, with its written colonial charters and state constitutions, the fundamental law gradually came to be understood as a text, just like regular legislative enactments. By 1787, therefore, the Philadelphia Convention could agree to assert (in Article VI of the Constitution): "This Constitution, and the Laws of the United States which shall be made in Pursuance thereof; and all Treaties made, or which shall be made, under the Authority of the United States, shall be the supreme Law of the Land; and the Judges in every State shall be bound thereby, any Thing in the Constitution or Laws of any State to the Contrary notwithstanding." It was not unreasonable to take this text to mean that federal judges bound by this supreme law would be compelled to reject or nullify both state and federal laws that contradicted it.

Hamilton's case for this practice went even further. In Federalist 78, he argued that the Constitution, once ratified by the public, should be understood as a direct enactment of the public so that when courts sought to resolve disputes between a statute and the Constitution, they would effectively be resolving a dispute between the people and the legislature and were compelled to side with the people—that is, with the Constitution. Hamilton wrote:

> It is not otherwise to be supposed, that the Constitution could intend to enable the representatives of the people to substitute their WILL to that of their constituents. It is far more rational to suppose, that the courts were designed to be an intermediate body between the people and the legislatures, in order, among other things, to keep the latter within the limits assigned to their authority. The interpretation of the laws is the proper and peculiar province of the courts. A constitution is, in fact, and must be regarded by the judges, as a fundamental law. It therefore belongs to them

to ascertain its meaning, as well as the meaning of any particular act proceeding from the legislative body. If there should happen to be an irreconcilable variance between the two, that which has the superior obligation and validity ought, of course, to be preferred; or, in other words, the Constitution ought to be preferred to the statute, the intention of the people to the intention of their agents.

In this view, the Constitution is just another kind of law but with a higher standing than regular statutes—not only because it is formally prior but also because it is the will of the people. "Where the will of the legislature, declared in its statutes, stands in opposition to that of the people, declared in the Constitution, the judges ought to be governed by the latter rather than the former. They ought to regulate their decisions by the fundamental laws, rather than by those which are not fundamental," Hamilton wrote. Thus the logic of republicanism, or at least its vocabulary, is used to justify judicial nullification of legislative acts that the courts take to contradict the Constitution. At the heart of that case, and that vision, was what we might call judicial republicanism—a mode of interpretation by which judges in hard cases make complex determinations by applying the underlying logic (or the "manifest tenor") of the Constitution to determining the meaning of its text.[14]

And yet, although this doctrine gave the courts enormous power to police the boundaries of constitutionalism, that power was nonetheless also constrained by the very nature of law. The Constitution is supreme, and as a *political* matter it is not like other laws. Among other things, it can only be revised with the backing of an extremely broad and varied consensus of the public. But as a *legal* matter, from the point of view of judges, it is to be interpreted in the same way as any other law, using the same tools judges would employ when applying regular statutes to cases and controversies.

Of course, as we saw in chapter 1, the Constitution is more than a legal framework, and we mistake its character and understate its significance when we treat it as only a matter of law. But it is, nonetheless, first and foremost, a legal framework, and in the hands of judges (as opposed to those of legislators, administrators, or citizens), it must be taken up as a legal framework. In court, the same modes of construction and analysis that judges use to interpret legal texts are applied to interpret the Constitution itself. According to Gordon Wood, "In various decisions from the 1780s into the early 19th century, [American judges] brought the higher law of the several constitutions into the rubric of ordinary law and subjected that higher law to the long-standing common law rules of exposition and construction, as if it were no different from a lowly statute." This led to the emergence of what we now think of as constitutional law, which is a peculiar hybrid to a degree we rarely grasp now. In this sense, the Constitution lowered rather than raised the status of the fundamental law and narrowed rather than broadened the scope of potential judicial action. Judges could apply the Constitution, but they could not alter it as common-law judges could alter and shape the common law.[15]

Indeed, a key part of the job of judges would be to prevent other constitutional actors from altering that fundamental law without going through the proper process of amendment. This was a further reason why the independence of the third branch was so important. The fact that a majority is known to want one of the elected branches to do something other than what the Constitution permits does not make such an action legitimate. The republican regime is ruled by the majority, but the majority rules through the regime, not around it. It is bound by the framework of the Constitution, and until the people change that framework in the appropriate way, which requires very broad consensus, they cannot simply act as they wish. And it is up to the judges to stop them. "Until the people

have, by some solemn and authoritative act, annulled or changed the established form," Hamilton wrote, "it is binding upon themselves collectively, as well as individually; and no presumption, or even knowledge, of their sentiments, can warrant their representatives in a departure from it, prior to such an act. But it is easy to see, that it would require an uncommon portion of fortitude in the judges to do their duty as faithful guardians of the Constitution, where legislative invasions of it had been instigated by the major voice of the community." Resisting the will of majorities is, therefore, an essential function of the courts. And to perform it reliably, judges need protections like lifetime tenure.[16]

Here we begin to see most clearly the distinct role of the federal courts in the advancement of the Constitution's capacity to form and sustain national cohesion. The crucial service they provide is not the resolution of the disputes that divide our free society. Courts do resolve disputes, of course, but they resolve disputes over what the law is, not what it should be, and so they are not the proper venue for mediating among competing visions of the public good. They also usually resolve disputes by designating a winner and a loser, which, as we have seen, is not generally an effective way to build common ground. Our great public disputes need to be resolved through the work of the legislature above all. The most valuable service the courts provide to the cause of national unity is in their policing of the rules and boundaries of constitutionalism, and their restricting of the power of majorities to break those rules and boundaries. The courts can do that by insisting on the adherence of officials and citizens to the structure and procedures of the Constitution, which, as we have seen, are designed to advance common action across lines of difference and to build public confidence in the outcome.

In this respect, moreover, the courts do more than act retrospectively to right wrongs that have already been committed. By providing a stable, predictable framework of constitutionalism and law, the

courts can also create strong disincentives to future misbehavior. If everyone knew that the courts would reliably strike down unconstitutional laws or administrative actions—to police constitutional boundaries and to protect constitutional rights—then those laws or actions would become much less likely to be attempted. Such "benefits of the integrity and moderation of the judiciary" are enormously important influences on the character of government, Hamilton argued. Having judges who reliably reject such laws "not only serves to moderate the immediate mischiefs of those which may have been passed, but it operates as a check upon the legislative body in passing them; who, perceiving that obstacles to the success of iniquitous intention are to be expected from the scruples of the courts, are in a manner compelled, by the very motives of the injustice they meditate, to qualify their attempts."[17]

In this way, the courts can act to reinforce the accommodative work of the legislature and the stabilizing work of the executive by insisting on the integrity of the constitutional structure that demands such work of the elected branches. They cannot serve the cause of constitutional cohesion by substituting themselves for legislators or administrators at the state or federal levels but, rather, by playing their own proper role and interpreting the law, including the Constitution as law.

The insight that won the day in the Philadelphia Convention's debates about involving judges in the exercise of the president's veto power—the insight that judges should be kept at some remove from politics—is, thus, essential to the capacity of the courts to facilitate greater unity. As Maryland delegate Luther Martin told his colleagues, "It is necessary that the Supreme Judiciary should have the confidence of the people. This will soon be lost if they are employed in the task of remonstrating against popular measures of the Legislature." They should be restricted to determining whether such measures are constitutional, not whether they are good policy. The

public's perception of judicial impartiality, which must be rooted in a reality of impartiality, is a necessary precondition for the functioning of the courts.[18]

But things are never quite this simple, because the line between form and substance is never perfectly clear. The complexity of life in a vast and diverse country presents endless fodder for thorny controversies and disputes, and these can often be fought out as debates about the meaning of the Constitution's words and not just the best way to pursue the common good. Because the courts offer combatants the prospect of total victory rather than an unsatisfying compromise, the temptation to settle political differences judicially is frequently irresistible. So, as the Supreme Court began to do its work of liquidation and interpretation, it was confronted with a seemingly endless parade of national controversies to consider. By 1835, Alexis de Tocqueville could observe after his visit to America that "there is almost no political question in the United States that is not resolved sooner or later into a judicial question." It was the power of judicial review and the development of constitutional law that often made such resolution possible. That power gradually evolved in ways that threatened the capacity of the courts to facilitate constitutionalism and, with it, greater cohesion.[19]

THE SUPREME COURT QUICKLY ESTABLISHED ITS PLACE IN THE EARLY republic as the authoritative interpreter of constitutional meaning. Although all three branches were expected to interpret the meaning of the text in the course of their own work, the resolution of disputes about that meaning was generally left to judges, and Americans implicitly came to agree with Chief Justice John Marshall's assertion in the landmark 1803 case *Marbury v. Madison* that

"it is emphatically the province and duty of the judicial department to say what the law is."[20]

Carrying out that duty, however, inevitably put the courts at the center of the most intense controversies in American political life, and in time, this meant that judges were pushed to engage in a kind of constitutional evolution and not just interpretation. This was especially true regarding the most heated controversy of the first half of the nineteenth century, the question of slavery and race. As we have seen, the Constitution intentionally left that question open, and this meant that, as slavery became the subject of ever more heated political disputes, the Supreme Court was called on to address questions that the Constitution as a legal framework gave the justices no clear way to resolve.

As the nation expanded, the slavery question came to be fought as a debate about the reach of that evil institution into new states. Congress tried to settle the question with the Missouri Compromise of 1820, which set a geographic boundary on slavery, permitting it in new states south of a line members drew on the map and prohibiting it north of that line. But what would become of enslaved persons taken across that line from the South into the North? This was just the sort of question courts exist to answer, and the case of Dred Scott put it before the federal judiciary. The result set a pattern that has recurred throughout the history of our system: the Supreme Court thought it could settle a divisive national issue rather than police the boundaries of the constitutional system to enable it to be resolved by the elected branches, and in the effort to settle that debate, it only made it far more divisive and dangerous. The *Dred Scott* decision, handed down in 1857, was perhaps the lowest moment in the entire history of the federal judiciary. The court ruled that people of African descent in America could not be citizens under the Constitution and also struck down the Missouri Compromise (which, by then, had been largely superseded) as a violation of the property rights of

slave owners. The decision was viciously racist and also unmoored from the court's constitutional foundations. And needless to say, it did not resolve the underlying dispute but only heightened it.

That dispute, of course, ultimately proved unmanageable by constitutional means. As we have seen, the Civil War that followed brought an unavoidable transformation of some core constitutional arrangements to better align the American political order with the nation's founding ideals. Among the most significant facets of that reordering was the Fourteenth Amendment, ratified in 1868, which clarified that citizenship was not restricted by race and expanded the constitutional role of the federal government to include the protection of the basic equal rights of all citizens. Among other things, the amendment launched a transformation of the role of the federal courts. Section 1 of the Fourteenth Amendment reads, "All persons born or naturalized in the United States, and subject to the jurisdiction thereof, are citizens of the United States and of the State wherein they reside. No State shall make or enforce any law which shall abridge the privileges or immunities of citizens of the United States; nor shall any State deprive any person of life, liberty, or property, without due process of law; nor deny to any person within its jurisdiction the equal protection of the laws."

This language was a vital civic achievement—finally aligning the Constitution with the most ambitious commitments and ideals of the Declaration of Independence so that the practice of American government might, in time, come to be aligned with them as well. But as actionable law, this language was also very vague, extending some protections that the Fifth Amendment had provided at the federal level to also apply at the state level, but without clarifying exactly what these protections were intended to include. In Section 5 of the amendment, Congress was empowered "to enforce, by appropriate legislation, the provisions of this article" in a way that might give greater definition to some of the glittering generalities of the

remainder of the amendment. But Congress never did so. Instead, Black Americans continued to confront abject discrimination and violent oppression, and the broader "liquidation" of the Fourteenth Amendment was left largely to the courts.

Therefore, just as the Fourteenth Amendment significantly increased the power of the federal government in relation to the states (as we saw in chapter 4), it also increased the power of the courts relative to the rest of the federal government. The amendment planted several seeds in our constitutional soil that would, in the course of time, bring the broad concepts of "privileges and immunities," "due process," and "equal protection" to the forefront of American constitutional law. These concepts relate less to constitutional structure than to personal rights, and they would function as an invitation to the courts to discover (or manufacture) rights with broad application in a variety of circumstances well beyond the racial discrimination and oppression that had necessitated the post–Civil War amendments.

This practice would evolve over decades, but it began with the Supreme Court's response to the ambitions of the progressive critics of the Constitution, whose arguments we have been tracing in the last several chapters. As state and federal policymakers began to regulate economic activity aggressively, the courts confronted more and more challenges to such regulation. The Supreme Court proved willing to permit the breakup of monopolies and trusts in various industries as exercises of the federal government's constitutional authority to regulate interstate commerce, but it nullified limits on working hours and requirements for minimal working conditions and pay in various states. The justices often did so on the premise that such laws violated workers' right to contract—a right articulated nowhere in the Constitution but which the court discerned as a substantive implication of the Fifth and Fourteenth Amendments' insistence that no American can be deprived of property without

due process of law. On its face, that protection is procedural, not substantive: it means these rights cannot be denied except through the normal processes of lawmaking, administration, and adjudication. But the court increasingly applied a doctrine that came to be known as "substantive due process," protecting a variety of economic and personal freedoms regardless of the procedures involved in government attempts to regulate them. The court deployed this doctrine in selective and, frankly, arbitrary ways, putting itself precisely in the position of rendering judgment on the "policy of public measures"—a position the framers had sought to avert in keeping judges out of political decision-making.[21]

Ironically, this practice was first used to frustrate the progressive constitutional revolution and then to advance it. In the late nineteenth and early twentieth centuries, this mode of jurisprudence meant that the court mostly acted as a break, thwarting progressive economic policies in an effort to protect individual property rights. These tensions came to a head in the 1930s, when the Supreme Court looked likely to reject significant portions of Franklin Roosevelt's Great Society agenda, and Roosevelt and the Democrats threatened to "pack" the court—increasing the number of justices by law so as to create a majority friendlier to their aims. That brazen threat worked, and the court backed down some and increasingly left economic policy to the elected branches. But the doctrine of substantive due process soon came to be applied in other arenas and, especially, to advance progressive social aims. As the great constitutional scholar Walter Berns put it, "Thanks in large part to the Court's Fourteenth Amendment jurisprudence, the Constitution came to be seen not as the embodiment of fundamental and clearly articulated principles of government but a collection of hopelessly vague and essentially meaningless words and phrases inviting judicial construction. In other words, it came to be understood as no more than an

invitation to these insulated judges to make constitutional law and, when necessary, remake it."[22]

This assertive judicial behavior defined our constitutional politics in the second half of the twentieth century. Especially regarding civil rights and social issues, the Supreme Court sought to drive the public agenda when it deemed the political branches were moving too slowly, to resolve divisive debates rather than allow them to be worked out legislatively, and to facilitate the evolution of the Constitution rather than its interpretation. Some of the ends it pursued were surely laudable and public-spirited, while others were misguided or partisan. But the ways it pursued these ends were not judicial means in the traditional sense. The doctrine of substantive due process was deployed to create rights to privacy, abortion, education, marriage, and more. By taking up divisive controversies in these terms, the court tended to close the paths to resolving them in more accommodative legislative terms. As Berns put this point, at the height of the court's era of rights-creation, "success in the legislature is measured by the extent to which one's interest is accommodated in the law adopted by the majority, and to achieve that success it is necessary to display a willingness to be accommodating oneself. . . . Success in the courts, however, is now measured by having one's interest declared a right, and with the right comes the freedom to be immoderate."[23]

The court in this period became an arena in which a narrow faction (backed by as few as five judges) could advance the kinds of changes that would previously have required major legislation or even a constitutional amendment and, thus, a broad national coalition.

Such judicially driven transformation grew intensely controversial and, ultimately, set off a powerful reaction that put the court and constitutional interpretation at the center of our partisan politics. Because the progressive court was focused on the discovery or

manufacture of personal rights, the conservative response was, at first, focused on restraining the capacity of judges to declare such rights without constitutional foundation. But this alternative to progressivism's judicial philosophy developed, in time, into a fuller constitutionalism of its own, which came to be called "originalism," and to revolutionize our understanding of the purpose of the courts.

ORIGINALISM BEGAN IN THE 1970S AS AN INTELLECTUAL AGENDA—A SET of arguments developed by legal scholars like Robert Bork, Antonin Scalia, Laurence Silberman, and others. They set out to show that the modern court had strayed from the original intentions of the Constitution and that judges had come to exercise essentially arbitrary policymaking power and to impose their own preferences over the will of democratic majorities and the text of the Constitution and the laws.

To correct the resulting deformations, the role of the judge would need to be dramatically constricted. The originalists argued that judges should interpret the Constitution and the laws based on their original public meanings, as best they can discern them, and should defer to those meanings over their own or others' preferences. The judge does sometimes need to limit the republican citizenry and its representatives when they threaten to trample rights explicitly protected in the Constitution or violate the structure of the constitutional system and its institutions. But the judge may not stand in for those citizens or their representatives as an active agent of political change. A judge must protect both the personal rights of individuals and the community's right to make laws for itself.[24]

Originalism thus champions an ideal of self-government rooted in the premise that legitimate public power is generally a function of popular sovereignty and, therefore, that the elected branches,

and especially the legislative branch, should be the moving forces in our system of government. The judiciary exists to interpret and apply the Constitution and the laws in particular cases, restraining or enabling public or private action as required. As the late Chief Justice William Rehnquist put it, in the early days of originalism, if judicial action were not fundamentally interpretive in this way, then judges would have to be understood as "a small group of fortunately situated people with a roving commission to second-guess Congress, state legislatures, and state and federal administrative officers concerning what is best for the country," and that is surely not what they ought to be. At the heart of this early form of originalism was, therefore, an ideal of "judicial restraint" connected to a Madisonian conception of the nature of the American system and its approach to resolving disputes and advancing cohesion.[25]

The originalist framework is, itself, a theory of interpretation. It was not simply a return to the practices of the courts before the age of progressive judicial activism. As Bork argued, the jurisprudence of the second half of the twentieth century had shattered the framework of those practices, and a recovery of constitutionalism would require a countertheory aimed at providing judges with a set of neutral interpretive principles.[26]

This restrained idea of the role of the judge quickly became more than an intellectual project. Particularly through the work of the Federalist Society (a professional organization of conservative and libertarian lawyers and law students), its influence soon reached the federal judiciary, and by the mid-1980s, Republican presidents could generally be counted on to appoint originalist judges to the federal bench. Soon the question whether judges should interpret the Constitution in accordance with their understanding of its original meaning or with their assessment of the desirability of its contemporary implications became the key dividing line in American constitutional law. By the early twenty-first century, the case for originalism

had become thoroughly dominant, and even its opponents had to acknowledge its force. There is certainly still a strong current of progressive ends-based judicial practice in American courts, but there is almost no intellectual argument for the role of the judge that is not either a variant of originalism or an attempt to respond to it within the framework it established. And as a majority of Supreme Court justices have been originalists in recent years, the court has taken some steps to reverse the creation of judge-made rights and looks likely to reconsider some of its substantive due-process jurisprudence in the coming years. In some important respects, the reaction against judicial progressivism has succeeded.

And yet, the conservative legal movement that produced that response is now divided about its future. Its successful ascendance in the courts has forced hard questions about the limits of a judicial philosophy focused on reversing past excesses. At its origins, modern originalism sought to be understood as a theory of judicial restraint, which would limit the role of the judge's own judgment in hard cases. But over time, as Supreme Court Justice Amy Coney Barrett has said, "originalism has shifted from being a theory about how judges should decide cases to a theory about what counts as valid, enforceable law. The Constitution's original public meaning is important, not because adhering to it limits judicial discretion, but because it is the law. And because it is the law, judges must be faithful to it."[27]

But in the hardest cases, which tend to matter most, judges may confront not only a lack of will to enforce the original meaning of the Constitution but a lack of clarity about that meaning in the circumstances before them. Those cases often reach the courts precisely because the Constitution or the laws are not clear and need somehow to be completed or extended to become applicable to a complicated real-world situation. Some principle, some substantive moral good that is taken to be inherent in the Constitution, has

to guide the judge's pursuit of the meaning of the text in such a situation.

The tendency of originalists to ignore or dismiss this problem and to insist on the possibility of entirely neutral textual analysis even in the hardest cases has driven two waves of conservative unease with originalism over the last several decades. Both have been founded in the sense that substantive neutrality alone is neither possible nor desirable as a principle of interpretation and that it renders the work of judges morally vacuous. The first wave proposed that individual liberty, rooted especially in a libertarian reading of the opening of the Declaration of Independence, ought to be the substantive interpretive principle in those hard cases. The second has argued that an ideal of the common good, rooted particularly in the classical and Christian legal traditions, should serve that purpose. In practice, the two would point in opposite directions in many particular cases, but they are remarkably similar as critiques of modern originalism and as arguments for a more assertive judicial interpretive role when the text is not decisive. Both chafe against the notion that a judge's role is to make himself scarce, which in hard cases, they view as an evasion of responsibility.[28]

That critique has real force. But it may ultimately only point toward a stronger argument for originalism and one that sheds light on the role the judiciary can play in the kind of solidarity-minded constitutionalism we have been sketching. The notion that genuinely hard cases require an organizing interpretive principle is persuasive, but the most persuasive candidate for that role is the very republicanism that underlays the constitutional thinking of the framers.

In truly uncertain cases, where the original public meaning of the constitutional text is not clear, judges might avail themselves of the political philosophy that most prominently motivated the authors of that text. That philosophy is not so much liberal as republican, and it

is far from neutral with regard to public morality. As we have seen, it is grounded in an anthropology of human fallenness and human dignity, a sociology of civic responsibility and communal self-rule, and a politics of solidarity and common action. Republicanism is attuned to the needs of moral and civic formation that require us to distinguish the community's moral priorities. But it also values self-rule and, therefore, looks to the legislature, in particular, as the source of such prioritization for the purpose of government action. As a practical matter, therefore, a republican interpretive principle would have a great deal in common with contemporary originalism, since it would prioritize the work of the legislature over the substantive preferences of judges; would value steady and effective administration; and would grasp the importance of accommodative consensus building, social peace, and the rule of law.[29]

A renewed judicial republicanism is the natural next phase of the originalist project. But such a renewal would require a lot of intellectual work to clarify the meaning of modern republicanism—as the framers understood it and as we should—and its relation to natural law, to liberalism, and to democracy. This would be constructive work for conservative-minded political and legal theorists in the coming years.

But such work must extend beyond the courts. Originalism is inherently limited as a constitutional doctrine not only because it prescribes a restrained role for the judge but also because it is almost exclusively *about* the role of the judge. A fuller constitutionalism would have to take up the proper roles of everyone else in our system and so would be far less constrained, even as it did restrict the reach of judges. Its republicanism would point it especially toward the first branch of our government. Judges must be faithful to the laws, and the executive must take care that those laws be faithfully executed, but legislators ultimately frame the laws on behalf of the public and so have much more latitude to take in deeper and broader

conceptions of the common good and to enable our political order to take shape accordingly. The legislature is where a desire to transform the government's role in American life within the bounds of the Constitution should be directed.

That this desire is now misdirected (to both courts and the administrative state) is an enormous problem, which almost by definition calls for more than a theory of judicial action. The original originalists, to quote Justice Barrett once more, "insisted that the Court needed to be reined in so that the democratic process could function." Implicit in their project was the assumption that if the courts ceased to intrude upon the space reserved for the people and their representatives, then the people and their representatives would act energetically to fill that space. In just this way, the Constitution's own emphasis on limitations on power seems rooted in the assumption that power and ambition will never be lacking in government, so that constructing limits on improper means of action is also a way to construct proper means of action.[30]

As we have seen, the modern deformations of the constitutional system cast doubt on that confidence. Congress now frequently declines to use its power, or at least to use it in the ways prescribed by the Constitution. And the states sometimes do too. More aggressive judges, however well-intentioned they might be, are not in a position to address that problem themselves. Some contemporary criticism of originalism is therefore at least in part a kind of chafing at the constraints of a judge-centered constitutionalism. It points to a genuine problem, but not one that can be legitimately or effectively addressed by the means it proposes. It proposes a more conservative judicial activism, as if replacing one unaccountable elite with another will restore our republic. But that expectation is itself a corruption of the republican form of government, and many friends of the Constitution have come to lack the vocabulary to properly describe and resist that corruption because

they have put so much of their hope in a transformation of the judiciary for so long.

Ironically, in arguing for a modest role for judges over the past half century, conservative constitutional thought has become too focused on judges—just like the progressive judicial activism it criticized. The felt need for a conservative theory of government action alongside conservative theories of government restraint should move conservatives to look beyond the judiciary, and especially to Congress and to federalism.

HAVING SEEN HOW THE REPUBLICANISM OF THE CONSTITUTION CAN advance the cause of national unity—by allowing our diversity to be lived out through federalism, enabling differences over national priorities to be negotiated in the legislature, and facilitating stability through the work of the executive—we can see how a judiciary guided by republican imperatives can reinforce that capacity for unity.

For much of the twentieth century, the courts served as an arena for expanding the scope of personal rights. Having reached too far and drawn a backlash, they may now be gradually restoring some sensible constitutional constraints on that front. But to truly serve their unifying purpose, the courts must recover a Hamiltonian conception of judicial republicanism, which would emphasize the judiciary's role in policing our constitutional structure at least as much as its obligation to protect personal rights. Neither progressive judicial activism nor conservative originalism has focused enough on the question of constitutional structure, and the contemporary battles between them risk taking an excessively assertive judicial role for granted. The next phase of judicial evolution in our system must emphasize the judge's obligation to police the structural boundaries that make republicanism possible.

This would require us to see beyond debates about originalism when we think about the courts. Originalism has succeeded beyond the wildest hopes of its founders, but that very success means that, as legal scholar William Haun said, "the relevant divide in American constitutional theory is not between originalism and non-originalism; it is between opposing characterizations of the nature of our political tradition, as applied through the Constitution's written guarantees." The basic divide between the constitutional ambitions of the framers and the powerful (even if misguided) rival vision of the progressives is again the vital question at the heart of our politics. Judicial activism can serve or disserve either side in that debate, and has in fact both served and disserved both. But it is that deeper, underlying debate to which we must now recur.[31]

To do that, we will need to recall that the Constitution is not only law so that the work of constitutionalism is not only work for the courts. The courts police the boundaries of our constitutional practice, but it is what happens within those boundaries—the work of citizens, legislators, and administrators in the states and in Washington—that is the substance of our constitutional politics and of the political life of our democratic republic. To think of the courts as the only real practitioners of constitutionalism is to let everyone else off the hook and to encourage a kind of civic dereliction that badly undermines constitutionalism and (therefore) now also badly undermines our society's cohesion. An overly broad notion of the judge's role inevitably involves an excessively narrowed notion of the roles of citizens, legislators, and executives. And such a narrowing can hardly help but be divisive.

Addressing that all too familiar problem requires a proper understanding of the role of the courts and of the larger system of which they are a part, more than it requires any particular reforms of the judicial branch. There may be some marginal ways the courts might be improved to help them better play their proper part. For instance,

the almost total discretion available to the Supreme Court in selecting its cases tends to politicize the court's work. As Adam White has
argued, "Legislation setting clearer standards for granting writs of
certiorari, or mandating judicial review of more kinds of cases, could
help to make the Court's caseload less a matter of judicial will and
more a matter of judicial duty." But it is, ultimately, serious attention
to that duty, in the spirit of republican self-restraint, which is most
required.[32]

The courts have done better than our other governing institutions at resisting the lure of performative politics and sustaining their
institutional character and sense of duty and responsibility. Indeed,
unlike those other institutions, the courts have actually undergone
a kind of constitutional renaissance in recent years and are much
closer to performing their proper role today than they were, say, half
a century ago. But to keep the ground they have gained, they must
resist the urge to inflate their own role and displace other key constitutional actors. And to gain more ground, they must rediscover their
responsibility to police the boundaries of our constitutional structure, and so to make the renewal of the rest of the constitutional system more plausible—by giving the law a clear and steady meaning,
and by guarding the rights of the people while enforcing the duties
of constitutional officers.[33]

A properly constrained vision of the role of the judge requires
a properly expansive vision of the nature of constitutionalism.
When we mistake mere legalism for constitutionalism, the judge's
role becomes supreme. But when we see that role in the context
of a broader cast of constitutional characters, we can more readily
understand that constraints upon the power of judges are meant
to empower them within their proper sphere and also to empower
republican citizens within their broader sphere. When we fully identify constitutionalism with legalism, we mistake what are properly
political differences for legal disputes and imagine that the rules of

the game alone can determine the outcome. But properly political disagreements happen within the rules. They are legitimate, even when they are divisive, and to be made less divisive, they must be resolved through the political process.

The structure of our Constitution can promote unity by enabling negotiation and engagement. End runs around that structure, therefore, tend to intensify division and bitterness, and the courts have a crucial role to play in preventing such end runs and sustaining a predictable, stable arena for constitutional action. It is easy to see why we want judges to do more than that—they seem like the only constitutional officers capable of doing much of anything now. But we must actually demand something harder of them than just doing more. We must ask them to do their proper constitutional work and nothing else so that we all can do ours. And we must ask for that with precisely the imperative of unity in mind. Our Constitution is law, but also more than law. The work of constitutional statesmanship and constitutional citizenship is not fundamentally legal work: it can bring us together because it is political.

Chapter 8

CONSTITUTIONAL PARTISANSHIP

THE FRAMERS OF THE CONSTITUTION HAD AN EXTRAORDINARILY sophisticated grasp of politics, but the particular role of political parties in the life of a democratic republic fell into a peculiar blind spot in their thinking. America's constitution-building moment came at a time when the core partisan alignments shaping both British and American politics were in flux. Britain had gone through a century-long evolution from a politics in which a party of royal authority faced off against a party of parliamentary prerogatives into a politics organized around competing visions of the appropriate character of social and political change. Whigs were becoming liberals, and Tories were becoming conservatives—a transformation that would be greatly clarified and intensified in the debates about the French Revolution and its implications in the course of the 1790s.

In the United States, the American Revolution had created a strange pocket of nonpartisan politics. The cause of independence could be justified on relatively radical and relatively conservative grounds, as the two portions of the Declaration of Independence demonstrate. That the circle of revolutionary leaders included both

Thomas Jefferson and John Adams—the foremost radical and conservative voices of their generation of Americans—is evidence that ideological categories were suspended for a time in the new nation. Here, too, the questions opened up by the French Revolution would illuminate deep partisan differences, but that had yet to happen when the Philadelphia Convention gathered in 1787. That summer, a politics without organized parties still seemed imaginable.[1]

And such a politics also seemed highly desirable. Precisely because the necessity of union and cohesion was so clear to the framers, the danger of rigid partisanship was much on their minds. They took themselves to be combating just that risk through the structure of the Constitution, as we have seen. James Madison could see that factions in some form were unavoidable, and even that they were ultimately a function of the very freedom of a free society. "When men exercise their reason coolly and freely on a variety of distinct questions, they inevitably fall into different opinions on some of them," he wrote in Federalist 50. Unanimity, in other words, was a bad sign—an indication that passion had overtaken reason, or that freedom had been stamped out. "Such an event ought to be neither presumed nor desired; because an extinction of parties necessarily implies either a universal alarm for the public safety, or an absolute extinction of liberty."[2]

But Madison understood this reality as a price paid for freedom, not a positive good. Some of his fellow framers even suggested that this price might be avoided or at least that they should see themselves as working to avert it. Alexander Hamilton articulated that ambition in a speech to his fellow New Yorkers at the state's ratifying convention: "We are attempting by this constitution to abolish factions," he said, "and to unite all parties for the general welfare."[3]

The framers' objections to partisanship were rooted in worries about faction and division and so had everything to do with the challenge of cohesion. But they underestimated the need to

organize political actors before those could constructively participate in the institutions of the new system. Formal political parties
ultimately exist not to embody divisions but to organize coalitions.
The unavoidable necessity of such organization led, in time, by the
first decades of the nineteenth century, to a party system that could
complement the constitutional architecture and reinforce its aims
of compelling accommodation and broadening majorities. Precisely
because it came to be aligned with the logic of the Constitution,
however, that distinctly American party system frustrated the ambitions of the early progressives, who proposed an alternative model
of parties.

American politics functioned as a kind of hybrid of those two
approaches for much of the twentieth century. But in our time, we
have largely lost sight of how parties could contribute to the functioning of the constitutional order and, therefore, to the cause of
greater cohesion in a diverse nation. We too easily forget that parties
exist to organize coalitions, and our parties have gradually lost the
ability to do that. Restoring that ability must be a primary goal of
political reform in the coming years. Our society's capacity for unity
and for a constitutional restoration will depend on our ability to
recover a practical sense of the coalitional purpose of parties—a sense
that the framers of the Constitution themselves mostly lacked, or
only arrived at through difficult experience.

THE EQUATION OF FACTIONS WITH PARTIES WAS KEY TO HOW THE FRAM-
ers approached this subject at the outset. Parties were viewed as
institutionalizing a division of society into subnational interests that
were opposed in some way to the national interest. Since a party represents a part of society, it is, by definition, not an advocate for the
interests of the whole. Madison emphasized that point in Federalist 10,

in defining factions: "By a faction, I understand a number of citizens, whether amounting to a majority or a minority of the whole, who are united and actuated by some common impulse of passion, or of interest, adversed to the rights of other citizens, or to the permanent and aggregate interests of the community."

Essentially every discussion of party and partisanship in the records of the Constitutional Convention reflects the sense that parties are interchangeable with factions in this respect—that they are groups organized in defense of partial interests and, therefore, in opposition to the overall interest of the nation.[4]

A different idea of party was emerging in Britain at around that same time and was given voice, in particular, by Edmund Burke, a conservative Whig who grasped earlier than most the nature of the transformation of British political categories. "A party," Burke argued, "is a body of men united for promoting by their joint endeavours the national interest, upon some particular principle in which they are all agreed." In this view, a party is a way for like-minded people to work together toward a shared ideal of the common good—not just their own good but that of the whole society. Opposing partisans don't differ about whose good should be advanced in politics but about what would advance the good of all; they don't disagree about *whether* to work toward the benefit of the entire nation but about *how* to do so.[5]

Doing so by "joint endeavors" was particularly important to this Burkean conception of party. The party was a way to build a coalition, both among elites and in the larger electorate, in order to bring about the election of like-minded officials and facilitate their work when in power. Parties connected actual people around concrete goals. It is that formation of coalitions that connects this idea of partisanship to the framers' constitutional logic. Partisans appeal to an idea of the common good, not because they are somehow pure of motive and above petty concerns, but because the politics of even

a modestly democratic society requires the formation of durable majorities.

As we have seen, James Madison displayed a sophisticated understanding of this dynamic when considering the structures of the institutions of government. But he did not at first apply the same logic to parties. He expected coalition building to happen in Congress above all and certainly assumed that this would mean that partisans of different interests, in an effort to build a majority, would appeal to concerns they had in common with others and to an ideal of the good of the whole when forming legislative coalitions. But majorities are needed not only to enact legislation in Congress but also to win office at election time. How would those majorities be built in the new republic?

The framers' approach to that question was sometimes exceptionally individualistic. They tended to think about officeholders, and especially legislators, as units, and so of the work of the legislature as a complex process of cooperative and competitive aggregation among them. But they did not have as much to say about what it would take to get to the point of election and to work toward reelection as a coalition.

That is not to say that the design of the constitutional system did not mean to account for the selection of able officeholders. As we have seen, this was actually a preeminent priority. "The aim of every political constitution is, or ought to be," Madison wrote in Federalist 57, "first to obtain for rulers men who possess most wisdom to discern, and most virtue to pursue, the common good of the society; and in the next place, to take the most effectual precautions for keeping them virtuous whilst they continue to hold their public trust." Since leaders in a republican government are obtained by means of election, this meant thinking about the rules of eligibility and reeligibility for office and about the character of the different electorates created around the different offices in the system. All of

these were high on the minds of the delegates in Philadelphia, as noted throughout the prior chapters.[6]

But they did not seem to think that electoral politics itself could offer much preparatory training in the art of coalition building. Burke's idea of party, rooted in his experience as a member of the British Parliament, assumed two broad national parties locked in conflict over differing visions of the nation's future. The party, in that conception, served to structure and prepare the sort of coalition building that might then happen in the legislature. It would also serve to moderate partisans, because they would need to make broad appeals, and it would serve to signal to voters which office seekers stood for what and with whom.

All of this should have made parties, understood in Burkean terms, an appealing, and perhaps even necessary, complement to the American constitutional system once that system became home to a politics alive with heated controversies. Indeed, the experience of actually governing under the new Constitution quickly persuaded the leading figures of the early republic (including Madison, Hamilton, and other critics of parties) of the necessity of some party apparatus. Jefferson and Madison took the lead in this regard. In the course of the Washington administration, as they sought to head off measures advanced by Alexander Hamilton that they believed would render the executive branch too powerful and would promote the interests of northern commerce over those of southern agriculture, they concluded that they needed a formal party organization around which to coalesce their supporters, at least temporarily. The Democratic-Republican Party took shape around their efforts, and the Federalist Party then arose, almost by default, as the home of their opponents.

There was still a lingering suspicion of parties in American politics in those years, however. In 1796, as George Washington prepared to leave office and retire from politics, he devoted a significant

portion of his farewell address to the dangers of partisanship and factionalism. Parties were particularly dangerous if they are founded on regional or geographic identities, he argued, but there was also reason to worry about "the baneful effects of the spirit of party, generally." Washington warned, "This spirit, unfortunately, is inseparable from our nature, having its root in the strongest passions of the human mind. It exists under different shapes in all governments, more or less stifled, controlled, or repressed; but in those of the popular form it is seen in its greatest rankness and is truly their worst enemy."

At its worst, party spirit can open the door to despotism, he argued. But even in less extreme forms, "the common and continual mischiefs of the spirit of party are sufficient to make it the interest and the duty of a wise people to discourage and restrain it." He continued, "It serves always to distract the public councils and enfeeble the public administration. It agitates the community with ill-founded jealousies and false alarms, kindles the animosity of one part against another, foments occasionally riot and insurrection. It opens the door to foreign influence and corruption, which find a facilitated access to the government itself through the channels of party."

And yet, even as he warned of these grave dangers—which touched, in particular, on the risks of disunity and division—Washington pointed toward an emerging sense not only of inevitability but also constructive potential regarding parties. "There is an opinion that parties in free countries are useful checks upon the administration of the government and serve to keep alive the spirit of liberty," he noted.

> This within certain limits is probably true—and in governments
> of a monarchical cast patriotism may look with indulgence, if not
> with favor, upon the spirit of party. But in those of the popular

character, in governments purely elective, it is a spirit not to be encouraged. From their natural tendency, it is certain there will always be enough of that spirit for every salutary purpose. And there being constant danger of excess, the effort ought to be by force of public opinion to mitigate and assuage it. A fire not to be quenched, it demands a uniform vigilance to prevent its bursting into a flame, lest instead of warming it should consume.

This is a subtle argument. While warning against the risks of excessive partisanship, Washington could also see how parties contained in a particular way could serve the cause of liberty and how the challenge of a free society was to contain their excesses rather than to extinguish them altogether.[7]

The hostility to parties that prevailed at the Constitutional Convention had moderated quite a bit in the republic's first decade. But a positive argument for party, and for the compatibility of partisanship with the constitutional framework, was still lacking.

IT WAS, ABOVE ALL, THE PECULIARITIES OF THE SYSTEM OF PRESIDENTIAL selection that paved the way for that argument, and that propelled the evolution of the American party system. The Electoral College never quite worked as intended, and it was reformed by constitutional amendment fairly quickly in a way that soon intensified the need for parties.

As originally conceived in the Constitution, each presidential elector chosen by the public was to have two votes and so would vote for two candidates. A candidate who got an absolute majority (that is, more than 50 percent) of all the electoral votes nationwide would be elected president, and then the person who got the second-highest number of votes would become vice president. If two

candidates tied or if no one got a majority of the votes, then the House of Representatives would choose the president, and again, the second-highest vote-getter would be vice president. But as the consensus of the founding era dissipated and broad ideological divisions began to emerge, it quickly became apparent that this system could result in some strange and undesirable outcomes. The individuals elected president and vice president would have been the two leading candidates in the election, so they would have run against each other and could well be political opponents not well suited to cooperating. Even if they were not opponents, and instead ran together or were attractive to the same electors, it was entirely possible that each of them would receive the same number of votes (since each elector could cast two votes), which would result in a tie that needed to be resolved by the House of Representatives. These two kinds of problems were not just arcane theoretical possibilities. As soon as George Washington departed the scene, they both materialized immediately. The election of 1796 produced a president and vice president (John Adams and Thomas Jefferson) who were opponents incapable of working together, and then the election of 1800 resulted in a tie (between Jefferson and Aaron Burr) that had to be resolved by the House of Representatives.

To address these problems, the Twelfth Amendment was ratified in 1804. It changed the system so that each member of the Electoral College would have just one vote for president, not two, and a separate single vote for vice president. The winner of a majority of electoral votes in each case would win the office, and if no one got a majority, then the presidential election would be decided by the House, and the vice-presidential election by the Senate. This meant that candidates for president and vice president would tend to run as a package, on a joint ticket, and so would be more likely to work together when elected. But because each elector now had only one vote for president, rather than two, this change also completed the

process of turning the Electoral College into a simple rubber stamp on the outcome of the popular vote in each state. Electors would be chosen based on their commitment to vote for a particular candidate, so that the mass of voters, in essence, were voting for president themselves, and the popular elections in the various states would determine the outcome.[8]

This altered system added significantly to the need for some coordination and organization in advance of presidential contests. The Electoral College would not provide a deliberative sifting or selection function, and if too many candidates ran, then presidential elections would routinely be decided by the House. Some process of winnowing would have to precede the presidential election—a process for which organized parties, and (because winning required an absolute majority of electors), ideally just two large, organized parties that each worked to build a national majority coalition, were all but essential.

For a time, the ad hoc party system that emerged around the controversies of the Washington administration seemed capable of taking up this work. But Jefferson's Democratic-Republicans soon became so dominant that the party system all but ceased to function. The federalists effectively disappeared by the time James Monroe succeeded Jefferson and Madison to become the third two-term Democratic-Republican president in a row. That stretch came to be known as the "era of good feelings," but by the end of it, with the party system vitiated, the risks inherent in the transformed Electoral College rules re-emerged with a vengeance.

The election of 1824 featured four major candidates—Andrew Jackson, John Quincy Adams, Henry Clay, and William Crawford—all of whom were Democratic-Republicans. They divided the vote, and none came close to a majority in the Electoral College, sending the election to the House, where Adams (who had come in second to Jackson in both the popular and electoral votes) won the

presidency. Without functional parties, the presidential selection process fell into chaos, and many observers worried that every subsequent election would devolve into a multicandidate contest of personalities, with factions gathering around high-profile figures rather than governing visions and every president being chosen by the House. These concerns pointed to a distinct inadequacy in the constitutional framework, and the man who most fully grasped how to fill that void was Martin Van Buren, the father of the American party system.

Van Buren was a politician's politician. Born in New York in 1782, he climbed every rung of the political ladder, serving as a county commissioner, state legislator, state attorney general, US senator (the job he held during the 1824 election), governor of New York, US secretary of state, ambassador to Britain, vice president, and finally the eighth president of the United States. This path through the system made Van Buren an expert in the practicalities of electoral politics, and it led him to grasp the danger implicit in the nonpartisan republic. He was himself a Democratic-Republican, but he understood that what revealed itself in 1824 was ominous. In a posthumously published memoir, Van Buren wrote of his sense of that moment: "In the place of two great parties arrayed against each other in a fair and open contest for the establishment of principles in the administration of Government which they respectively believed most conducive to the public interest, the country was overrun with personal factions. These having few higher motives for the selection of their candidates or stronger incentives to action than individual preferences or antipathies, moved the bitter waters of political agitation to their lowest depths."[9]

That kind of personalism, which pointed the way toward the sorts of demagoguery that had undone many republics throughout history, was a foremost fear of the framers of the Constitution, and they hoped the Electoral College would help avert it. In the absence

of "two great parties arrayed against each other," it seemed the constitutional system alone could not do so.

Therefore, Van Buren argued for the development of two broad parties of national scope, each of which would seek to become a majority coalition and so to advance its chosen candidates for the presidency, the vice-presidency, and the Congress, as well as state and local offices. These must not be regional parties, so as not to exacerbate geographic divisions. And they ought not be factional parties that represent narrow interests or (as we would say now) single-issue platforms with an aim to then join governing coalitions upon being elected. Rather, each party would define itself by a general governing approach and agenda but appeal to persuadable, moderate voters from one direction or the other.

Implicit in this vision was the idea that the politics of a democratic society would fall relatively naturally into two broad camps—or that the Left and Right, in our vernacular, had some genuine significance as ways of thinking about the great questions of the day. But although these broad visions might each speak with some force to a portion of the population inclined to approach politics intellectually or ideologically, large numbers of voters might swing back and forth between them, based on their sense of the country's needs at the moment and of the appeal of the particular ideas and candidates each party offered.

Van Buren thought these general ideological camps were real but permeable. Their names would change over time, but their broad approaches to political questions had a meaningful continuity. "Men of similar and substantially unchanged views and principles have, at different periods of English history, been distinguished as Cavaliers or Roundheads, Jacobins or Puritans and Presbyterians, as Whigs or Tories," he wrote. And something of that pattern had already emerged in America in its first half century. "Here, with corresponding consistency in principle, the same men have at different

periods been known as federalists, federal Republicans, and Whigs, or as anti-federalists, Republicans, and Democrats." These were truly national parties. Their differences had to do with how to best advance the interest of all, not whose narrow interest should prevail. But they were divided over a core sense of what mattered most in politics—a party of social order confronted a party of social justice, very roughly speaking. This core division would not be imposed on American society; it was already present in a general sense. The parties merely institutionalized it in a particular way, and it was time for them to think more carefully and explicitly about just what that way ought to be, and so how to use party committees, conventions, and other mechanisms to sift and select candidates and to facilitate electioneering and governing.[10]

This ideological framework inclined American politics toward breaking into two parties, but there were also strong structural reasons for our two-party politics. As we've seen, the design of the Electoral College rules means that our parties must be built to produce national majorities in presidential elections. American legislative elections generally use plurality voting, or first-past-the-post rules, by which there is only one seat at stake in each election and the top vote-getter wins that seat, rather than dividing several seats among several parties in proportion to their share of the vote, as some other democracies do. This encourages parties to seek absolute majorities at the congressional level, too, and in state and local elections, which creates a strong incentive for just two broad parties all the way through the system.

And a two-party system, Van Buren argued, could be particularly well aligned with the aims of the Constitution. Because both parties would need to win moderate voters to expand their coalitions and each would seek to achieve an absolute majority in the electorate, the parties' particular ways of institutionalizing political differences would involve their effectively functioning as moderating

institutions, tempering their own core voters to increase their appeal to more marginal voters and, in the process, tempering our electoral politics more generally. Partisans would have to build coalitions between ideologically compatible but distinct factions within their party in order to win, which would prepare them to build coalitions beyond their party in order to govern. Just like Madison's constitutionalism, Van Buren's approach to partisanship leaned into the diversity of American society as a way to restrain extremism and thought about institutions as means of facilitating political action while creating pressures and incentives for accommodation. Such parties, as Josiah Lee Auspitz has put it, "impose institutional discipline upon popular will," just like the formal institutions of the Madisonian system.[11]

In this sense, Van Buren's party system was a kind of missing piece in the constitutional puzzle. Its logic was distinctly Madisonian: the party would subsume personal ambition beneath institutional purpose, moderate potentially divisive differences, use the selection process for an office as a means of forming people to perform that office well, and pave the way for an accommodative mode of governing in both of the elected branches. Party conventions and similar nominating processes that Van Buren pressed the parties to adopt would allow for some elite management of the options to be presented to the mass democracy, ensuring that candidates were both qualified and broadly appealing. And by controlling the number of candidates for the presidency in particular, they would also avoid sending elections to the House—and indeed, so far not a single election has gone to the House since 1824, thanks in no small measure to the parties adopting the sorts of processes Van Buren and his allies proposed.

Van Buren's key insight was one that contemporary Americans still find difficult to wrap our heads around, though it remains as true as ever: parties as institutions actually restrain partisanship and

CONSTITUTIONAL PARTISANSHIP

moderate its ill effects. Weaker parties or a politics without functional parties would mean more intense partisanship. Stronger parties tend to result in a more temperamentally moderate politics and in more bargaining and compromise. To achieve the framers' goal of restraining partisan zeal, Van Buren proposed to employ a means they had repudiated and to strengthen and formalize the roles of two broad, institutionally assertive yet ideologically multifaceted national parties.

That two huge parties will inevitably each be fractious and messy was a feature, not a bug, in such a system. The existence of intraparty factions, and so of a range of views within each party, means that while the substantive division between the parties is meaningful, it is often dull rather than sharp. This can go too far, rendering party differences meaningless and leaving the two parties fighting only about power or about individual leaders. But it is also possible to go too far in the other direction and turn our parties into weaponized ideological purifiers. Between the two is a kind of moderate partisanship that tends to suit the often ideologically nebulous American electorate. And factions within the parties tend to drive change in the system, allowing for substantive activism to advance political transformations but in ways that are moderated by the larger party institutions. As political scientist Daniel DiSalvo has shown, such faction-driven agitation is how the most significant and durable policy reforms on all sides of our politics have tended to materialize.[12]

The appeal of Van Buren's approach to party structure and process was not only its compatibility with the logic of the Constitution but also its ability to facilitate the elevation of candidates and leaders in the absence of broadly admired national figures. As the generation that had won the Revolutionary War departed the scene, Americans found themselves with politicians who were merely normal human beings, and they needed some way to organize the system by which such politicians would compete for prominence and

position that would be answerable to public priorities but not subject to every momentary whim of the masses and would plausibly select for qualified candidates. By the middle of the nineteenth century, Van Buren's vision was a reality.

THAT PARTY SYSTEM, LIKE SO MUCH OF THE CONSTITUTIONAL ORDER, DID not hold up in the face of the slavery debate and the buildup to the Civil War. The Democratic Party divided over the issue into regional parties, the Whigs all but disappeared, a new Republican Party arose to take their place and champion the fight against slavery's expansion, and American politics broke down just as the nation did. But the party system, like the constitutional system, reintegrated itself remarkably quickly after the war, and its basic logic was not lost.

That logic of American partisanship came under a more sustained and ultimately more effective assault in the Progressive Era, however, precisely because of its relation to the logic of the Constitution. As we have seen, the early progressives critiqued the American system for lacking coherence and sacrificing responsiveness, energy, and effectiveness in government for the sake of stability, safety, and cohesion in society. They argued that this trade-off was neither successful nor necessary, and that unity could be achieved by unified leadership, especially presidential leadership, not by aimless negotiation. So they sought a politics in which different parties offered thoroughly distinct and comprehensive policy programs, the public selected among them on Election Day, and then the winning party would have essentially unlimited power to pursue its program until the public voted for someone else. The competition among factions in society would not be resolved by their bargaining within the institutions of government but by voters choosing among them at the ballot box and letting whichever won a majority

deploy all the powers of government in the service of its vision. The Westminster model works more or less along such lines. It is a legitimate and democratic approach to government, geared more to the demands of administration and accountability than deliberation and social peace, and the progressives thought it would better serve modern America. Just as that model required a very different conception than Madison's of the purpose of Congress and the executive, so it demanded a very different notion than Van Buren's of what parties should be.

Woodrow Wilson was, again, the clearest early champion of that alternative. He believed the two vast, sloppy parties of the American system offered voters no clear choice among policy directions. Their disagreements just were not stark enough, which meant that election victories did not empower any clear governing agenda. In a short newspaper essay in 1886, Wilson argued that the nature of the American party system, which elevated coalition building above any clear goals, made it impossible for voters to know who to support. He offered an example:

> Does anyone favor civil service reform? The present act establishing competitive examinations and a commission was proposed by a democratic senator to a republican senate, was passed by that body and a democratic house, and signed by a republican president. The senator who proposed it was afterward cast aside by his constituency because of his reform sentiments. His measure is now administered with full sympathy for its purposes, by a democratic president elected because of his record on this question; but it is covertly attacked in a democratic house, and openly sneered at in a republican senate; and the democratic chairman of the house committee on civil service reform fails renomination in North Carolina because of his fine reform work on that committee. Which party, then, advocates civil service reform?

This scenario would have pleased Madison or Van Buren, but it struck Wilson as a failure of the political system.[13]

What was required instead was a sharper set of distinctions between the parties. Wilson and his acolytes wanted elections to produce clear popular mandates that would enable energetic leadership. They did not think government should move on the basis of accommodations reached by bargaining among elected officials but on the basis of the public will, discerned by elections and framed by clear party platforms. Leaders would build public support and then act on it decisively rather than facilitate accommodation to reduce tensions.

This would require leaders with real vision. Wilson's conception of party politics was, like his conception of politics more generally, particularly focused on the presidency and its capacity to move the public. "Policy—where there is no arbitrary ruler to do the choosing for the whole nation," Wilson wrote, "means massed opinion, and the forming of the masses is the whole art and mastery of politics." The party system should facilitate, and then serve such formation of mass public will. A party should be arranged to enable some competition among potential leaders, and then to follow the lead of the one who won its presidential nomination. As political scientist James Ceaser summarized it, Wilson's goal in reforming the parties was "an open nominating process in which each contender presented his program directly to the people. The winners would then earn the right to 'own' their parties."[14]

For this purpose, the progressives proposed selecting candidates (for the presidency and other offices) through primary elections rather than conventions, committees, or behind-the-scenes negotiations among party elites. Ideally, these primaries would be open to all voters who wanted to take part, not just members of the party. Candidates for Congress and for state-level offices would follow the lead of the party's presidential aspirant. The purpose of the party

apparatus would then be to support and reinforce the winners of those primaries to help them win the general election and advance the agenda they had put before the public.

Wilson himself was not originally a champion of primaries, but he had come to that view (which had long been promoted by other progressives) by the time he entered politics himself, as a candidate for governor of New Jersey. And he did so not out of any great faith in (or naïveté about) the public's knowledge or political acumen. He championed primaries not so much as a way to enable voters to control politicians but as a way to move politicians to put clear and distinct policy ideas before voters, to bring voters together around those ideas, and then to be held accountable for pursuing them in office. Such "responsible party government," rather than governing through an indecipherable fog of deal making that lets everyone avoid responsibility, seemed to the progressives both more democratic and more likely to yield genuine change.

This idea of the purpose of parties was very much in line with Wilson's proposals for transforming the American constitutional system more generally, which we have seen from several angles in prior chapters. His responsible parties would populate his more polarized and leadership-driven Congress and elevate his more policy-assertive president, who could serve as the focal point of popular will.

In fact, as their proposals for reforms of the formal institutions of the constitutional system met with resistance, progressives came to see that reforms of the parties made possible a kind of end run around that system—a way to drive changes in the Madisonian architecture without having to amass the arduous supermajorities needed for formal constitutional amendments. By changing the sorts of people the parties would elevate and the expectations both officeholders and voters would have, you could transform the function of American government, even without transforming its structure. Party reforms

thus became a preeminent focus of progressive political action at all levels of government.

But those did not take hold all at once. Rather, the twentieth-century American party system was a kind of evolving and unsteady hybrid of Van Buren's and Wilson's visions, combining elements of party-elite management and radical democratization in ways that were not fully thought through. By the middle of the century, progressive intellectuals and political scientists had formulated a thoroughgoing case for party reform along Wilsonian lines, and that argument—often without even acknowledging the case for the alternative approach—became the commonsense view of parties in the American elite, and not only on the Left. That view came to be embodied in a highly influential 1950 report by a special committee of the American Political Science Association, titled "Toward a More Responsible Two-Party System." The commission, chaired by political scientist E. E. Schattschneider of Wesleyan University, argued that the parties should sharpen their ideological appeals, better highlight their differences, nationalize their internal infrastructure, and work to make their core voters more energized and engaged.

Some critics could see the risks of such an approach, and they focused precisely on the threat it posed to the capacity of our system to engender cohesion. Political scientist James Q. Wilson warned in 1962 that such reforms would "mean that political conflict will be intensified, social cleavages will be exaggerated, party leaders will tend to be men skilled in the rhetorical arts, and the parties' ability to produce agreement by trading issue free resources will be reduced." In retrospect, he was prophetic.[15]

And he was not alone. As Daniel Stid has recently shown, there was a cadre of Madisonian political scientists in that midcentury moment warning about precisely the imperative of cohesion and the need to allow the party system to perform its accommodative

work. Austin Ranney and Willmoore Kendall wrote in defense of Van Buren's model of parties and warned their colleagues not to take social cohesion for granted. "By sustaining and refreshing the consensus on which our society and governmental system are based," they argued, the American party system "makes possible our characteristic brand of pluralistic bargaining-compromising discussion of public issues, which is probably about as close to the model of creative democratic discussion in the nation-state as a community like the United States can hope to get." Edward Banfield, Pendleton Herring, and a handful of others made similar cases. These scholars, as Stid noted, "recognized the American party system could be messy and homely—especially compared to the ideal-type, Westminster-style party systems that had animated reformers from Woodrow Wilson's day to their own." Yet they also believed that, as Stid wrote, "surface appearances and ungrounded trans-Atlantic comparisons missed an underlying reality. The traditional American parties they studied and defended had developed in ways that were fit for purpose in the American regime. As a result, the country continued to enjoy the modicum of consensus and unity it needed to prosper. That, they knew, was no small thing."

But the progressive core of the political science profession dismissed this concern about unity. "There is no real ideological division in the American electorate," the American Political Science Association report argued. "Hence programs of action presented by responsible parties for the voter's support could hardly be expected to reflect or strive toward such division." Those assurances have not worn well with time, to put it mildly.[16]

The party system has evolved in a progressive direction, slowly but surely, for many decades. Party primaries had come to be used by both parties to select nominees for Congress and many local offices by the middle of the twentieth century. In presidential elections, both parties have chosen their candidates almost exclusively by binding

state primary elections or caucuses since the 1970s, essentially handing off their most important function to mass electorates—which, in some states, even include voters who aren't registered members of the party. These changes did not only happen because of progressive intellectual and political pressure. There were also real problems with the machine model of party politics. It was too tolerant of corruption and, worse yet, of organized racial exclusion and segregation. The Democratic Party, in particular, had arranged itself around the accommodation of Jim Crow and needed to be rearranged. It was not a coincidence that party reform happened first among Democrats. But the sorts of changes pursued in response to these justified frustrations in both parties were very much a function of decades of progressive intellectual work and activism and were not sufficiently thought through.

The system, at first, seemed to digest these changes without a major transformation of political culture. But that could not last. As the parties increasingly took a more Wilsonian shape, greater tensions arose between the aims of the party system and those of the constitutional system. Were elections meant to settle key issues by a decisive choice or to decide who would have a seat at the table when they were settled by incremental negotiation? The gradual adoption of progressive reforms of the parties meant that the people running for office increasingly tended to have one set of expectations on that front while the system of government they populated when they won was built in light of another. The resulting frustration led to growing dysfunction over time and to a political culture ill at ease with our political system and increasingly inclined to reject its emphasis on cohesion. Americans have grown keenly aware of the polarization of our politics but increasingly unaware of the constitutional tools at our disposal for responding to division. Instead, as we have seen in prior chapters, the core institutions of the Madisonian system have gradually (and mostly informally)

been transformed and deformed in the same Wilsonian direction as the party system.

It is now painfully obvious that the reforms that disempowered party professionals in both parties were a catastrophic mistake, which has sown bitter division throughout our political system and beyond it in the broader culture and done terrible harm to our country. This was not the intent of the reformers who advanced such changes in both parties. They sought to democratize the parties' internal procedures and so to give the public more of a voice in the earliest stages of the political process. But the result has been a less democratic American party system, because it is one that empowers only the most active fringes of both parties—and especially the small percentage of voters who participate in party primaries. Those tend to be the voters least interested in bargaining and compromise and least inclined to see the point of the accommodationist structure of our system's core institutions. Primaries have actually empowered elites—elites who are amateur activists with a lot of time for politics, not those who are party professionals but elites nonetheless, and not the broad public. By making office seekers most attentive to those voters rather than to the marginal voters essential for broader coalition building and who had been the focus of party professionals, the modern primary system has drawn into politics a type of politician who is not well suited to the work of the institutions, and so to the office to which he or she is seeking election. Indeed, in many cases, winning a primary now involves effectively committing not to negotiate or bargain with the other party and, therefore, in essence, not to do the job of a member of Congress or a governor or president.

Primaries have pushed our presidential politics, in particular, in a demagogic direction, encouraging our parties to take shape around the personalities and ambitions of individual candidates rather than constraining and containing those ambitions for the

sake of a broader public purpose and set of principles. Presidents now implicitly (and sometimes explicitly) understand themselves to be accountable to a narrow segment of their own party's base, and the demands of winning the presidential nomination of either party are now deeply at odds with the demands of both winning a presidential election and governing.

Primaries have been used to select congressional candidates for far longer, but in combination with the broader Wilsonian transformation of the party infrastructures, today's primary system interacts in ruinous ways with the polarization of the electorate. Many members of both houses represent relatively safe partisan constituencies, which means they now consider their primary electorates their only relevant set of voters. But those voters make demands on them that are in great tension with the requirements of legislative bargaining and negotiation. The primaries are not the reason those districts or states are not competitive, but they create unhealthy disincentives to constructive cross-partisan accommodation. Primaries have made core legislative work politically risky for members of Congress—which is a truly crazy way to structure the incentives confronting our national legislators.

The primary system has also driven both parties to neglect winnable voters in the middle of the electorate. The parties exist to build broad coalitions and win majorities. But individual politicians in both parties now have strong incentives to, instead, only satisfy their party's most devoted voters. As a result, both parties now appeal to the fringes and leave the ideological core of the electorate oddly underrepresented. It is no coincidence that the thirty years since the logic of the primary system became deeply embedded in our political culture have been a time of exceedingly narrow majorities, with both parties essentially stuck at 50 percent of the vote and doing very little to change that. Our society really is polarized, but it is not as deadlocked as the political system; that system is stuck because

it seeks to represent mostly those elements of both party coalitions that are not interested in getting unstuck.

The primaries have also exacerbated our sense that our society is bitterly divided by persuading Americans that the loudest and most extreme supporters of each party are the essence of that party and, therefore, that our politics consists of two camps of vociferous extremists who differ fundamentally and intensely about the basic character of our society and its future. The party system is intended to compel more radical activists into coalitions with more moderate copartisans before they mount the electoral stage, but the dominant role of primary elections has meant that this no longer happens, and both parties approach voters in the guise of their worst selves.

In all these ways, our increasingly Wilsonian party system is poorly aligned with the Madisonian constitutional system. That misalignment leads political partisans to view our governing institutions as hopelessly unsuited to their ends and, therefore, to approach those institutions with hostility and invest their hopes in various end runs around them. But durable political change in our country happens through the institutions of our system, not around them. Our party system now more or less ignores the nature and structure of those institutions, and that has created an enormous gap between our electoral politics and our constitutional practice—between the demands of our system of government and the demands of primary voters.

That gap has worsened the dysfunction of our governing institutions. Many members of Congress and several recent presidents have used the institutions to which they were elected as mere platforms for political performance art for the sake of their most devoted voters. From the point of view of the constitutional system, such behavior seems like dereliction and failure. But from the point of view of the modern primary system, it is both rational and effective. A party system with incentives so thoroughly out of alignment with

the constitutional system is a recipe for disaster—and disaster is just what we have experienced.

That gap could be closed by altering the constitutional system, and there are certainly some reformers who would make the case for that, arguing that we should reduce the need for cross-partisan bargaining in our system rather than increase the likelihood of such bargaining. But such reforms would only intensify our divisions. By seeing *why* our constitutional system is set up to incentivize and facilitate competition, accommodation, and constructive tension, we can see that undermining its capacity to do so has contributed mightily to today's polarized and bitter political culture. That suggests that we should seek to close the gap in the other direction—by altering our party system so as to better align it with the imperatives and structures of the constitutional system and by reforming our practice of constitutionalism in ways that better align with those as well. We have seen what such reforms of constitutional practice could involve in prior chapters. But what reforms of the party system might be compatible with them?

This is no easy question, but it is a crucial one. As Josiah Lee Auspitz wrote, "It is a symptom of our own constitutional disarray that we must look to Van Buren with renewed respect and consider again the standards implicit in his hopes for the party system."[17]

It is probably not possible to go back to the pre-primary era of meaningful party conventions and behind-the-scenes candidate selection. Getting from here to there would require politicians to tell their most active and engaged voters that they are the problem in our broken politics and must be made less influential over candidate selection. That isn't just hard to imagine, it's effectively impossible to do. So while it is certainly possible to give party elites more of a role, some form of the primary process is likely here to stay.

Changing the incentives created by primaries is therefore essential. One way to do that may be to arrange primary elections in ways

that require office seekers to build coalitions within the party to succeed. Ranked-choice voting in primary elections is worth considering for that reason. A ranked-choice election allows voters to vote for multiple candidates in order of preference, and then have their vote count on behalf of their second or third choice if their first or second choice is not among the top vote-getters. In most forms, it is essentially an automatic runoff system. From the point of view of candidates, such a system creates a strong reason to be many voters' second choice, as well as the first choice of some. That naturally invites an accommodating, coalition-building mind-set, of just the sort that the Van Buren party system intended to encourage and that the Madisonian Constitution values and depends on. Our system now encourages candidates with the wrong disposition to run for office, and there is nothing wrong with rethinking the incentives involved to attract a better sort of politician. The framers of the Constitution devoted much thought to the question of how to appeal to the sort of people who would best perform the roles of officeholders in the system, and we should too.

If ranked-choice methods were deployed in primaries, there would be no particular reason to deploy them in general elections, since the problem to be solved is the character of the candidate pool in our political system and the attitudes those candidates are encouraged to have—a problem to be solved within the parties much more than between them. Indeed, political reformers should keep in mind the appeal and advantages of our two-party system and pursue reforms that enable that system to serve its sifting and selection functions, rather than those that undermine that system. Ranked-choice general elections would tend to undermine the parties, while ranked-choice primary elections would strengthen them, as we should want to do. The diversity of American political life should be represented by intraparty factions that negotiate with one another within and between the two broad parties.

Such constructive factions could be encouraged by changes in party rules that give durable intraparty groups some meaningful role in the process of candidate selection, and also (as discussed in chapter 5) by giving them a more formal and significant role in the workings of both party conferences in both houses of Congress. As Daniel Stid has put it, "By intensifying conflict within the parties, we can reduce the negative effects of polarization between them. While the clash of disparate and competing factions inside the parties runs counter to ideals of responsible partisanship, it creates more leeway for creative coalition-building and policy-making."[18]

The expansion of "fusion voting," in which small parties (often representing factions within our two larger parties) use their access to the ballot to endorse and support major-party candidates, and so gain leverage over the larger parties and help facilitate their internal coalition building, is also worth some experiments. Fusion voting has mostly been limited to New York and Connecticut in our day, and growing its reach could help shape and strengthen our two-party system in the right way. This kind of party-focused (rather than voter-focused) reform is crucial to building a more Madisonian party system. Along similar lines, both parties should also look for ways to expand the candidate selection process, combining primaries with some formal role for current officeholders and other party leaders—particularly in presidential selection, but also perhaps to some degree in choosing congressional or statewide-office candidates. Political scientist Elaine Kamarck has proposed such an approach, which she dubs "peer review," for the presidential nomination process. The parties have ceased to function as venues for deliberation about political choices and so to play their crucial part in keeping the constitutional system functional. It is vital to find ways to help them play that part again.[19]

It is also important for both parties to invest in their local and state infrastructures to help them become venues for organizing

and acting politically on an interpersonal level again rather than just serving as brands and communications platforms for national candidates. Local party organizing is inherently coalitional and could help to refocus the parties on work that better aligns them with the constitutional system. In a sense, the advent of primaries has encouraged us to confound voting with political engagement, within the parties just as in the larger system. We now conflate the party organizations with the act of voting once every few years, and as a result, the actual organizations have withered and cannot perform their function—which is a fundamentally moderating function. The parties no longer teach us the art of associating, and that could and should change.[20]

Reforms like these, and especially some moderation of the ruinously divisive logic of the primaries, are essential prerequisites to the kinds of structural renewal of the constitutional system discussed in earlier chapters. Those other changes have to be advanced by elected officials, and the deformations of our parties now stand in the way of electing men and women inclined to do the sort of work our constitutional system demands—and, therefore, to help that system work better in its own terms.

NO SUCH AGENDA FOR REFORM COULD BE A SILVER BULLET, AND THERE IS no simple path to restoring the Constitution's capacity to bring us together. The American party system can help the American constitutional system serve its unifying goals, but it can only do that by understanding itself as directed to such goals and by understanding our society as in need of greater and more sustainable cohesion.

Such cohesion is possible, but today's party system increasingly obscures rather than clarifies that fact by persuading Americans that their political opponents are much more radical than they really are.

The fact that our parties are called Democrats and Republicans is a sign of our cohesion, more than our division. We live in a democratic republic, and both parties stand for the principles of that republic, even when they see its promise and potential in quite different ways. Both have their roots in the truths and commitments of the Declaration of Independence, even if they view human nature and political life through somewhat different lenses. The conflict between them, which is very real, is, for the most part, fought between boundaries that allow our society to endure and thrive. There are exceptions: both parties do contain some elements that are genuinely hostile to the aims and principles of our regime. Those are not the essence of either party, but they are elevated and magnified within both by what has become of our party system. To address that, it is necessary to advance a more moderate understanding of the conflict between the parties, and that will require thinking institutionally about the form and purpose of the party system.

Americans transformed that system over the past half century and more because we assumed, at least implicitly, that our national cohesion would not be a problem. We can no longer assume that, and so we have to rethink some of the changes we've made and learn from our mistakes about how we might better enable our system of government to perform its crucial functions. That does not mean going backward, but it means grasping the problems to which the Madisonian system is a solution and seeing how that solution could work now. For that reason, it must also mean better understanding just what unity should look like and involve.

Chapter 9

WHAT IS UNITY?

THE DECLARATION OF INDEPENDENCE, WHICH LAUNCHED OUR nation into existence, announced an act of separation. It did not proclaim the birth of a new people but rather asserted that Americans had found themselves in a situation in which it had become "necessary for one people to dissolve the political bands which have connected them with another." It implied that the British and the Americans were already two peoples and, therefore, that the Americans were already one.

But after winning independence, as they gradually turned their attention from the struggle for separation to the work of self-government, the people of the United States came to see that simply saying they were one people was not enough. Unity would take even more work than separation and would require a structure of government built for the task. So in the summer of 1787, they sent a group of their best politicians back to Philadelphia, to the very room where separation from Britain had been proclaimed, to formulate a framework for governing their new republic, rooted in the principles they had declared a decade earlier and geared to holding a dynamic,

fractious, growing society together. We have seen that unity was much on the minds of the delegates who took on that work. But just what did they mean by unity? And what might we mean by it now, as we confront some of the same daunting challenges they did, and some they could not quite have imagined? Those questions are not nearly as simple as they might seem. Ironically, the meaning of unity has always been a contentious question in America.

But the Constitution does point toward an answer. It offers up an ideal of unity that is rooted in the practical nature of political life and that works to make common action possible. Such unity requires some agreement about who we are and what we believe as a society, but that very general agreement is only a starting point for political life. Ultimately, politics in every society exists to deal with differences, and so assumes disagreement. Politics is hardly necessary where we all agree. And in a free society, where politics cannot involve the coercive quashing of differences, it exists instead to facilitate common action despite differing beliefs and priorities. That means unity is less a condition than a way of life. It does not need to be tranquil in order to be genuine, does not need to be calm in order to be productive, and has at least as much to do with disagreeing better as with agreeing more. The various capacities of the Constitution to facilitate greater cohesion, laid out in all the prior chapters, therefore point us to a distinct idea of unity with much to teach us now. They suggest that unity is less about thinking alike than about acting together and, therefore, also that unity is more within our grasp than we might think.

ALTHOUGH THEY DID NOT SIMPLY DEFINE UNITY, THE FRAMERS WERE forthright about two assumptions related to it that seem, at first, to contradict each other but that ultimately illuminate their particular

conception of the term. On the one hand, they assumed that unanimity of views was not an option for a free society. On the other hand, they assumed that political union, marked by genuine cohesion and togetherness, was an absolute necessity for their new nation and that this must be a union of the people, not just of the states.

James Madison, who reflected most deeply on this challenge, was adamant on both points. He resisted assurances that the American people were already a highly cohesive and unified whole. As noted in chapter 1, for instance, he waved away South Carolina delegate Charles Pinckney's insistence at the Philadelphia Convention that the absence of a formal aristocracy in America would help the new nation avert deep divisions. Maybe the United States did not have precisely Europe's kinds of social divisions, Madison responded, but it was a profoundly fractured society in its own ways. And disunity was not just the result of America's particular political, cultural, or demographic circumstances. It would always be a challenge in any genuinely free society. In Federalist 10, Madison put the point bluntly: "As long as the reason of man continues fallible, and he is at liberty to exercise it, different opinions will be formed."[1]

But this reality, sobering as it was, did not need to mean that the American people could not sustain a unified society. Just a week after Federalist 10 was published, Madison, writing in Federalist 14, warned his readers away from the lure of division and of fragmentation of the union, insisting with unusual passion and intensity: "Hearken not to the unnatural voice which tells you that the people of America, knit together as they are by so many cords of affection, can no longer live together as members of the same family; can no longer continue the mutual guardians of their mutual happiness; can no longer be fellow citizens of one great, respectable, and flourishing empire."[2]

So unanimity was not an option, but unity was both possible and necessary. How could that work? Madison's gesture toward

affection is surely one part of the answer. American life is not simply politics, and discrete disagreements need not loosen what Alexander Hamilton, in Federalist 15, called "that sacred knot which binds the people of America together." Even within politics, there were some crucial shared commitments that contributed to civic affection across much of American society, not least the experience of having recently fought for independence together. But the idea of union at the forefront of the Constitution's ambitions is not merely an outgrowth of affection and sympathy. Indeed, the fear of disunion was, for the framers, maybe above all, a fear of political disaffection that would undercut Americans' warm sentiments toward one another. Averting bitter fracture in an often-fragmented society would have to be a central purpose of American political life, so that the heterogeneity of American society did not make a shared political existence impossible. In this sense, unity would have to be at least as much a product as a premise of American politics.[3]

That distinction, which clarifies the complicated tension between Madison's assumption of permanent differences and his insistence on a robust union, amounts to the beginning of a definition of unity. Cohesion would be produced by common action, more than it would be evinced in shared opinions. In a complex and free society, unity would consist less of thinking alike than of acting together. Some degree of agreement on fundamentals is necessary for common action, but that agreement is fairly broad much of the time. It can define the boundaries within which legitimate political life can happen, but it is too general to really constitute a foundation for specific political actions. Most of political life involves acting together across and despite disagreements—acting together in negotiated ways to address common challenges and take up common efforts and, through such common action, also forging common aims, a common identity, and real affection.

But how can people act together when they don't think alike? That is the question that most troubled James Madison. It is the question that motivated a great deal of the work of the Philadelphia Convention. Indeed, it is one way to formulate the question to which the United States Constitution was, and remains, an answer. Much of what is mysterious and frustrating to many Americans about our system now is a function of its being an answer to that question. Some of our most divisive constitutional debates are about whether we need to ask that question and, if so, how we ought to answer it. A great deal of the dysfunction of our contemporary political culture is a consequence of failures of constitutional practice that stand in the way of putting the Constitution's distinct answer to that question into effect.

THAT ANSWER, AND THE DEFINITION OF UNITY THAT IT IMPLIES, HAS roots that run deep in the political tradition of the West. It can be hard to pin down because it combines classical, Christian, and modern insights with republican and liberal aspirations. Teasing these apart just a little could help us clarify the character of Madisonian unity and appreciate the complex roots of our regime.

It is natural and appropriate for us to see the US Constitution as, in large part, the embodiment of a particular kind of modern liberal political outlook. But it is a modern constitution that owes a great deal to premodern political ideas, and this is particularly true of its conception of social cohesion. We have already seen that a number of ideas we tend to attribute to James Madison or to his immersion in the thinking of the Scottish Enlightenment were, in fact, prefigured in Aristotle's political thought. Most notably, that a larger polity is more likely to be stable and less riven by faction than a smaller one, that economic differences are the primary drivers of factional

division, and that statesmen would best deal with such divisions by setting factions off against one another in the structure of the regime, are all proposed in Aristotle's *Politics*. The approach to political unity that characterizes Madison's defense of the Constitution is not as explicitly prefigured in classical political philosophy, but it owes a great deal to two concepts that Aristotle illuminates: the idea that politics (and political unity) is best understood as a mode of activity and the related complex concept of civic friendship.[4]

For Aristotle, the essence of politics is common action, and political speech is ultimately best understood as speech about how to act collectively. "The political orator aims at establishing the expediency or the harmfulness of a proposed course of action," he argued in the *Rhetoric*. Political speech in this respect begins from the assumption that there are multiple possible courses of action and that there are diverging views among the polity (or those with the power to rule) about which to pursue. The process of determining which course to pursue or what action to take together is at the core of political life. To make such decisions is to rule; to live by them is to be ruled. And politics is the combination of the two.[5]

Political engagement is, thus, a way of dealing with difference and assumes heterogeneity. Modern political thought makes that heterogeneity much more prominent in its vision of social life, but it was very much an element of classical political thought as well. Political philosopher Pierre Manent summarizes Aristotle's view on this front as insisting that every genuine political community contains some underlying social division, and politics is unavoidably organized around that division. Political action is not exactly a means of effectuating agreed-upon plans; it is a means of forging agreement regarding a course of action where before there was disagreement. Manent describes that process as "the production of the common," so that, in this sense, common ground is the result and not the setting of political action. Politics turns disagreement into common action

and, in the process, brings the people involved closer to one another as fellow citizens. As we have seen, Madison thought this kind of process, in the form of the sorts of negotiation made necessary by the structures of the institutions of our system, could change how people understood their own aspirations. In being forced to describe our aims in terms of the general good of society, we come to actually understand our aims in those terms. By being forced to work together toward common goals, we come to understand ourselves as sharing a life in common.[6]

The idea of a production of the common assumes that the common is not fully present to begin with. But that does not mean that citizens start out as foes. Political life produces common ground on specific matters of contention, but it does begin with some common assumptions about the general character of civic life. Politics does not turn enemies into friends; it brings citizens closer. They are citizens to begin with, so they do share in common some mutual acceptance of some fundamental principles. Politics is generally not *about* those principles; it unavoidably comes to be organized around questions regarding which there is disagreement. Otherwise, it would be unnecessary. But its ability to point toward common action regarding those disputed matters depends on its foundation in shared agreement. A political community, even one as capacious as a modern nation, shares a common life. Its politics is not just a venue for negotiating treaties among hostile, unconnected individuals or groups, and its form of government is not just a framework of procedural rules. Citizens also share a general sense of what their life together aims to do. But that sense is often just a starting point for disagreement.

This is surely true in the United States, where that sense is actually unusually explicit, in no small part because it is articulated in the Declaration of Independence and pervades our political rhetoric. The Declaration puts forward a set of truths about the human

person: that we are all created equal and that we are all endowed with certain basic rights. That set of truths commits our society to a politics of equal citizens, where the answer to the question of who rules is not "the one," "the few," or even "the many," but "all citizens." That means our consent is the root of the government's legitimacy. Our commitment to these principles is, in fact, very widely shared. The framers of the Constitution had to take it for granted in doing their work, and people involved in American politics ever since have too. There are a few people on the fringes of our two broad political camps who would deny these principles and openly reject the Declaration of Independence, but they are broadly perceived as radical outliers. For the most part, our political differences are about what these principles actually mean or demand, not whether they are true. We implicitly understand them to define the foundation of our common life and in a decisive way. President Calvin Coolidge articulated this point with exceptional clarity in a speech marking the 150th anniversary of the Declaration in 1926:

About the Declaration there is a finality that is exceedingly restful. It is often asserted that the world has made a great deal of progress since 1776, that we have had new thoughts and new experiences which have given us a great advance over the people of that day, and that we may therefore very well discard their conclusions for something more modern. But that reasoning can not be applied to this great charter. If all men are created equal, that is final. If they are endowed with inalienable rights, that is final. If governments derive their just powers from the consent of the governed, that is final. No advance, no progress can be made beyond these propositions. If anyone wishes to deny their truth or their soundness, the only direction in which he can proceed historically is not forward but backward toward the time when there was no equality, no rights of the individual, no rule of the people. Those who wish to

proceed in that direction can not lay claim to progress. They are reactionary. Their ideas are not more modern, but more ancient, than those of the Revolutionary fathers.[7]

It is easy to wave away such talk in modern America and insist that we no longer think this way, but our political life suggests that we certainly do. Americans commonly accuse their political adversaries of rejecting or denying these principles, while insisting they themselves embrace them. Sometimes activists or critics say the founders didn't really believe these principles or that they lived in ways that rendered their assertion of them hypocritical. A great deal of law and policy throughout the history of our country, especially involving the question of racial equality, could in fact be shown to have failed and contradicted these ideals in practice. But very rarely, at least since the end of the slavery debates of the nineteenth century, have significant swaths of our society openly rejected these ideals themselves. The very popularity of arguments accusing political opponents of betraying the Declaration's core principles testifies to the hold those principles still have on us.[8]

But although those principles describe the general boundaries of American political life, there is room for quite a lot of legitimate disagreement within those boundaries. This includes intense and serious disagreements about just how we should understand the Declaration's principles and their implications, both theoretical and practical, let alone disagreement about the more mundane sorts of political and policy choices that always confront us.

The Constitution looks to organize the political life of a nation marked by this broad agreement and these deep disagreements. That is a combination that characterizes what Aristotle called civic friendship. As Paul Ludwig has argued in an important recent book on the subject, civic friendship is a kind of friendship by analogy. Common citizenship doesn't give all citizens enough

in common to truly make them friends. Aristotle did not think that a political community could be fully unified around a truly comprehensive vision of the good. Some groups of citizens would share such visions in common and would be friends of the highest sort, but their relations to other citizens would be friendly in a thinner way. Their common citizenship would give them a foundation of very basic agreement about the ends of their society that can create room for a political life that facilitates practical agreement—that is, agreement achieved through and regarding common action—even in the absence of the sort of comprehensive alignment regarding the deepest questions that Aristotle takes to be required for the highest sorts of friendships. "The result," Ludwig writes,

> is a tension between society-wide friendship (which, for him is analogical) and his plural civic friendships of smaller associations (which are literal, but partial). The smaller friendships tend to have stronger bonds, forged as they are among citizens who know each other better and share parochial interests with one another that they do not share with the mass of fellow citizens. Aristotle lives with this tension, sometimes relying on rationality to make society-wide interests prevail over parochial interests, at other times attempting to harness the parochial passions to put them to work for the common good.[9]

Aristotle did not shy away from describing such thinner civic friendship as a way of rendering citizens useful to one another. "Civic friendship," Ludwig writes, "grows up around shared utility and supplements it." But that supplementing can involve the gradual emergence of genuine affection and community. Civic friendship, thus, connects to a politics of common action because what holds civic friends together is practical agreement more than comprehensive

alignment regarding the deepest questions. Citizens are able to agree about how to act together.[10]

The persistence of intense political division is, therefore, not an argument against the presence and power of civic friendship. In fact, the intensity of disagreement within a political community seemed to Aristotle to be evidence that citizens *do* hold some core ideals in common. Our anger at fellow citizens who champion views we disagree with is often greater than our anger at outsiders who do so precisely because we expect more of our fellow citizens—they are like friends who have disappointed us.[11]

The vocabulary of civic friendship therefore should not cause us to expect the political arena to be friendly, or polite. It is a venue for contention. But it does mean that it would be a grave mistake to think of the domestic politics of any functional society as an arena for distinguishing between friends and enemies, as some in our politics now suggest. Politics is where we decide how to act jointly. That's not what enemies do. As Aristotle noted, "Enemies would not even want to go on a journey together." Abraham Lincoln was not being naïve when he insisted in his first inaugural address, "We are not enemies but friends, we must not be enemies." Even amid deep divisions, citizens are friends of a sort. Lincoln's warning was not heeded, of course. Southerners decided they would, in fact, make themselves enemies of the Union and of the Declaration of Independence and its principles, and so they became outsiders to the North and not fellow citizens. Such moments do come. But they are rare, and we should want to keep them rare. The ideal of friendship that Lincoln was defending was not utopian. He did not have in mind a politics of calm and quiet agreement but of citizens resolving their resolvable differences by finding ways to accommodate one another and deal with one another. The alternative to a politics of friends and enemies is not an impossible politics of unanimity but a politics of civic friendship or, we might say, of constitutional unity—of acting

together even when we do not think alike. It is by no means easy to attain or sustain, but it is possible.[12]

This difficult but attainable goal describes a crucial facet of the sort of civic unity the Constitution has in mind. But the framers were not simply Aristotelians, to be sure. For one thing, Madison and others supplemented that classical conception with a kind of modern realism about human nature, rooted in a Christian understanding of the fallenness of the human person but, at times, also pointing toward a darker and more Machiavellian skepticism of human moral potential. The Constitution may be liberal, but it is not utopian. Its sense of the limits of politics informs its approach to political action and to its pursuit of the ambitious goals set forward in its preamble.

As we have seen, Madison articulated a kind of middling view of the virtues of his fellow citizens. He thought there was no escape from self-interest and ambition but that Americans, nonetheless, did take freedom, equality, and personal honor seriously. "As there is a degree of depravity in mankind which requires a certain degree of circumspection and distrust," he argued in Federalist 55, "so there are other qualities in human nature which justify a certain portion of esteem and confidence." Recognizing the depravity of mankind had made possible a new and modern science of politics, which Hamilton and Madison believed had developed means of organizing a regime and holding it together that could secure a republican polity against its worst excesses, and which were not known to classical philosophy. But acknowledging the other, higher possibilities of human nature meant the framers nonetheless remained committed to a republicanism that was only partially modern.[13]

That republicanism calls upon a civic ethic of communal self-rule. It fosters unity by inculcating a sense of common ownership and responsibility and a tendency to see public needs as sources of citizen obligations. It, therefore, willfully blurs the line between ruling and being ruled. This republican ethic has always been difficult for

Americans to articulate, but it exerted a powerful pull on the thinking of the framers of the Constitution and is particularly relevant to their conception of political unity. Republican unity is a patchwork of mutual obligations, but the framers' republicanism also assumes a society characterized by multiplicity, not unanimity. It demands an enormous amount of acting together, but it does not presume an enormous amount of thinking alike.

For this reason, the republicanism implicit in the Constitution's conception of unity is intertwined with a form of modern liberalism too. The definition and nature of liberalism is a complicated and contested question, and is exceptionally controversial in our time. But broadly speaking, liberalism implies a commitment to equal individual rights secured by procedural legal protections backed by a government rooted in a limited conception of the purpose of the state and an expansive conception of the freedom of the individual. Liberalism is sometimes justified by reference to a set of philosophical principles that amount to a radical individualism. This view implies that the purpose of liberal politics is to more and more fully apply those principles and so to approach more and more closely an ideal of personal liberation. But liberalism is sometimes justified instead by reference to a gradually evolved set of political forms that, by the time of the Enlightenment and especially in Britain, had, in practice, achieved an extraordinary balance between individual freedom and social order. This view implies that the purpose of liberal politics is to conserve those practices and institutions in an effort to sustain and reinforce that balance so as to attain the best of both political freedom and political order to the greatest extent possible. Both the more radical and the more conservative justification for liberalism are present in the American tradition and, indeed, in the Declaration of Independence itself. The tension between them has often given shape to some of the deepest divides in our politics.

The Constitution's liberalism is perhaps most evident in its attempts to balance majority will and minority rights by recourse to procedural protections, structural constraints, and institutional mechanisms. But it would be a mistake to see these as purely procedural: Madison's concern about faction, and therefore his prioritization of unity, was above all a concern about the injustice of majority factions abusing minorities. In this sense, his concern was with justice as much as with unity. But he argued that majority factions would only treat minorities justly if they were somehow drawn into a process of negotiation and consensus building with them. This is another crucial respect in which Madison's concern with unity is practical: it is a failure to act together, more than a failure to think alike, that threatens gross injustice in a republic. But this practical-mindedness serves a substantive moral end: it is about more than unity for the sake of avoiding conflict. It is a concern about the danger of injustice rooted in the underlying reality of diversity, which creates the possibility of majority tyranny.

The Constitution assumes that there will always be majorities and minorities in America, divided by serious differences and contesting over matters they take to be of the greatest importance. It establishes a pluralistic framework for this contestation, not because the differences involved somehow matter less than social peace or are merely subjective or relative, but precisely because of the underlying moral and political presumptions that Americans do hold in common. Pluralism is a necessary implication of our society's broadly shared commitment to equality, which is a more than liberal commitment rooted in the Jewish and Christian grounds of our civilization. When people are free and equal, they will form different opinions, including different opinions about the meaning of freedom and equality. In the resulting disagreements, we tolerate people who differ from us because we are confident that every person, including those who are terribly wrong about important

questions, is our equal in humanity and dignity and is equally made in a divine image.[14]

This kind of republican liberalism is, therefore, ultimately founded in a substantive vision of human flourishing and demands respect for human dignity and recognition of human needs. Its purpose is not just social peace but social order—a mode of living together so as to enable all to better thrive. For that reason, it pursues social peace, understood less as a concordance of views than as a mutuality of action. And it looks for ways to make that possible by encouraging habits of moderation—not in ideological terms but in practical terms, as a disposition toward the complexity of social life and a willingness to abide some contradiction for the sake of higher goods. That willingness is the root of the kind of toleration that is bound up with the Constitution's conception of unity. Toleration, in this sense, means allowing people to be wrong, not denying that there is a right. It means grasping that the fact of equality proscribes the means that would be required to enforce a unanimity of opinion.

Proscribing those means is the work of many of the procedural protections in our Constitution. The Constitution's proceduralism is, thus, a liberal means to liberal but more than merely liberal ends. And it is one means among several. It works to establish a framework for political contestation that keeps minorities safe, keeps majorities responsible, and allows for some production of the common—for forging genuine unity through unending engagement.

The common good that orients society, in this understanding, is not so much a set of ideas about which we are all agreed as a way of life through which we are able to thrive—individually and together. The two are not entirely distinct, of course. Human beings flourish by living in light of the truth. But precisely how to understand the truth and live in light of it are questions about which we will continue to disagree, and how to flourish given that fact is the challenge to which the Constitution's approach to unity is directed.

The structure of the Constitution is a function of the framers' view that forging and sustaining unity under these circumstances will be extremely difficult and could well be the most daunting challenge our society confronts. Forging unity is the ongoing work of American life, and in a sense, it is the forging that describes the unity. This view assumes that cohesion isn't always calm, and unity isn't always harmonious. Our politics compels us to act together but does not guarantee that we will, therefore, come to think alike. After an election, after an arduous legislative process, after more than two centuries of producing the common together, we are far from done negotiating and competing, pushing and pulling. The Constitution's distinct idea of unity has made sure of that.

THIS COMPLEX CONCEPTION OF UNITY CAN BE VERY ATTRACTIVE, BUT IT has its downsides and its adamant detractors. It is a form of unity that involves a lot of friction and confrontation, which doesn't always feel like togetherness. And by prioritizing this kind of cohesion, to be achieved by endless coalition building, the Constitution cannot help but de-emphasize efficient public action. It assumes that unity will be hard to come by and sustain and so looks to avert dangerous division more than facilitate responsive government. It does seek both, but its worries about social division run deeper than its hopes for public policy. This has always meant that the elements of the constitutional system work against one another as much as they work with one another, in order to check one another's excesses and broaden the circle of voices involved in making decisions. And some critics of the system have long found that kind of politics by internal tension to be counterproductive and self-defeating.

As we have seen throughout the prior chapters, this view was particularly characteristic of the powerful progressive critique of

the Constitution. Arising in the wake of industrialization and the enormous social and economic dislocations of the nineteenth century, the constitutional program of progressivism began from the view that American government was too focused on restraint and not conducive enough to action and, therefore, was just not up to the challenges of modern life.

Like many of the most profound critiques of our system, this progressive case is essentially integralist. It argues that the parts of a system of government (and indeed the various institutions of a society) ought to all work together, guided by the same vision and pulling in the same direction. As we have seen, Woodrow Wilson made this point particularly clearly. In his 1908 book *Constitutional Government in the United States*, Wilson insisted that Madison's mechanistic conception of politics was misguided. "Government is not a machine but a living thing," he wrote. This meant that separating powers and setting interests off against one another made no sense: "No living thing can have its organs offset against each other as checks and live. On the contrary, its life is dependent upon their quick cooperation, their ready response to the commands of instinct or intelligence, their amicable community of purpose."[15]

In other words, Wilson doubted that it was even possible to act together without thinking alike in politics. Contemporary progressivism is similarly integralist, insisting that every institution in our society, private and public, must be engaged in the same social crusade—no exceptions, no exemptions—and implicitly that there can be no society without a single, comprehensive common project. Some contemporary conservatives agree.

Taken to its logical conclusion, this would mean that no sort of free society was possible, at least if we assume that Madison was broadly right to believe that as long as human beings are free, they will form different opinions on key questions. But Wilson was only calling for an incremental step in this direction, which would

require a different form of democracy, based on a more thorough-going ideal of majority rule that allowed for more decisive action. Ideally, he thought, the differences among factions in society should not be resolved by bargaining among them in the institutions of government but by a competition between them at election time, after which the party that wins a majority may deploy all the powers of government in the service of its vision.

This kind of progressive approach was far from blind to the need for unity. In fact, it took itself to be advancing a more comprehensive form of national unity better suited to modern life. Some early progressives believed not only that the American system of government was inadequate to governing the modern economy but also that the Civil War had shown that the Constitution's approach to national unity was insufficiently assertive. In the wake of the war, they suggested, cohesion needed to be understood and advanced in a much more aggressive and consolidated way. In part, this meant an emphasis on unitary leadership and, therefore, above all, presidential leadership, as the president alone has the national mandate to speak on behalf of the whole society. Wilson and other early progressives tended to downplay the potential of achieving cohesion by representing plurality and to emphasize, instead, the potential of achieving cohesion by representing all of society at once, and in a form that allowed it to speak in one voice. Such leadership required a president who could focus, guide, and then express the will of society. It sought a way to move Americans to think alike, not just act together.

Underlying this ideal is the belief that our society does have one unified, coherent interest that good leadership could advance, and that it is opposed in our politics by private interests—"special interests," as the progressives liked to say—pursuing their own good at the expense of the good of society. Such powerful interests could only be overcome by an even more powerful champion of the public interest.

This idea of the unifying leader clarifies the nature of the progressive critique of the Constitution, because it combines two related conceptions of unity. One views unity as submission to a common authority, and the other as commitment to a shared understanding of the good. Both are essential to any functional political community, of course, and are part of the Madisonian conception of politics too. But Madison's critics are right to contend that his vision of unity downplays both submission to authority and substantively thick, shared ideological commitments. This is one common cause of the unease that some Americans have always felt toward our constitutional system and the sense of inadequacy that underlies every serious criticism of that system.[16]

That perception of inadequacy is multifaceted. For some critics, the trouble with the Madisonian system is that it lacks urgency and accountability—it doesn't move assertively enough or respond sufficiently to public wishes. For some, it is that it lacks moral purpose and a common social vision, and so it evinces the suffocating open-mindedness of modern liberalism. It refuses to say, on behalf of society, what is right and best and highest. These are serious objections. They should not be dismissed, and at the very least, they should be given room to criticize our political order, from within and without, so as to improve it and correct its excesses. But they systematically diminish the challenge of cohesion and of social peace and so end up focusing on the Constitution's inadequacies without crediting its core achievement.

That means that this alternative or counter-Madisonian approach to unity, which looks to express and represent a unified national purpose through focused acts of government power rather than to create common ground through accommodative negotiation, should serve as a corrective in our system but cannot substitute for traditional constitutionalism. Because it prioritizes action over negotiation, this approach tends to empower narrow majorities. And because it

values unitary executive action over plural legislative bargaining, it tends to raise the stakes and the temperature of our politics. In other words, it threatens to exacerbate our divisions. In fact, it more than threatens: it has plainly exacerbated our divisions.

OUR POLITICS HAS GROWN MORE BITTERLY DIVIDED IN RECENT DECADES less because these two competing visions of constitutionalism have faced off against each other than because the more progressive vision has been adopted in many arenas of our public life and has pulled our system in its desired direction. We have not been fighting about how to understand the Constitution, for the most part. We have been fighting because our understanding of the Constitution has left the Madisonian prescription for unity behind. We have grown less capable of dealing with one another because we have embraced an approach to American government that de-emphasizes dealing with one another.

This change has not been driven by a desire for disunity. It has been driven by impatience with American government and by a passion for democracy that is both understandable and well-intentioned. But we have reviewed the sorry results in the last several chapters. American federalism has been reconfigured to combine state and national power in pursuit of national ends, leaving less room for states and communities to differ and compete. The Congress has been centralized and consolidated to better enable party leaders to stage-manage performative party conflict, making narrow majorities more cohesive but giving them less reason to seek broader coalitions and to legislate. The presidency has moved to fill the vacuum and, in the process, has become the focal point of ideological conflict—embodying the exaggerated hopes and fears of opposing camps but becoming less capable of steady administration and durable action.

The courts are called on to resolve political and cultural conflicts rather than to police the boundaries of constitutionalism. The parties have lost their roles as facilitators of coalition building and have, instead, become mere brand names for two opposing camps keen to remain terrified of each other at a distance.

These constitutional transformations are, by no means, the only reason our society is polarized and divided. The causes of our fracture reach far beyond politics, to the fragmentation of our common culture and the decay of some core institutions in American life. But although it is not all that explains why we are more divided, the counter-Madisonian evolution of our constitutional system is why we think our Constitution can't help us address our divisions and why we no longer quite grasp its conception of unity.[17]

The progressive program is not senseless, and its critique of the Madisonian vision of political life is not crazy. But it has been profoundly unhealthy for our fractured polity, because it ignores the imperative to build cohesion in a free society. Progressives have long insisted that the American system is not up to the challenges of modern life. But their critique has understated what may well be the preeminent challenge of modern life: the challenge of multiplicity and diversity and, therefore, of division, which James Madison saw far more clearly than they have. The result of de-emphasizing that challenge has been deeper and more bitter division. This is not because Americans have forgotten how to agree with one another but because we have forgotten how to disagree and how to accept the simple fact that those we disagree with are not going away and must be accommodated if our own views are to be accommodated too.

The desire to see our opponents go away tends to express itself in excessive expectations of elections and in an impatience with the constraints our system imposes on narrow and ephemeral majorities (which are the only majorities our elections have produced for a generation). Majority rule is essential to republican government, of

course. As Abraham Lincoln expressed in his first inaugural address, "Unanimity is impossible. The rule of a minority, as a permanent arrangement, is wholly inadmissible; so that, rejecting the majority principle, anarchy or despotism in some form is all that is left." But precisely for that reason, it is crucial that we try to expand and complicate majorities before empowering them. Not simply a majority, Lincoln insisted, but "a majority held in restraint by constitutional checks and limitations, and always changing easily with deliberate changes of popular opinions and sentiments, is the only true sovereign of a free people." Restraining and reshaping majorities in that way is the work of the Madisonian system. But when we insist that simple, narrow majorities are all that is required for legitimacy, we remove the incentive to broaden appeals and, instead, create strong reasons to intensify the purity and internal cohesion of narrow majorities—which tends to make our parties less appealing to voters who are not already on board, and so prevents majorities from growing larger. This leaves restrained majorities intensely frustrated, and that frustration has moved many Americans to see restraints on narrow majorities as illegitimate rather than essential and, therefore, to see the work of forging common ground as a betrayal of party principle and, ultimately, a betrayal of democracy and a failure of nerve.[18]

This puts us all at risk of losing our patience with normal political life. We now all too easily persuade ourselves that *this* moment, unlike past ones in our politics, is an emergency—that we are on the edge of an abyss so that the normal rules must be put aside, and the imperative to compromise and bargain must be suspended. We cannot stomach another round of incremental adjustments. We want this to be the moment of the decisive showdown. But that desire is misguided, and we have not reckoned with its stakes. We still can't quite grasp the danger of genuine disunity—of a fundamental and violent breakdown of our political order. All those who call

for breaking the boundaries of our constitutional framework and for throwing away the restraints on majority power are minorities themselves, and yet they act as if they do not see that. They insist that the policy action they seek is more important than the framework that makes it possible for us to act together in the first place. We have forgotten that the only real alternative to a politics of bargaining and accommodation in a vast and diverse society is a politics of violent hostility. That forgetfulness now crosses lines of party and of ideology. It is pervasive in our politics. And it is genuinely terrifying.

But it is not irredeemable. By grasping that our divisions have been deepened, in part, by our abandonment of the constitutional system's core approach to unity, we could find our way toward a constitutional restoration and, with it, a recovery of both our capacity for unity and our desire for it.

This need not be—indeed, it cannot be—a partisan enterprise. The Madisonian system does not imply a specific policy agenda in the traditional sense. It exists to facilitate our political disagreements and so does not belong to one side or another of those disagreements. But it does require us to understand the purpose and the character of the Constitution's prioritization of unity. That means it also requires us to take the anthropological assumptions that underlie the Constitution seriously—its insistence on the limits of human knowledge, the importance of social order, the connection between institutional structure and political culture, and the republican ideal of the citizen. The Constitution rests on these foundations, but it also teaches us to understand them by habituating us in a set of civic practices built upon them. And so, given the condition of American politics now, renewal and revitalization call for recovering our practice of constitutionalism so that we may also recover our understanding of it.[19]

That does not mean going backward. As we have seen in the preceding chapters, reforms of our institutions would have to take

account of how and why they have changed, and of how our society has changed too. They would have to help those institutions serve their proper purposes—including their unifying and accommodative purposes—while learning from the ways in which they have failed in the past. Repairing our institutions does not mean assuming they were perfect to begin with. Plainly they were not. They are the products of compromise, and have been strained and stretched and sometimes broken in ways that we should learn from. They have also often failed to accommodate important swaths of our society and facilitated accommodations among some by excluding and oppressing others (and especially Black Americans, again and again). Strengthening the capacity of our system to unify our society must mean insisting that our conception of that society include all Americans.

It must also mean making some effort to learn from the insights of the framers regarding the question that bedevils our country now: How can a diverse and divided nation hold together and govern itself? That would have to involve a recovery of our appreciation of the beneficent complexity of our institutions—and of their potential to facilitate competition, negotiation, and constructive tension. By thinking about our system of government as existing in part to form us to better live together and not just to count heads and use power, we can come to see how civic action can facilitate not only greater social peace but also genuine cohesion. And by revitalizing the republicanism of the framers, we can better understand how to pursue the common good in practice, as a way of life lived together despite our variety and multiplicity.

Our era of disunity has taught us that part of what must be rebuilt for any of this to work is mutual trust. And here, too, the Madisonian approach to unity can serve us well. Trust, and particularly trust in those with power, is a function of a combination of evident competence and evident restraint. To trust our institutions

and those who lead them, we need to be persuaded that they are capable of performing their core work and that they will not abuse their power. That is a difficult balance to strike. The deformation of our politics has made Americans particularly (and understandably) skeptical about the possibility of restraint—restraint of majorities, of public officials, of the opposite party. We increasingly think that any-one with power will use it without restraint. But our constitutional system is built to achieve precisely a combination of empowerment and restraint and, therefore, to enable us to better trust one another. The particular ways in which we have deformed that system, which have prioritized majoritarian policy action above the imperative to pursue greater consensus, have been distinctly damaging to mutual trust in our society, especially in a time of narrow majorities, because they have neglected the importance of restraint. A recommitment to the structure of our institutions and of the relations among them could let us gradually rebuild that depleted confidence.

Key to that trust must be the sense that the stakes of our elec-tions are not absolute. As we have seen, the constitutional system is designed to reduce those stakes. Keeping some essential questions beyond the reach of majorities (through the protection of essential rights and through the decentralization of many governing deci-sions) helps avert the impression that everything depends on the next election. Multiplying power centers and setting them against one another ensures that no particular election outcome alone can determine the fate of our society. But even more crucially, creating a space for open and competitive debate within the boundaries of a general agreement about basic principles helps ensure that political change is restrained and contained. A great deal of our loss of trust in recent decades has had to do with a sense that these boundaries no longer hold and that our politics has become unmoored from its restraints. Perhaps it is ironic that this has happened in an era of close elections and narrow majorities—when the actual potential for

radical departures from the status quo is relatively limited. But this is no coincidence. For one thing, close elections tend, unavoidably, to undermine the legitimacy of their own outcomes, and each of our major parties has lately denied the legitimacy of some of the other's election victories. But for another, the stakes of our elections have, in fact, increased, as presidential power has ballooned and as policy durability and continuity have been radically de-emphasized.

In such a moment, it is vital that we find ways to lower those stakes again by restoring the structure of the Constitution. It is vital, too, that we grasp that our debates do generally happen within the bounds of relatively broad (if sometimes shallow) agreement. Each party must resist the urge to see the other as an enemy of American democracy. This is not easy, but it is vital. As the great political philosopher Harry Jaffa put it, "We must recognize the necessity of preventing the enemies of liberty from gaining power in the regime of liberty; but we must also recognize the extreme difficulty, and the danger, in the possible confusion of those whose interests differ from ours within that regime, and those who in truth stand outside of it."

There is no simple way to avoid confusing the two, Jaffa continued: "They have in fact been confused to some extent, at every point in our political history, save one. If slavery was right (as distinct from expedient), then free government itself was wrong." But most debates, he concluded, do not run so deep to the core of our regime, and we must work, especially in divided times, to acknowledge the legitimacy of our political opponents and see how they, too, could understand themselves as advancing the principles underlying American life. We must work to see that our fellow citizens are not our enemies.[20]

We have something of an advantage over the framers of the Constitution in overcoming the temptation to vilify our opponents and

dismiss them as anti-American. We have the shared memory of a common national life that has now extended over two and a half centuries. We do not depend purely on reason, or fear, in our effort to believe that our society can thrive together. We can fall back on our national experience too. That experience can help us avoid the inclination to approach our politics abstractly. It can also help us grasp the weight of our responsibility as Americans. We know something the founding generation of our country did not know: we know their experiment can succeed. We know that the nation they launched can endure through extreme hardships and can prosper and thrive and grow and evolve. That means that if it all falls apart on our watch, the fault will be ours and not theirs. We can learn something from them about how to bear this burden of responsibility and what tremendous blessings can result from our doing so. But in the end, the burden is ours to bear together, just as the blessings are ours to enjoy in common. We have a choice to make as citizens about how to respond to this moment of division in our society.

The choice we face is not a "yes" or "no" question about the Constitution. It is rather a question about how the frustrations of this period will be translated into an agenda of constitutional reform. Those frustrations are likely to motivate action, one way or another. There is very broad agreement now that something important in our political system has broken down. But beneath that agreement, there is a profound dispute about what it is that American politics is failing to do. Some reformers argue that our system is failing to act decisively on behalf of the majorities who win elections. Others argue that it is failing to hold our society together and that we need to broaden majorities to build greater trust and cohesion in American life.

Those two diagnoses point in opposite prescriptive directions as a practical matter. Reforms to empower narrow majorities would

exacerbate division and mistrust in our society. Reforms to compel more cross-partisan bargaining to broaden majorities would make it harder to take decisive and clear public-policy action. The direction we choose must be a function of our understanding of the chief problems our society faces, and so of which of those trade-offs is better for America on net.

There are times when the deliberate recalcitrance of our system of government is among our foremost problems: when large majorities of Americans express a clear set of desires for an extended period of time but are denied what they seek by the institutional rigidity of our system of government. There are other times, however, when strife and discord in our society are among our foremost problems: when Americans are bitterly divided and view one another more as enemies than friends. We are plainly now living in one of the latter moments. There is no broad and durable American majority advancing a coherent agenda that is obstructed by our institutions. Rather, our politics overflows with partisan bile, and each of our major parties views the other as the country's biggest problem.

That suggests that we will need to choose to prioritize cohesion, coalition building, and the forging of trust. And to do that, we should begin by recognizing that these are among the original aims of our Constitution and that today's intense disunity has been driven in part by our broken constitutional practice, which has undermined the means by which these aims are pursued in our system. To recover those means and better pursue those aims, we will need to recover the understanding of unity that undergirds the Constitution, grasp its appeal and its truth, and think about reforms in its light.

That aspiration suggests not only an agenda of reform but also a particular spirit in which to approach the work. Citizens who want to see our society grow stronger should approach its institutions in a spirit of repair—informed by a sense of what is missing and has gone wrong and inspired by a sense of what is good in what

we have and could serve us well. Our era tempts us to repudiate our inheritance, but it requires us to renew it. Americans are frequently angry at our Constitution now because we sense that it has broken down. But if we grasped that we have broken it, we could see that it needs us if it is to serve us. By rising to repair it, we could enable it again to repair our society and bring us closer together, as it was made to do.

CONCLUSION

O N AUGUST 8, 1787, THE CONSTITUTIONAL CONVENTION TOOK UP
the question of the formula for representation in the House of
Representatives. In his notes from that day, James Madison recorded
that, while he himself was making a point about how one proposed
approach might play out over many decades, Massachusetts delegate
Nathaniel Gorham rose to object that thinking so far ahead was a
waste of time. "It is not to be supposed that the government will
last so long as to produce this effect," Gorham insisted. "Can it be
supposed that this vast country, including the Western territory, will
150 years hence remain one nation?"[1]

It was a reasonable question. And Madison made no mention in
his notes of offering any reply to Gorham. But the Constitution that
the convention ended up producing was itself a reply in the affir-
mative. The system of government it created could last, and it has
lasted, with amendments and adaptations, far longer than even the
century and a half that was the furthest that Gorham's imagination
could stretch. We have remained one nation, thanks in no small part
to the Constitution's distinct approach to keeping us together.

That approach has involved pushing, plying, and pressuring Americans to engage with one another and so also to understand themselves as engaged in a common enterprise. The Constitution forces insular factions to forge coalitions with others and, thereby, to expand their sense of their own interests and priorities. It forces powerful officeholders to govern through negotiation and competition rather than through fiat and pronouncement and so to align their ambitions with those of others. It forces Americans to acknowledge the equal rights of fellow citizens, and has (gradually, and thanks to the heroic efforts and sacrifices of many) come to better align the definition of "fellow citizen" with the ideals of the Declaration of Independence. None of this is easy or simple. All of it happens through politics and so through contention, competition, pressure, and negotiation. It's a struggle. But the Constitution is rooted in the insight that this very struggle is, itself, a source of solidarity and an engine of cohesion.

We have become too divided in contemporary America, not because we engage in that struggle too intensely but because we avoid it too readily and so have lost some of our knack for disagreeing constructively. The factions in our politics tend to talk about one another rather than to one another, and therefore, we too rarely talk in ways that could point to common action. Recovering our grasp of why it is important to pursue ways of acting together across difference, and then recovering the habits of doing so, is the path toward a more cohesive society, a more responsive government, and a more responsible citizenry. That grasp could be renewed by coming to know the Constitution again. And those habits could be revitalized by a better practice of constitutionalism.

That practice could be aided by the sorts of practical reforms and repairs considered in these pages, but it ultimately requires a restoration of the spirit of our political and civic life. Structural reforms—changes to the rules of the House of Representatives or rebalancing

state and federal administration of various programs—naturally feel small and petty in relation to the sorts of problems that bedevil our political culture now. But the Constitution reflects the insight that institutional structure shapes political culture. By structuring incentives, channeling power, and forming habits, we can influence the spirit of our politics. Our civic culture and our governing institutions affect each other in a cyclical way, which can be either virtuous or vicious. Institutions that function well and achieve their ends tend to encourage more responsible citizenship and leadership and to restrain our worst impulses and more responsible citizens, and leaders then, in turn, enable institutions to function better. But when our institutions are dysfunctional or deformed, our habits and behavior become broken as well, and we grow cynical and wary of one another, which further harms our institutions. How to break the vicious cycle and initiate a virtuous one is in the end a practical question. We have to ask not only what we wish to achieve but also what we can plausibly change. Institutions and culture shape each other, but institutions are much more readily changeable, and so it makes sense to begin to approach deep cultural problems by considering what institutional reforms might be of use and work from there. The structure of the Constitution and the insights of its framers have a lot of wisdom to offer us on that front.

This is not because the Constitution is somehow perfect. Far from it. As Alexander Hamilton wrote in the final Federalist essay, "I never expect to see a perfect work from imperfect man. The result of the deliberations of all collective bodies must necessarily be a compound, as well of the errors and prejudices, as of the good sense and wisdom, of the individuals of whom they are composed. The compacts which are to embrace thirteen distinct States in a common bond of amity and union, must as necessarily be a compromise of as many dissimilar interests and inclinations. How can perfection spring from such materials?"[2]

There is insight in that sentiment not only about the process involved in producing the Constitution but about its substance too. The Constitution approaches political life with a peculiar mix of high and low expectations. It evinces humility about the potential of a vast and complex society to govern itself efficiently. It prioritizes comity and legitimacy, because these are hard to achieve and sustain, and because they are the preconditions for policy progress. But it also recognizes that comity and legitimacy are starting points for the kind of virtuous self-government to which republicanism aspires.

That is why the means by which our Constitution seeks greater social peace are not properly understood as empty procedures. At the heart of our republicanism is an ambitious, demanding ideal of the human being and citizen, which recognizes not only our fallenness and our limitations but also our dignity and our potential. It insists on our obligations to one another, and habituates us to recognize them through the practice of our citizenship. That ideal should be the starting point of any constitutional restoration. It calls on not only our institutions and our elites but also on every one of us to take on the responsibilities of citizenship and accept the duties that come with the high privilege of calling ourselves Americans. It gives us each something to do individually and gives us all a lot to do in common. For all our divisions, that is an ideal we will need to take seriously together. The Constitution does not speak of social peace in terms of quieting an angry mob but of seeking an amicable common life. It asserts the need to "insure domestic tranquility," which brings to mind something like the peace of a household. It seeks to form a people who will join together in calling this nation their home. That we have made of ourselves such a people is little short of miraculous, and we should never take it for granted.

I am an immigrant to the United States. My family came here from Israel when I was a young child, and I became an American

citizen at the age of nineteen. I took the oath, together with a group of several dozen new citizens from all over the world, at the Federal Building in Newark, New Jersey, in the spring of 1996. After the ceremony, the retired federal judge who had presided told us he had just a few words of advice. I was already enough of a patriotic history buff by then to hope he might quote Lincoln or the founders. But he didn't. Instead, he told us that from that day on we should think about America in the first-person plural: in terms of *we* and *our* and not *them* and *their*. That was it. I distinctly remember being disappointed with his very brief remarks. Yet here I am, almost three decades later, recounting them. His point was profound, and it was one we all need to hear all the time.

We is the first word of the Constitution. It is the first word of the glorious second paragraph of the Declaration of Independence. Both documents speak in the first-person plural, because they both speak for a people taking joint ownership of their common fate. This is no easy feat, especially in a society that is, as every free society always must be to some degree, divided over what direction we should all take together. The Declaration of Independence helps us understand why it is worth the effort to make that "we" a reality. And the Constitution helps us see just how that could be done. We now need to be reminded of both the "why" and the "how." That reminding will need to take the form of civic practice and of constitutional renewal. But its purpose is ultimately to let us see one another as belonging together again.

American politics is an endless argument among people who share a history, a geography, a culture, a national character, and a set of broad commitments in common and who owe one another something. We sometimes disagree intensely, but what we disagree about is how to live out the shared promise of our country together. Those with whom we disagree in our society are not our enemies; they are our neighbors. They are not out to do harm to our country;

they differ with us about what would be good for it. To love our country is to love them too—even when they do not make it easy. We should not allow ourselves to fall into hysterical fear of the supposed advances and victories of these ideological adversaries. They are struggling and mostly failing, just as we are. Our system of government makes sure that they have to persuade a substantial portion of our society for an extended period of time before they could get their way on any matter of real substance, just as we do. This helps us keep our balance as a nation, and avoid large mistakes. And it forces us to act together, even when we do not think alike.

The Constitution thereby offers us the hope of greater unity. We should be cheered by that hope. And we should be profoundly grateful for the glorious fact that we all get to be Americans together.

ACKNOWLEDGMENTS

T HIS BOOK IS A WORK OF GRATITUDE, YET ALONG THE WAY, IT HAS left me in even deeper debt to a number of people whose support, guidance, and goodwill really made it possible.

These debts are particularly concentrated at the American Enterprise Institute (AEI), an extraordinary island of sanity, honesty, collegiality, and rigor in Washington, which has been my professional home since 2019. Robert Doar, the institute's president, had the wisdom to see that AEI should become a gathering place for scholars of social, cultural, and constitutional questions in this moment and determined (less wisely, no doubt) that I should help lead that work. This has put me in the middle of a dream team of scholars of the very questions taken up in this book, as well as scholars of many other subjects and other leaders and staff around the institute who have contributed enormously to making this work possible.

The greatest of these debts is easily to Adam White, a friend and colleague whose wisdom and insight on constitutional matters are simply unmatched in our generation and whose good sense, good humor, and judgment have been a gift to me and many others. Every

facet of this book took shape in conversation with Adam, even if he ultimately could not talk me out of a few notions we do not share in common (and regarding which I am, therefore, likely wrong). He also read the first draft of the manuscript and made sure the second was better.

Benjamin Storey and Jenna Silber Storey, two wonderful colleagues and longtime friends, also read the manuscript with great care and improved it by their characteristically wise attention to the deepest questions. Their remarkable capacity, individually and together, to see clearly to the heart of things never ceases to impress me. Nicole Penn, another extraordinary colleague and friend, gave careful attention to the manuscript as well and helped me avoid confounding history and political theory, which a work like this must strive to distinguish, even while drawing on both.

Many other AEI colleagues helped me enormously—both by their work and in conversation—to think through particular portions of the argument or to clarify its broader purposes. These include Matthew Continetti, Philip Wallach, Ramesh Ponnuru, Kevin Kosar, John Fortier, Gary Schmitt, Jonah Goldberg, Christina Kopp, Dan Wiser, Howe Whitman, Christine Rosen, Will Haun, Joel Alicea, Chris Scalia, Joshua Katz, Tim Carney, Jeffrey A. Rosen, John Yoo, and Jay Cost, among others. I am also immensely grateful to countless supporters of AEI's work, and especially to Ravenel Curry and to Roger Hertog, whose backing and encouragement have made my own work possible.

Several other wise friends read through all or parts of the manuscript or otherwise helped me to think through and improve it. Daniel Stid, whose scholarship on parties and on Congress has been formative for me, provided essential comments and corrections on an early draft. And conversations about portions of the argument with Daniel Burns, Jon Ward, Reihan Salam, Jonathan Rauch,

Robert George, Diana Schaub, Harvey Mansfield, Adam Keiper, Andy Smarick, and John Bridgeland were invaluably helpful. Leon Kass, my teacher and mentor, helped me see this work in its fullest context and properly broaden the scope of the project.

I have also had the opportunity to deliver a number of lectures on the themes of the book along the way and to draw guidance and wisdom from the responses of knowledgeable audiences, especially at Yale University, Benedictine College, and Ursinus College. I am grateful, as well, to a number of magazine editors who have allowed me to think out loud in their pages in recent years about some of the broad themes taken up in this book. These include Rich Lowry, Ramesh Ponnuru, and Philip Klein of *National Review*; John Podhoretz of *Commentary*, and Brian Smith and John Grove of *Law & Liberty*. The latter publication also did me the great honor of running a symposium on a portion of the thesis of the book, through which I benefited from learned responses by James Stoner, Stephanie Slade, John Inazu, and Andrew Beck—all of whom contributed a great deal to improving the argument of the book.

At Basic Books, I have been particularly fortunate to work with Lara Heimert, whose unerring judgment and skill are a marvel. This is the fourth book that I have had the honor of publishing with Basic, and my esteem for Lara and the entire team she has assembled—throughout the process of editing, production, publicity, and beyond—has only grown. I am very grateful to them all and never take for granted the privilege of being a Basic Books author.

All these individuals have improved this book immeasurably. The many faults it nonetheless retains despite their best efforts or thanks to my stubborn refusal to accept their good advice are, of course, my fault alone.

My greatest debt, however, is as always to my family. I am grateful to my parents for more than I could ever say. I am grateful to

my children, Maya and Sam, for giving me endless causes for hope. But above all, I am grateful to, and grateful for, my wonderful wife, Cecelia, who is so much more than I deserve. She is a model of how to live a life of flourishing devoted to making it possible for others to flourish too. I dedicate this book to her with love and admiration, and with a smile.

NOTES

INTRODUCTION

1. The text of the Constitution is not contested, so it hardly seems necessary to cite a particular version as a source. I will generally cite specific provisions in the text when quoting the Constitution, and readers looking for an authoritative version can consult, for instance, the official transcription of the document provided online by the National Archives at https://www.archives.gov/founding-docs/constitution-transcript.

2. The coming chapters will make reference to the Federalist Papers more than any other single source except for the text of the Constitution itself. But I will do so with some care to distinguish among the three authors (Alexander Hamilton, James Madison, and John Jay) because, with regard to my particular subject, they actually differ in some significant respects, even though they clearly share some core views and often echo one another. Most notably, Madison and Hamilton identify different kinds of problems as the core challenge for modern republicanism. Hamilton sees the essential problem as disorder and chaos and seeks a means to a more reliable and steady political order. Madison is alert especially to the problem of division and factionalism, and so seeks social peace without resort to tyrannical power. Both are ways

of thinking about the problem of unity, as both chaos and diversity are modern challenges to unity. But they yield different priorities and emphases, as we shall see. It is also worth saying that I cite the Federalist not so much because it was influential—it was only modestly influential in the debates it sought to shape—as because it is perceptive, brilliant, and persuasive, and because it speaks to a set of questions that are pertinent and timely now.

3. George Washington, "Letter to the President of Congress," in *The Records of the Federal Convention of 1787*, Vol. 4, ed. Max Farrand (New Haven and London: Yale University Press, 1937).

4. Abraham Lincoln, "Seventh and Last Debate with Stephen A. Douglas at Alton, Illinois," in *Collected Works of Abraham Lincoln*. Vol. 3, ed. Roy Basler (New Brunswick, NJ: Rutgers University Press, 1953).

CHAPTER 1: WHAT IS THE CONSTITUTION?

1. I use the term *regime* throughout this book advisedly, as it sometimes carries dark overtones. I mean to use it descriptively and without those overtones to refer to more than the system of government as such and to describe something of the spirit of a polity, combining its guiding principles, its practice, and its collective political instincts.

2. Thomas Paine, *The Complete Writings of Thomas Paine*, ed. Philip Foner (New York: The Citadel Press, 1969, Vol. I), 29. *Nomocratic* is a term particularly identified with the British political philosopher Michael Oakeshott, who considered it in contrast to the term *telocratic*, which is discussed below. See especially Michael Oakeshott, *Lectures in the History of Political Thought*, ed. Terry Nardin and Luke O'Sullivan (London: Imprint Academic, 2006).

3. On this point see, Gordon Wood, *Power and Liberty: Constitutionalism in the American Revolution* (Oxford: Oxford University Press, 2021).

4. For instance, in his famous "Speech on Conciliation with the Colonies," delivered in Parliament in 1775, Edmund Burke noted of America that "in no country perhaps in the world is the law so general a study," that "all who read, and most do read, endeavour to obtain some smattering in that science" there, and that this renders the Americans "stubborn

and litigious." [Edmund Burke, *The Works of the Right Honourable Edmund Burke*, Vol. I (London: Henry G. Bohn, 1854), 467.]

5. For instance, when President George W. Bush signed the McCain-Feingold Campaign Finance Reform Act in 2002, he noted in a signing statement that he had some "reservations about the constitutionality of the broad ban on issue advertising." But rather than refuse to sign a bill he deemed constitutionally dubious, he concluded, "I expect that the courts will resolve these legitimate legal questions as appropriate under the law." This kind of equating of the constitutional with the legal is now rampant, and the resulting constitutional passivity afflicts Congress, the executive branch, and the broader citizenry in ways we shall explore. [George W. Bush, "Statement on Signing the Bipartisan Campaign Reform Act of 2002," *Weekly Compilation of Presidential Documents*, Volume 38, Number 13 (Washington, DC: Government Printing Office, 2002), 518.]

6. James Madison, *The Papers of James Madison*, Vol. III, ed. William T. Hutchinson (Chicago: University of Chicago Press, 1964).

7. See Michael Oakeshott, *Lectures in the History of Political Thought*, ed. Terry Nardin and Luke O'Sullivan (London: Imprint Academic, 2006).

8. Karen Orren and Stephen Skowronek, *The Policy State: An American Predicament* (Cambridge, MA: Harvard University Press, 2017).

9. The importance of the simple fact of structured decision-making, even apart from its capacity to build consensus, should not be underestimated. As James Madison wrote in Federalist 64, structure and process are vital to making good decisions. "Although the absolute necessity of system, in the conduct of any business, is universally known and acknowledged, yet the high importance of it in national affairs has not yet become sufficiently impressed on the public mind." Alexander Hamilton, John Jay, and James Madison, "Essay 64," in *The Federalist*, ed. Clinton Rossiter (New York: Mentor Books, 1999). (Further references to this edition will be cited as "Federalist" and the essay number.)

10. Federalist 41.

11. Federalist 37; Federalist 48.

12. This is another way to distinguish an institutional from a legal framework. And it is a distinction with deep roots not only in the modern liberal effort to guard against abuses of power but also in the ambition of

classical political philosophy to understand the nature of political authority. Aristotle, in book IV of the *Politics*, argued that "a constitution is the regulation of the offices of the state in regard to the mode of their distribution and to the question of what is the sovereign power in the state and what is the object of each community, but laws are distinct from the principles of the constitution, and regulate how the magistrates are to govern and to guard against those who transgress them." [Aristotle, *Politics*, Book IV, Chapter 3, (1290a).]

13. Walter Berns, *Taking the Constitution Seriously* (New York: Simon & Schuster, 1987), 184. Herbert Storing made a similar point, arguing that "in thinking about limited government, the basic limitations cannot be found in governmental powers—in what the government can do—but must be found in the way the government is organized and the way it acts." [Herbert Storing, *The Founding of the Democratic Republic* (New York: Cengage Learning, 1981), 366.]

14. Aristotle, *Politics*, Book III, Chapter 1 (1274b32–41); Book IV, Chapter 11 (1295a40–b1); Book VII, Chapter 8 (1328b1–2).

15. James Ceaser, "Restoring the Constitution," *The Claremont Review of Books*, Spring 2012.

16. Charles-Louis de Secondat, Baron de Montesquieu, *The Spirit of the Laws* (Cambridge: Cambridge University Press, 1989); Federalist 83.

17. Thomas Jefferson and James Madison seemed to hold this view of the distinction between the Declaration of Independence and the Constitution. In an 1825 exchange about texts to be included in the curriculum of the University of Virginia's law school, Madison wrote to Jefferson: "Sydney & Locke are admirably calculated to impress on young minds the right of Nations to establish their own Governments, and to inspire a love of free ones; but afford no aid in guarding our Republican Charters against constructive violations. The Declaration of Independence, tho' rich in fundamental principles, and saying every thing that could be said in the same number of words, falls nearly under a like observation." In his reply, Jefferson expressed agreement with the general point. [James Madison to Thomas Jefferson, February 8, 1825; and Jefferson to Madison, February 12, 1825, *The Papers of James Madison*, Retirement Series, vol. 3, 1

March 1823–24 February 1826, ed. David B. Mattern, J. C. A. Stagg, Mary Parke Johnson, and Katherine E. Harbury (Charlottesville: University of Virginia Press, 2016), 471–473.]

18. Gordon Wood, in particular, has advanced the argument that the Constitution amounted to a pulling back from the more radically democratic character of American politics in the revolutionary era. Martin Diamond (particularly in "The Declaration and the Constitution: Liberty, Democracy, and the Founders," *The Public Interest*, Fall 1975) responded persuasively.

19. Federalist 10. Madison goes on in the next paragraph to double down on this minimalist definition of the term, writing, "The two great points of difference between a democracy and a republic are: first, the delegation of the government, in the latter, to a small number of citizens elected by the rest; secondly, the greater number of citizens, and greater sphere of country, over which the latter may be extended."

20. Federalist 55.

21. James Madison, "Notes from June 25," in *Notes of Debates in the Federal Convention of 1787* (Athens, Ohio: Ohio University Press, 1966). (Further references to this edition of Madison's notes on the convention will be cited as "Madison's Notes on the Convention," and the date of the relevant quotation); Federalist 2.

22. Madison's Notes on the Convention, June 26.

23. See Charles Kesler, *Crisis of the Two Constitutions* (New York: Encounter Books, 2021).

24. Federalist 71.

25. Herbert Agar, *The Price of Union* (New York: Houghton Mifflin, 1950).

26. It's worth seeing that the Left and Right in the United States have, in some respects, switched sides in this debate in the course of the past generation. The Left used to be much more invested in counter-majoritarian institutions like the courts and the Bill of Rights, while the Right would dismiss them as undemocratic elite impositions. The Right used to be much more invested in empowering majorities, while the Left insisted on minority protections.

CHAPTER 2: MODES OF RESOLUTION

1. Federalist 9.

2. James Madison, "Notes from June 18," in *Notes of Debates in the Federal Convention of 1787* (Athens, Ohio: Ohio University Press, 1966).

3. Federalist 10.

4. Aristotle, *Politics*, Book IV, chapter 11 (1296a).

5. Christopher DeMuth, "Competition and the Constitution," *National Affairs*, Fall 2011.

6. "Winner take all" refers to an election in which the winner, regardless of how narrow his or her victory, wins the entirety of the office in question. The alternative would be a more proportional approach in which a range of offices is divided among competing parties based on their portions of the overall vote. A number of parliamentary democracies employ such proportional representation. "First past the post" means the candidate who receives the most votes wins, even if his or her share is only a plurality of the electorate. This is the practice in most American elections, although a number of states (particularly in the South) have runoff elections between the two leading candidates if no candidate in a multicandidate race wins more than 50 percent of the vote.

7. The Electoral College is often assailed for being insufficiently democratic, but along with the advantages it offers by focusing presidential races on undecided portions of the electorate, the system also does not stand out from those of other democracies to the extent many critics imply. Very few democracies elect their chief executives directly. In parliamentary systems, prime ministers are generally chosen by their parties' parliamentary majorities, rather than directly by voters, and so are selected by an even less representative process than the Electoral College. (As of this writing, for instance, the United Kingdom has been through three prime ministers since the last general election, so that two of them were chosen by their party without consulting the voting public.) And in more mixed systems, there is generally a structured process for selecting chief executives. This is, in part, because the job of the chief executive (especially in our system, where the president is not a legislator) is not fundamentally representative but administrative and, in part, to moderate the risks of demagoguery. This subject will be taken up at greater length in chapter 6.

8. Federalist 51.

9. Madison plainly argues that the legislative branch is a danger to the others in Federalist 49: "The tendency of republican governments is to an aggrandizement of the legislative at the expense of the other departments." The three branches are "coordinate" in the sense that each is housed in its own branch and is relatively independent, but the legislature is certainly the primary branch, for good and bad.

10. DeMuth, "Competition and the Constitution." This point is further discussed in chapter 4.

11. On the views of some framers that commerce was supportive of social peace, see for instance, Walter Berns, *Taking the Constitution Seriously* (New York: Simon & Schuster, 1987), 177–180.

12. James Madison, "To Thomas Jefferson from James Madison, 27 June 1823." Founders Online, National Archives, https://founders.archives.gov /documents/Jefferson/98-01-02-3597.

13. It is worth noting that the framers were not of one mind on the value of such mechanisms. In Federalist 22, for instance, Alexander Hamilton is sharply critical of supermajority requirements. Among much else, he says, "When the concurrence of a large number is required by the Constitution to the doing of any national act, we are apt to rest satisfied that all is safe, because nothing improper will be likely to be done, but we forget how much good may be prevented, and how much ill may be produced, by the power of hindering the doing what may be necessary, and of keeping affairs in the same unfavorable posture in which they may happen to stand at particular periods."

14. This point clarifies an important trend in our contemporary politics. The system is designed to prioritize and empower its mechanisms of consensus building, and particularly Congress and federalism. But because we find this frustrating, we tend to look to empower those mechanisms that don't operate by consensus—especially the courts and administrative agencies. This plainly contributes to the divisiveness of our politics. If we were to prioritize social peace, as we need to in times when that peace is threatened, we would want to empower those institutions of our system that prioritize it too.

15. Harry Jaffa, *Equality and Liberty* (New York: Oxford University Press, 1965), 82–83. As Abraham Lincoln expressed in his first inaugural

address, "Unanimity is impossible; the rule of a minority, as a permanent arrangement, is wholly inadmissible, so that, rejecting the majority principle, anarchy or despotism in some form is all that is left."

16. Daniel Bell, *The Coming of Post-Industrial Society* (New York: Basic Books, 1973), 351. Of course, there exists in American politics a deep and long-running countertradition to this approach, a tradition of moralism that implicitly views compromise as impure and corrupt. That tradition continues to find recurrent and vibrant expression in our politics in every generation, on both the Left and Right, and is behind a great deal of the tension surrounding constitutionalism and liberalism in American life in the twenty-first century. For a brilliant exposition of this tension, see Seymour Martin Lipset, "The Paradox of American Politics," *The Public Interest*, Fall 1975, 142–165.

17. Federalist 51.

18. Alexis de Tocqueville, *Democracy in America*, trans. Harvey Mansfield and Delba Winthrop (Chicago: University of Chicago Press, 2000), 379. On this point, see also Greg Weiner, *Madison's Metronome: The Constitution, Majority Rule, and the Tempo of American Politics* (Lawrence, KS: University Press of Kansas, 2012).

19. Herbert Storing, *Toward a More Perfect Union* (Washington: AEI Press, 1995), 20–21.

20. Martin Diamond, *The Founding of the Democratic Republic* (New York: Cengage Learning, 1981), 35. Some elements of the system were, in fact, just functions of a desire to find a middle ground or of splitting the difference between competing views. In Federalist 62, Madison suggests that the particular formulas of representation in the House and Senate express a general agreement about the republican character of the system but that their details are not applications of any pure theory. Quoting the words of Washington's letter to Congress submitting the Constitution to their consideration, Madison writes, "It is superfluous to try, by the standard of theory, a part of the Constitution which is allowed on all hands to be the result, not of theory, but 'of a spirit of amity, and that mutual deference and concession which the peculiarity of our political situation rendered indispensable.'" But by no means were all the compromises involved of this sort.

21. Madison's Notes on the Convention, June 30.

22. This approach runs deeper than the study of the Constitution. A certain kind of conservative view of social life tends to deny the antinomies that define a certain kind of philosophical view of the political. Distinctions between the natural and the artificial, the ancient and the modern, philosophy and poetry, Athens and Jerusalem, all insist on lines that are clearer than reality. To see that these opposing possibilities are commingled in fact—that their commingling is what creates our political tradition—is to perceive the complexity of the political and to glimpse one source of its potential. What is enabled by these durable contradictions is a dynamic stability, which, paradoxical as the term may seem, is an essential purpose of political order. This is not because the truth that underlies the political is somehow contradictory or relative, but because our ability to grasp that truth is frequently imperfect and because its character is not always best described by the categories put at our disposal by modern social science. (On this point, see particularly Book I, Chapter 3 of Aristotle's *Nicomachean Ethics*.)

23. Joseph Cropsey, *Political Philosophy and the Issues of Politics* (Chicago: University of Chicago Press, 1977), 130.

24. Federalist 10.

25. Madison's Notes on the Convention, June 18.

26. Madison's Notes on the Convention, June 29.

27. Federalist 39.

CHAPTER 3: THE CONSTITUTED PUBLIC

1. In Federalist 55, Madison described the different institutions and their different forms in terms of a "combination of the several members of government, standing on as different foundations as republican principles will well admit, and at the same time accountable to the society over which they are placed." In this sense, the elected branches each create a different electorate too.

2. Federalist 63 (Madison offers this argument specifically in defense of the US Senate); Federalist 55.

3. Robert Nisbet, "Public Opinion vs Popular Opinion" *The Public Interest*, Fall 1975.

4. Federalist 10.

5. Federalist 49.

6. Federalist 51.

7. Federalist 10; Federalist 9.

8. James Madison, *The Papers of James Madison*, Vol. 11, ed. Robert A. Rutland and Charles F. Hobson (Charlottesville: University Press of Virginia, 1977), 158–165.

9. Federalist 76.

10. Federalist 57.

11. Federalist 55.

12. Not all the Constitution's champions called themselves republicans—in fact, early in the Philadelphia Convention, Alexander Hamilton championed a plan of government that included lifetime tenure for the national government's chief executive and Senate. According to James Madison's notes, at the start of his remarks in favor of that plan, he "acknowledged himself not to think favorably of Republican Government," though he "addressed his remarks to those who did think favorably of it." But all of them, including Hamilton, argued that the system of government proposed in the ultimate Constitution was republican in character. (Madison's Notes on the Convention, June 26.)

13. The anti-federalists certainly prioritized the formative power of the small republic, but it would be a mistake to try to force their disagreement with the federalists into the contemporary categories of our debates about liberalism. As Herbert Storing ably showed, the anti-federalists were not less liberal than the federalists, in our sense of the term. They did defend the need for the formation of a certain kind of citizen, and worry that a republic that was too large would have trouble with that crucial task. But ultimately, their purpose was individual liberty, and not the submergence of the individual into the community. Their aims were not premodern; they disagreed with the Federalists about how best to achieve a durable liberalism. [See especially, Herbert Storing, *What the Anti-Federalists Were For* (Chicago: University of Chicago Press, 1981).]

14. Federalist 10. Madison continued, "The two great points of difference between a democracy and a republic are, first, the delegation of the government, in the latter, to a small number of citizens elected by the rest;

secondly, the greater number of citizens, and greater sphere of country, over which the latter may be extended." He was not alone in insisting on such a narrow definition, and it may well be that this is all that was intended by the Constitution's guarantee of "a republican form of government" to all the states in Article IV, Section 4.

15. Martin Diamond, *The Founding of the Democratic Republic* (New York: Cengage Learning, 1981), 68–69.

16. Michael C. Hawley, *Natural Law Republicanism: Cicero's Liberal Legacy* (Oxford: Oxford University Press, 2022).

17. Andy Smarick, "Recovering the Republican Sensibility" *National Affairs*, Winter 2024.

18. Herbert Storing, *Toward a More Perfect Union* (Washington: AEI Press, 1995), 121.

19. Leo Strauss, *Liberalism Ancient and Modern* (Chicago: University of Chicago Press, 1995), 29. Both republicanism and liberalism have premodern roots, but the classical foundations of republicanism are more familiar to us than the premodern (and even Christian) roots of liberalism and of individualism. The argument of contemporary critics of liberalism that liberal individualism amounts to a rejection of the Christian anthropology involves a radical oversimplification of the profoundly intertwined histories of Christian and liberal thought. This is partly a function of an overemphasis of the radicalism of Enlightenment political thought, and partly a function of an underappreciation of the radicalism of Christian political thought. Alexis de Tocqueville's brief history of political egalitarianism in the introduction to *Democracy in America* offers the beginning of a correction of this view. Critics of liberalism too readily accept the triumphalist Whig narrative of liberal history peddled by liberalism's shallowest champions. Its deeper champions have more to offer.

20. Federalist 50. This is why defenders of this view must be defenders of the Constitution and its forms, even when some of those who wield the powers of our institutions reject the republican anthropology. It is why constitutional conservatives sometimes find themselves in the peculiar position of defending the courts from judges, the presidency from presidents, and the Congress from the hideous vices of its own members.

21. Federalist 51.

22. Charles Kesler, *Crisis of the Two Constitutions* (New York: Encounter Books, 2021), 68.

23. Federalist 57.

24. Bryan Garsten, "How to Protect America from the Next Donald Trump," *The New York Times*, November 10, 2020, A23.

25. The Bill of Rights was certainly not always understood legalistically. As Walter Berns noted, there were almost no First Amendment cases in the federal courts until well into the twentieth century. [Walter Berns, *Taking the Constitution Seriously* (New York: Simon & Schuster, 1987), 127.]

26. Michael P. Zuckert, "Madison's Consistency on the Bill of Rights," *National Affairs*, Spring 2021.

27. Article IV's Republican Guarantee Clause is notoriously mysterious, and it is far from clear what its practical purpose is meant to be. John Adams spoke for many subsequent interpreters when he wrote (in an 1807 letter to Mercy Otis Warren) that "I confess I never understood it, and I believe no other Man ever did or ever will."

CHAPTER 4: FEDERALISM

1. "Compound republic" was James Madison's term for the system of American federalism in Federalist 51.

2. Madison's Notes on the Convention, May 30.

3. Madison's Notes on the Convention, May 30.

4. On Madison's proposal, see especially Alison LaCroix, "What if Madison Had Won? Imagining a Constitutional World of Legislative Supremacy," 45 *Indiana Law Review* 41 (2011): 41–42. For Hamilton's remarks, see Alexander Hamilton, *The Papers of Alexander Hamilton*, Vol. 4, ed. Harold C. Syrett (New York: Columbia University Press, 1962), 195–202.

5. Martin Diamond, *The Founding of the Democratic Republic* (New York: Cengage Learning, 1981), 50.

6. The terms *federalist* and *anti-federalist* to describe the parties to this dispute were coined by the federalists and were much detested by their adversaries. As the prominent pseudonymous anti-federalist essayist known as the Federal Farmer put it: "We might as well call the advocates and opposers Tories and Whigs, or any thing else, as

federalists and anti-federalists. To be for or against the constitution, as it stands, is not much evidence of a federal disposition; if any names are applicable to the parties, on account of their general politics, they are those of republicans and anti-republicans. The opposers are generally men who support the rights of the body of the people, and are properly republicans. The advocates are generally men not very friendly to those rights, and properly anti republicans." [Herbert Storing, *The Complete Anti-Federalist* (Chicago: University of Chicago Press, 1981), 258–259.) Storing also notes a further crucial point: that while the anti-federalists championed sustaining the preconditions for the formation of a certain kind of citizen, their underlying purpose remained the protection of individual liberty. Their aims were not premodern; they were liberals, and their disagreements with the federalists had much more to do with means than ends.

7. Federalist 10.

8. Federalist 39.

9. Federalist 16. Madison makes much the same argument in Federalist 20.

10. Federalist 45. Article I, Section 10 of the Constitution describes the limits on state powers, which answer directly to the specific authorities delegated to the national government. It is worth noting that the argument that the states precede the union was not universally accepted. Some federalists argued that the states came into existence only with the Declaration of Independence, and therefore never had an existence outside the union. Abraham Lincoln later repeated this argument in his case for union during the Civil War, arguing, for instance, in his July 4, 1861, address to Congress that "the union is older than any of the states, and in fact it created them as states." But this argument did not have much purchase in the early republic, or after.

11. James Madison, *The Papers of James Madison*, Vol. 14, ed. Robert A. Rutland and Thomas A. Mason (Charlottesville: University Press of Virginia, 1983), 217–219.

12. James Madison, *The Writings of James Madison*, Vol. 9, ed. Gaillard Hunt (New York: G. P. Putnam's Sons, 1910), 351; Federalist 37.

13. Federalist 51.

14. Federalist 10. Madison makes a similar argument in Federalist 14, where he answers the objection that the new national government will have too much to do by arguing: "In the first place it is to be remembered that the general government is not to be charged with the whole power of making and administering laws. Its jurisdiction is limited to certain enumerated objects, which concern all the members of the republic, but which are not to be attained by the separate provisions of any. The subordinate governments, which can extend their care to all those other subjects which can be separately provided for, will retain their due authority and activity. Were it proposed by the plan of the convention to abolish the governments of the particular States, its adversaries would have some ground for their objection; though it would not be difficult to show that if they were abolished the general government would be compelled, by the principle of self-preservation, to reinstate them in their proper jurisdiction."

15. Herbert Storing, *Toward a More Perfect Union* (Washington: AEI Press, 1995), 38.

16. Madison's Notes on the Convention, August 25.

17. The Three-Fifths Clause is often attacked as treating an enslaved person as three-fifths of a human being rather than a full person, but this gets the moral tragedy involved roughly backward. It was the slave-holding states that wanted to count enslaved individuals as full persons to enlarge their congressional delegations and, thereby, entrench the power of slaveholders. Opponents of slavery at the convention wanted to not count slave populations at all. For a helpful discussion of this question and of the roots of the three-fifths rule in the Articles of Confederation, see Michael Zuckert, "Slavery and the Constitution," *National Affairs*, Spring 2023.

18. Madison's Notes on the Convention, August 25.

19. Abraham Lincoln, *The Collected Works of Abraham Lincoln*, Vol. 2, ed. Roy P. Basler (New Brunswick, NJ: Rutgers University Press, 1953), 255–256.

20. Abraham Lincoln, *Speeches and Writings, 1832–1858* (New York: The Library of America, 1989), 427–428.

21. On this point, see especially Walter Berns, *Taking the Constitution Seriously* (New York: Simon & Schuster, 1987), 238–239.

22. This argument is made most explicitly in Herbert Croly's *The Promise of American Life*, originally published in 1909, especially in chapters 2 and 3.

23. Theodore Roosevelt, *The New Nationalism* (New York: The Outlook Company, 1910), 28.

24. Roosevelt, *New Nationalism*, 28–29.

25. Federalist 17.

26. This discussion is not meant as a comprehensive overview of American progressivism (let alone of American debates about race) but only as a brief examination of the intersection of those crucial questions with the federalism of the Constitution. Progressive critiques of the Constitution will also be taken up in the next several chapters from several different angles.

27. Whether localities are merely creatures of the states or should be understood as an additional layer of sovereignty in America is a contested question, of course. We need not take it up here, but for a good sense of the debate, see Paul R. DeHart and Ronald J. Oakerson, "Are Local Governments Mere Creatures of the States?" *National Affairs*, Spring 2022.

28. Peter Berger and Richard John Neuhaus, "To Empower People," in *The Civil Society Reader*, ed. Don Eberly (New York: Rowman & Littlefield, 2000), 180.

29. Michael Greve, "Judicial Federalism Without Romance," *Law & Liberty*, January 5, 2022. Greve's superb book *The Upside-Down Constitution* (Cambridge, MA: Harvard University Press, 2012) is an essential resource on all the questions taken up in this chapter.

CHAPTER 5: CONGRESS

1. Federalist 51.

2. Federalist 48; Federalist 49.

3. Federalist 15.

4. Madison makes the point that setting the two houses against each other will prevent mischief more frequently than it prevents essential measures in Federalist 62, for instance, as does Hamilton in Federalist 70.

5. Federalist 71.

6. John Adams, "Defence of the Constitution of the Government of the United States," in *The Works of John Adams*, Vol. 5, ed. Charles Francis Adams (Boston: Little, Brown & Co., 1856), 457.

7. Madison emphasizes the refining potential of representative institutions in Federalist 10 and Federalist 63. Joseph Bessette, *The Mild Voice of Reason* (Chicago: The University of Chicago Press, 1994), 35.

8. Federalist 10. Adam White, "The Turn Against Religious Liberty," *Commentary*, January 2021.

9. Federalist 57.

10. Jay Cost, *Democracy or Republic?* (Washington: AEI Press, 2023), 64.

11. Federalist 85. Hamilton was referring to the work of the Constitutional Convention itself.

12. Federalist 70.

13. Walter Berns, *Taking the Constitution Seriously* (New York: Simon & Schuster, 1987), 151. Philip A. Wallach, *Why Congress* (Oxford: Oxford University Press, 2023).

14. Federalist 10.

15. Wallach, *Why Congress*, 263.

16. As Walter Berns argued, "Success in the legislature is measured by the extent to which one's interest is accommodated in the law adopted by the majority, and to achieve that success it is necessary to display a willingness to be accommodating oneself. Immoderate and outrageous demands especially are not likely to be successful, which explains why immoderate politicians are disdainful of legislative assemblies." (Berns, *Taking the Constitution Seriously*, 224.)

17. As Alexander Hamilton wrote, "Those politicians and statesmen who have been the most celebrated for the soundness of their principles and for the justice of their views, have declared in favor of a single Executive and a numerous legislature. They have with great propriety, considered energy as the most necessary qualification of the former, and have regarded this as most applicable to power in a single hand, while they have, with equal propriety, considered the latter as best adapted to deliberation and wisdom, and best calculated to conciliate the confidence of the people and to secure their privileges and interests." (Federalist 70.)

18. John McGinnis, "Defending the Consensus Constitution," *Law & Liberty*, January 13, 2022.

19. Alfred Frederick Pollard, *The Evolution of Parliament* (London: Longman, Green, & Col, 1926), 133.

20. On congressional response to national emergencies, see especially Philip A. Wallach, "Crisis Government," *National Affairs*, Summer 2020.

21. William Howell and Terry Moe, *Relic: How Our Constitution Undermines Effective Government and Why We Need a More Powerful Presidency* (New York: Basic Books, 2016).

22. Daniel Stid, "Two Pathways for Congressional Reform" (Menlo Park, CA: The William and Flora Hewlett Foundation, March 11, 2015), https://hewlett.org/wp-content/uploads/2018/01/Two-Pathways-for-Congressional-Reform_March-2015.pdf. Woodrow Wilson, *Congressional Government: A Study in American Politics* (Boston: Houghton Mifflin, 1885), 93.

23. Ironically, the staunch conservative Newt Gingrich, who served as Speaker of the House from 1995 through 1998, was, as a practical matter, the most Wilsonian leader in the history of the Congress. But his successors of both parties, and especially Democratic leader Nancy Pelosi (who served as Speaker and Minority Leader over a twenty-year period at the beginning of this century), only reinforced his approach.

24. Frances Lee, *Insecure Majorities* (Chicago: University of Chicago Press, 2016), 199.

25. For a more detailed discussion of the decline of institutional formation in Congress (and elsewhere) and on the costs of transparency, see Yuval Levin, *A Time to Build* (New York: Basic Books, 2020).

26. Daniel DiSalvo, *Engines of Change: Party Factions in American Politics, 1868–2010* (Oxford: Oxford University Press, 2012). Steven Teles and Robert Saldin, "The Future Is Faction," *National Affairs*, Fall 2020.

27. On this point see, for instance, "Consolidating Intelligence Appropriation and Authorization in a Single Committee," a report of the Congressional Research Service, October 29, 2004. While that report is focused on the intelligence domain in particular, it offers a useful history of the boundary between authorization and appropriation and of past reforms and proposals along these lines.

28. Hamilton made this remark in a letter to the *National Gazette* on September 11, 1792. (The letter was submitted under the pseudonym Amicus but has been authoritatively attributed to Hamilton.) Sparks recorded Madison's remark in a journal entry describing a visit with Madison on April 19, 1830. See H. B. Adams, *Life and Writings of Jared Sparks*, II, 31. For more on this point see my essay "Transparency Is Killing Congress," *The Atlantic*, February 9, 2020.

29. Regarding this idea, see Lee Drutman, Jonathan Cohen, Yuval Levin, and Norman Ornstein, "The Case for Enlarging the House of Representatives," a report of the American Academy of Arts and Sciences, published in June 2020, and available at https://www.amacad.org/ourcommonpurpose/enlarging-the-house.

30. Federalist 51.

CHAPTER 6: THE PRESIDENCY

1. Max Farrand, ed., *The Records of the Federal Convention of 1787*, Vol. 1 (New Haven, CT: Yale University Press, 1966), 71. (This quotation is from the notes on the convention kept by delegate Rufus King, rather than James Madison's notes, which are used for most other references to the convention.)

2. Madison's Notes on the Convention, June 1. Joseph Bessette and Gary Schmitt, *Crafting a Republican Executive* (Washington: The American Enterprise Institute, 2023), 3.

3. Madison's Notes on the Convention, June 1.

4. Federalist 76; Federalist 70.

5. Federalist 72.

6. Madison's Notes on the Convention, June 1; June 2. Federalist 71.

7. Federalist 70; Federalist 77.

8. Harvey Mansfield, "The Ambivalence of Executive Power," in *The Presidency in the Constitutional Order*, ed. Joseph Bessette and Jeffrey Tulis (New York: Routledge, 2010), 331.

9. Federalist 47.

10. It is worth remarking that these various concerns remain common in the democratic world. Very few democracies elect their chief executives

directly. In fact, in most parliamentary systems, that individual is selected by the parliamentary majority party or coalition alone. The public selects a party, but that party's members of parliament select its leader (before general elections, but sometimes also between general elections), who is then prime minister. This is a far less direct and less democratic mode of selection of the chief executive than the Electoral College.

11. Federalist 68.

12. Federalist 68; James Q. Wilson, "Rise of Bureaucratic State," *The Public Interest*, Fall 1975.

13. James Madison, *The Papers of James Madison*, Vol. 9, ed. William T. Hutchinson (Chicago: University of Chicago Press, 1975), 354–355; Federalist 44. Federalist 10.

14. Federalist 37.

15. Federalist 72.

16. Federalist 73.

17. Federalist 62.

18. Federalist 27; Federalist 62. Hamilton also makes a similar argument in Federalist 17.

19. Harvey Flaumenhaft, "Hamilton's Administrative Republic and the American Presidency," in *The Presidency in the Constitutional Order*, ed. Joseph Bessette and Jeffrey Tulis (New York: Routledge, 2010), 71.

20. Madison's Notes on the Convention, May 31; Herbert Storing, ed., *The Complete Anti-Federalist*, Vol. 2 (Chicago: University of Chicago Press, 1981), 214.

21. Federalist 10.

22. Woodrow Wilson, *Congressional Government: A Study in American Politics* (Boston: Houghton Mifflin, 1885), 318.

23. Federalist 47. Woodrow Wilson, *Constitutional Government in the United States* (New York: Columbia University Press, 1908), 56. It is hard to avoid hearing in Wilson's language about the parts of a body working together an echo of St. Paul's letter to the Corinthians (specifically 1 Corinthians 12:12–26), but Wilson offers no reason to think this was his intention.

24. This very brief history is indebted to the work of Susan Dudley, and particularly to Susan Dudley, "Milestones in the Evolution of the Administrative State," *Daedalus*, Summer 2021.

25. *City of Arlington v. Federal Communications Commission*, 569 U.S. 290 (2013). Neomi Rao, "Why Congress Matters: The Collective Congress in the Structural Constitution," *Florida Law Review* 70, no. 1.

26. Consider some administrative actions by our last several presidents—to grant a path to normalized status to illegal immigrants brought to America as children or to divert funds from the defense budget to build a wall at the border or to forgive student loans on a vast scale. There is a case for each of these measures, but it is a highly partisan case, which could not gain sufficient support in Congress even when the party that supports it held majorities in both houses. Rather than allow that to mean that it was too partisan to be enacted, each was pursued by presidential action, and each intensified a divisive partisan battle. Each is an example of a measure our system of government was intended to prevent.

27. A large and growing portion of what Congress does now involves facilitating that dereliction of its own responsibility and empowering the administrative state to take its place. Most of what members of Congress call "constituent services," for instance, involves them or their staffs playing the role of a kind of concierge to the work of executive agencies on behalf of their constituents.

28. Barack Obama, "Remarks by the President on College Affordability," October 26, 2011.

29. Jeffrey Tulis, *The Rhetorical Presidency* (Princeton, NJ: Princeton University Press, 1987), 4.

30. Woodrow Wilson, "Abraham Lincoln: A Man of the People, Chicago, Illinois, February 12, 1909," in *The Papers of Woodrow Wilson*, Vol. 19, ed. Arthur S. Link (Princeton, NJ: Princeton University Press, 1975), 42.

31. Mikael Good and Philip Wallach, "The Emotive Presidency," *National Affairs*, Spring 2023.

32. Madison's Notes on the Convention, June 1.

33. Madison's Notes on the Convention, June 1.

CHAPTER 7: THE COURTS

1. Gordon Wood, *Power and Liberty: Constitutionalism in the American Revolution* (Oxford: Oxford University Press, 2021), 127–129.

2. Federalist 22; Federalist 37; Federalist 78.

3. Federalist 22.

4. Federalist 81.

5. Federalist 78.

6. Madison's Notes on the Convention, May 31.

7. Federalist 78.

8. Federalist 78.

9. Herbert Storing, ed., *The Complete Anti-Federalist*, Vol. II (Chicago: University of Chicago Press, 1981), 437–442.

10. Federalist 16; Federalist 44. For a superb overview of Hamilton's novel argument in Federalist 78–83, see William Treanor, "The Genius of Hamilton and the Birth of the Modern Theory of the Judiciary," in *The Cambridge Companion to the Federalist*, ed. Jack Rakove and Colleen Sheehan (Cambridge: Cambridge University Press, 2020), 464–514.

11. Madison's Notes on the Convention, June 4. James Wilson, when raising this idea again on July 21 at the convention, insisted that judicial review would not be enough, in a way that plainly showed he did want judges to exercise political power: "It had been said that the Judges, as expositors of the Laws would have an opportunity of defending their constitutional rights. There was weight in this observation; but this power of the Judges did not go far enough. Laws may be unjust, may be unwise, may be dangerous, may be destructive; and yet may not be so unconstitutional as to justify the Judges in refusing to give them effect. Let them have a share in the Revisionary power, and they will have an opportunity of taking notice of these characters of a law, and of counteracting, by the weight of their opinions the improper views of the Legislature." (Madison's Notes on the Convention, July 21.)

12. Madison's Notes on the Convention, July 17.

13. Larry Kramer, *The People Themselves: Popular Constitutionalism and Judicial Review* (Oxford: Oxford University Press, 2004). Kramer's book is a spectacularly insightful study of the relation between the democratic elements of the American system and the role of the judiciary.

14. Federalist 78.

15. Wood, *Power and Liberty*, 140.

16. Federalist 78. This is not only a point about judges but also a broader point about the limits of majority power. It suggests that the power of the majority is framed and bounded by the structure of the Constitution, so that, in this sense, legitimate majorities must have a certain shape, a certain mode of action, in order to be legitimate. This is another way in which the Constitution shapes majorities, constituting the public rather than simply responding to its wishes.

17. Federalist 78.

18. Madison's Notes on the Convention, July 21.

19. Alexis de Tocqueville, *Democracy in America*, trans. Harvey Mansfield and Delba Winthrop (Chicago: University of Chicago Press, 2000), 257.

20. *Marbury v. Madison*, 5 U.S. 137 (1803).

21. Madison's Notes on the Convention, July 21.

22. Walter Berns, *Taking the Constitution Seriously* (New York: Simon & Schuster, 1987), 214.

23. Berns, *Taking the Constitution Seriously*, 224–225.

24. On this point, see William Haun, "The Virtues of Judicial Restraint," *National Affairs*, Fall 2018.

25. William Rehnquist, "The Notion of a Living Constitution," *Texas Law Review* 54 (1976), 693.

26. On this point, see Robert Bork, "Neutral Principles and Some First Amendment Problems," *Indiana Law Journal* 47 (1971).

27. Amy Coney Barrett, "Countering the Majoritarian Difficulty," *Constitutional Commentary* 32 (2017).

28. Regarding the first, see especially Randy Barnett, *Our Republican Constitution* (New York: HarperCollins, 2016). Regarding the second, see especially Adrian Vermeule, *Common Good Constitutionalism* (New York: Polity, 2022).

29. This is not to suggest that there is no place for natural-law considerations in the work of the judge, only that these do not argue for confidence in the judgment of a judge above those of other constitutional actors. The common good is an objective reality, but we do not know the whole of it directly. Parts can be known to us only through the medium of experience, history, culture, experimentation, and negotiation, and all these

must have a role in our pursuit of it. Moreover, natural-law arguments for the legitimacy of law involve an assessment of both the substance and the form of state action. To suggest that a judge should respond to his assessment that a law is unjust by overturning that law is to promote an unjust action, at least in cases where the judge lacks the legitimate authority to act and when the public or the legislator had that authority. That does not mean that unjust laws are legitimate, but it means that there are limits to the proper sphere of judicial action. Many natural-law critics of originalism ignore this element of the natural-law justification of state action. For further discussion of this point, see Joel Alicea, "The Moral Authority of Original Meaning," *Notre Dame Law Review* 98 (2022).

30. Barrett, "Countering the Majoritarian Difficulty."

31. William Haun, "Tradition-Based Originalism and the Supreme Court," *National Affairs*, Spring 2022.

32. Adam White, "Separate Statement of Commissioner Adam White," as published by the Presidential Commission on the Supreme Court of the United States, December 2021. At https://www.whitehouse.gov/wp-content /uploads/2021/12/White-Statement.pdf.

33. In the long political struggle between progressives and conservatives, the courts have always been a little out of sync. The courts became aggressively progressive thirty years after the first peak of progressivism but then helped to enable and reinforce a second peak of progressivism in the 1960s and '70s. The courts are now more conservative than they have been in a century, thirty years after American conservatism was at its most recent intellectual and electoral apex. And maybe now they can help enable and reinforce a second conservative peak, by helping to facilitate a constitutional restoration, if conservatives prove able or willing to pursue it.

CHAPTER 8: CONSTITUTIONAL PARTISANSHIP

1. On the character of the early Left–Right divide in the latter years of the eighteenth century, see my book *The Great Debate* (New York: Basic Books, 2013). The two portions of the Declaration of Independence—a more radical statement of principles and a more conservative catalog of

grievances—might be said to be divided and marked by the words "Prudence, indeed, will dictate."

2. Federalist 50.

3. Alexander Hamilton, *The Papers of Alexander Hamilton*, Vol. V, ed. Harold C. Syrett (New York: Columbia University Press, 1962), 83.

4. Federalist 10.

5. Edmund Burke, *The Writings and Speeches of Edmund Burke*, Vol. III, ed. Paul Langford (Oxford: Oxford University Press, 1981), 163.

6. Federalist 57.

7. George Washington, *The Writings of George Washington*, ed. Worthington Chauncey Ford (New York: G. P. Putnam's Sons, 1892), 304–305.

8. For a detailed discussion of this history, see James Ceaser, *Presidential Selection: Theory and Development* (Princeton, NJ: Princeton University Press, 1979).

9. Martin Van Buren, *Inquiry into the Origin and Course of Political Parties in the United States* (New York: Hurd and Houghton, 1867), 3.

10. Van Buren, *Origin and Course of Political Parties*, 7–8.

11. Josiah Lee Auspitz, "A 'Republican' View of Both Parties." *The Public Interest*, Spring 1982, 96.

12. See Daniel DiSlavo, *Engines of Change: Party Factions in American Politics, 1868–2010* (Oxford: Oxford University Press, 2012).

13. Woodrow Wilson, "Wanted—A Party," *Boston Times*, September 27, 1886.

14. James Ceaser, "Presidential Selection," in *The Presidency in the Constitutional Order*, ed. Joseph Bessette and Jeffrey Tulis (New York: Routledge, 2010), 236–237.

15. James Q. Wilson, *The Amateur Democrat* (Chicago: University of Chicago Press, 1962), 358.

16. Daniel Stid, "A Madisonian Party System," *National Affairs*, Fall 2023. See also: Pendleton Herring, *The Politics of Democracy* (New York: Norton, 1940); Austin Ranney and Willmoore Kendall, *Democracy and the American Party System* (New York: Harcourt Brace, 1956); Clinton Rossiter, *Parties and Politics in America* (Ithaca, NY: Cornell University Press, 1960); Edward Banfield, "In Defense of the American Party System," in *Political Parties, U.S.A.*, ed. Robert Goldwin (New York: Rand McNally, 1961).

17. Auspitz, "A 'Republican' View of Both Parties."

18. Stid, "A Madisonian Party System."

19. Elaine Kamarck, "Re-Inserting Peer Review in the American Presidential Nomination Process" (Washington: The Brookings Institution, April 27, 2017).

20. On this point, see Daniel Stid, "Political Parties and the Problem of Union," *National Affairs*, Fall 2023.

CHAPTER 9: WHAT IS UNITY?

1. "It was true as had been observed," Madison said of Pinckney's comment, that "we had not among us those hereditary distinctions of rank which were a great source of the contests in the ancient governments as well as the modern States of Europe." And yet, "we cannot however be regarded even at this time, as one homogeneous mass, in which every thing that affects a part will affect in the same manner the whole." Moreover, and perhaps more important, Madison concluded, "in framing a system which we wish to last for ages, we should not lose sight of the changes which ages will produce" on this front. (Madison's Notes on the Convention, June 26.) Federalist 10.

2. Federalist 14.

3. Federalist 15.

4. Aristotle's "Madisonian" case for the larger polity, the fundamentally economic character of factionalism, and the need to set such factions off against one another may be found in Book IV, Chapters 11 through 14 of the *Politics*.

5. Aristotle, *Rhetoric*, Book I, Chapter 3 (1358b). In this respect, political speech, as Jenna Silber Storey and Benjamin Storey have argued, "is not just any kind of talk about politics. It asks and answers a specific question: 'What shall we do?' Its aim is not speculative inquiry or self-expression, but the proposal of a possible course of action in which all might plausibly join. It addresses itself to the community, and assumes that its other members will have a say—that they are fellow citizens who must be persuaded to act. In so doing, it opens the speaker to the response of his auditor, summoning all parties forth from their passivity and engaging them

in common work that often transforms their self-understanding." (Jenna Silber Storey and Benjamin Storey, "Political Speech in Divided Times," *National Affairs*, Fall 2022.)

6. Pierre Manent, *Metamorpheses of the City*, trans. Marc LePain (Cambridge, MA: Harvard University Press, 2013), 14.

7. Calvin Coolidge, "Address at the Celebration of the 150th Anniversary of the Declaration of Independence in Philadelphia, Pennsylvania." Available online at The American Presidency Project, https://www.presidency.ucsb.edu/node/267359.

8. A good example is Nikole Hannah-Jones, the chief organizer of the "1619 Project," published by the *New York Times*. The project aims to put America's racial history at the center of its broader history, and it must be said that, while it deploys some important historical research in that effort, it also deploys a great many distortions and lies about our country and ultimately does an enormous disservice to its readers, the larger society, and its own stated purposes. But even amid her fiercest critiques of the founders, Hannah-Jones herself praises the ideals of the Declaration of Independence and points to the extraordinary commitment to those ideals evident in the lives and struggles of those Americans who were most cruelly and violently denied their benefits. "Through centuries of black resistance and protest, we have helped the country live up to its founding ideals," she writes. This is plainly true. And her writing it is evidence of the way in which the core commitments of the Declaration describe the boundaries of even our most intense disputes. (Nikole Hannah-Jones, "Our Democracy's Founding Ideals Were False When They Were Written. Black Americans Have Fought to Make Them True," *New York Times*, August 14, 2019.)

9. Paul Ludwig, *Rediscovering Political Friendship: Aristotle's Theory and Modern Identity, Community, and Equality* (Cambridge: Cambridge University Press, 2020), 15.

10. Ludwig, *Rediscovering Political Friendship*, 7. See especially Aristotle's *Nichomachean Ethics*, Book IX, Chapter 6 (1167a22–32).

11. Aristotle, *Politics*, Book VII, Chapter 7 (1328a).

12. Aristotle, *Politics*, Book IV, Chapter 11 (1295b). Abraham Lincoln, "First Inaugural Address," in *Abraham Lincoln: Speeches and Writings, 1859–1865* (New York: Library of America, 1989), 223.

13. Federalist 55.

14. It is crucial to see, in this respect, that pluralism often refers to ways of life and not just to personal opinions. Pluralism, thus, frequently describes a relation among communities, not just individuals.

15. Woodrow Wilson, *Constitutional Government in the United States* (New York: Columbia University Press, 1908), 56.

16. The idea of unity as submission to a common authority might seem, at first, to particularly characterize religious critics of Madisonian liberalism, but it is, perhaps ironically, also at the root of the political thought of Thomas Hobbes and other early-modern liberals. The idea of unity as a shared commitment to a substantive ideal of justice may seem more like the progressive critique, but of course, it is also central to religious modes of integralism. These two notions of unity are inexorably tied together.

17. For my own sense of those larger causes of disunity and fragmentation, see my last two books: *The Fractured Republic* (2016) and *A Time to Build* (2020).

18. Lincoln, "First Inaugural Address," 219.

19. Americans have never been in anything like full agreement regarding this underlying anthropology, and we likely never will be. But the Constitution embodies what I take to be the sensible truth about it, and our practice of constitutionalism can implicitly convey and teach that truth. Our constitutional order is, in this sense, a teacher of the truth, even as it leaves a great deal of room to debate it. That suggests the political Right (which tends to be the side of our politics that embraces this anthropology and believes it is true) will always be more protective of that order, and that our constitutional order would be especially endangered by a sustained assault from the Right.

20. Harry Jaffa, "The Nature and Origin of the American Party System," in *Political Parties, USA*, ed. Robert Goldwin (New York: Rand McNally, 1965), 82.

CONCLUSION

1. Madison's Notes on the Convention, August 8.

2. Federalist 85.

INDEX

MOSHE ZUSMAN

YUVAL LEVIN is the director of Social, Cultural, and Constitutional Studies at the American Enterprise Institute (AEI), where he also holds the Beth and Ravenel Curry Chair in Public Policy. The founder and editor of *National Affairs*, he is also a senior editor at *The New Atlantis*, a contributing editor at *National Review*, and a contributing opinion writer at *The New York Times*. His previous books include *The Fractured Republic* and *A Time to Build*. A former member of the White House domestic policy staff under George W. Bush, he lives in Maryland.